LTL

001.
Cole
Cryptozoology A to Z

F

A FIRESIDE BOOK
Published by Simon & Schuster

CRYPTOZOOLOGY
A to Z

The Encyclopedia of Loch Monsters,
Sasquatch, Chupacabras, and Other
Authentic Mysteries of Nature

LOREN COLEMAN AND JEROME CLARK

Allen County Public Library
900 Webster Street
PO Box 2270
Fort Wayne, IN 46801-2270

FIRESIDE
Rockefeller Center
1230 Avenue of the Americas
New York, NY 10020

Copyright © 1999 by Loren Coleman and Jerome Clark
All rights reserved,
including the right of reproduction
in whole or in part in any form.

FIRESIDE and colophon are registered trademarks
of Simon & Schuster Inc.

Designed by Gretchen Achilles

Manufactured in the United States of America

10 9 8 7 6 5 4 3 2 1

Library of Congress Cataloging-in-Publication Data
Coleman, Loren.
    Cryptozoology A to Z : the encyclopedia of loch monsters, Sasquatch,
    Chupacabras, and other authentic mysteries of nature / Loren Coleman
    and Jerome Clark.
        p.   cm.
    Includes bibliographical references (p.   ).
    1. Cryptozoology Encyclopedias.   2. Monsters Encyclopedias.   I. Clark, Jerome.
    II. Title.
    QL88.3.C65   1999
    001.944'03—dc21   99-31023
                                                                        CIP

ISBN 0-684-85602-6

For **CALEB** and **MALCOLM**,
new explorers of the wild country

For **ALEX**, **EVAN**, and **MOLLY**,
who will be there
when the next century learns
what we don't know now

CONTENTS

3 1833 03700 4667

Cryptozoological research should be actuated by two
major forces: patience and passion.

—DR. BERNARD HEUVELMANS, 1988

Cryptozoology Timeline

Milestones	Year	Animal Discoveries
1812 Cuvier's "Rash Dictum"	1800	
1817–1819 "New England Sea-Serpent" sightings peaked	1810	**1819** American tapir
	1820	**1834** first chimpanzee brought to Europe
	1830	**1847** lowland gorilla
	1840	**1856** giant squid
1860 Philip Henry Gosse's *The Romance of Natural History*	1850	**1869** giant panda
	1860	
1892 A.C. Oudemans's *The Great Sea Serpent*	1870	
1896 "Giant Octopus" of St. Augustine, Florida	1880	
	1890	**1901** okapi
	1900	**1902** mountain gorilla
	1905	**1903** dwarf siamang
	1910	**1904** giant forest hog
		1906 pygmy elephant officially described; now in dispute
1913 First Mokele-mbembe expedition	1915	**1912** Komodo dragon/pygmy hippopotamus
1913–1914 "Nandi Bear" sightings peaked		**1913** water civet
	1920	**1916** Chinese river dolphin
1920s "Sasquatch" coined	1925	
1921 "Abominable Snowman" coined		**1928** bonobo (pygmy chimpanzee)/crocodile lizard
1922 "Patagonian plesiosaur" expedition/"Mngwa" sightings peaked	1930	**1929** New Guinea crocodile
1930 Rupert T. Gould's *The Case for the Sea-Serpent*	1935	**1936** first "live" giant panda/Congo peacock
1933 "Loch Ness Monster" sightings begin		**1937** kouprey
1934 Rupert T. Gould's *The Loch Ness Monster and Others*	1940	**1938** coelacanth/Selevin's dormouse
1937 Gandar Dower's *The Spotted Lion*	1945	
1941 Willy Ley's *The Lungfish and the Unicorn*		
1944		

Upper timeline (new animal discoveries):

- ○ **1949** Andean wolf
- ○ **1951** water-loving mink
- ○ **1952** "second" coelacanth
- ○ **1954** pygmy otter shrew
- ○ **1955** golden langur
- ○ **1959** dwarf brocket muntjac
- ○ **1960** woodland bison
- ○ **1964** ufiti
- ○ **1965** yameneko
- ○ **1967** long-footed potoroo
- ○ **1974** Chacoan peccary (tagua)
- ○ **1975** king cheetah
- ○ **1976** megamouth
- ○ **1977** Prosperine rock wallaby
- ○ **1984** bondegezou
- ○ **1985** Bilkis gazelle
- ○ **1986** bamboo lemur/hairy Sumatran rhinoceros
- ○ **1988** black tree kangaroo
- ○ **1992** saola (Vu Quang ox)
- ○ **1994–1998** four new muntjacs
- ○ **1997–1998** Indonesian coelacanth
- ○ **1998** megamouth #11
- ○ **1999** blue Timor monitor

Axis markers: 1955 · 1965 · 1975 · 1985 · 1995

Axis markers: 1950 · 1960 · 1970 · 1980 · 1990 · 2000

Lower timeline (cryptozoology events):

- Charles Barrett's *The Bunyip*
- **1948** ○ Ivan T. Sanderson's "There Could Be Dinosaurs" inspires Bernard Heuvelmans
- **1951** ○ Ralph Izzard's *The Hunt for the Buru*/Eric Shipton's photographed Yeti attacks
- **1954** ○ *Daily Mail* Snowman Expedition
- **1955** ○ Bernard Heuvelmans's *On the Track of Unknown Animals* (in French)
- **1957–1959** ○ Slick-Johnson Snowman Expeditions
- **1958** ○ Soviet Snowman Commission founded/"Bigfoot" coined
- **1959** ○ "cryptozoology" coined
- **1960** ○ Loren Coleman inspired by *Half Human*, Sanderson, and by Heuvelmans/"globster" coined
- **1961** ○ Sanderson's *Abominable Snowmen: Legend Come to Life*
- **1966** ○ "Napes" coined
- **1967** ○ Patterson Film
- **1968** ○ Heuvelmans's *In the Wake of the Sea-Serpents*/"Minnesota Iceman" described
- **1978** ○ John Green's *Sasquatch: The Apes Among Us*
- **1982** ○ International Society of Cryptozoology formed
- **1983** ○ "cryptid" coined
- **1984** ○ CryptoQuest Expedition, Idaho
- **1986** ○ Heuvelmans's "Annotated Checklist" published
- **1989** ○ British Columbia Scientific Cryptozoology Club founded
- **1995** ○ "Chupacabras" coined
- **1997** ○ Vietnam Cryptozoic and Rare Animals Reasearch Center
- **1998** ○ Chad Arment's first cryptozoology e-mail list

The word **cryptozoology** first appeared in print in 1959, when Lucien Blancou dedicated his new book to "Bernard Heuvelmans, master of cryptozoology." Four years earlier, when Heuvelmans first published *On the Track of Unknown Animals,* the term "cryptozoology" as such did not exist. It was not until the publication of *On the Track of Unknown Animals* and the sensation it created that Heuvelmans began to call his lifelong pursuit "cryptozoology," and a new discipline was born. Since then it has become part of modern vocabulary, and appears in nearly all standard dictionaries.

But what exactly is cryptozoology?

It is not, Heuvelmans insists, an "arcane or occult zoology." It fuses three Greek words: *kryptos, zoon,* and *logos,* which mean, respectively, hidden, animal, and discourse. Thus cryptozoology is the science of "hidden animals." Heuvelmans prefers "hidden" to "unknown" because to those people who live near them, the animals are not unfamiliar; if they were, there would be no native accounts, and we would never have heard of them. They are, however, undetected by those who would formally recognize their existence and catalogue them.

In 1982, when the International Society of Cryptozoology (ISC) was founded at a meeting held at the Smithsonian Institution, an effort was made to produce a sharper, clearer definition. Cryptozoology, the assembled scientists and investigators agreed, also concerns "the possible existence of *known* animals in areas where they were not supposed to occur (either now or in the past), as well as the unknown persistence of presumed extinct animals to the present time or to the recent past. . . . What makes an animal of interest to cryptozoology . . . is that it is *unexpected*." This further definition failed to address one crucial aspect: the minimum size. In subsequent reflection on the subject, Heuvelmans insisted that "a minimum size is essential," though he left the precise dimensions open to further discussion. Nonetheless, he wrote, for an animal (or alleged animal) to be of cryptozoological interest, it must have at least one trait "truly singular, unexpected, paradoxical, striking, emotionally upsetting, and thus capable of mystification."

To most persons familiar with the term, cryptozoology is seen as the study of such spectacular and disputed creatures as Sasquatch, the Yeti, and the Loch Ness Monster. These legendary beasts do interest crypto-zoologists, but such "cryptids" (as cryptozoologists call them) comprise only a fraction of the hidden, uncatalogued, or out-of-place animals that have intrigued and frustrated cryptozoologists before cryptozoology as such existed.

Writing in 1988 in *Cryptozoology* (Vol. 7), Heuvelmans underscored the aims of cryptozoology:

> Hidden animals, with which cryptozoology is concerned, are by definition very incompletely known. To gain more credence, they have to be documented as carefully and exhaustively as pos-sible by a search through the most diverse fields of knowledge. Cryptozoological research thus requires not only a thorough grasp of most of the zoological sciences, including, of course, physical anthropology, but also a certain training in such extra-neous branches of knowledge as mythology, linguistics, archae-ology and history. It will consequently be conducted more extensively in libraries, newspaper morgues, regional archives, museums, art galleries, laboratories, and zoological parks rather than in the field!

CUVIER'S RASH DICTUM

In 1812 Baron Georges Cuvier, the revered French biologist considered the father of paleontology, declared the end of the age of zoological dis-covery. "There is," he said, "little hope of discovering new species" of large animals. From now on, he continued, naturalists ought to focus their attention on extinct fauna. As for fabled creatures such as Sea Ser-pents, which some of his colleagues held to merit further investigation, Cuvier had these words: "I hope nobody will ever seriously look for them in nature; one could as well search for the animals of Daniel or for the beast of the Apocalypse."

In 1819, a mere seven years later, the American tapir was found, only the first of thousands of "new" animals to be uncovered in the past two centuries. They include the giant squid (1870s), okapi (1901), the Komodo dragon (1912), the kouprey (1937), and the ultimate "living fossil," the coelacanth (1938). The largest land mammal to be documented since the kouprey is the extraordinary saola (*Pseudoryx nghetinhensis*), a new bovine species. Since the startling discovery in 1992 of a "lost world" of animals stretching sixty-five square miles near the Laotian border, Vietnam's Vu Quang Nature Reserve has produced evidence of two previously unknown bird species, at least one new fish, an unknown tortoise with a striking yellow shell, and two other mammals besides the Vu Quang ox.

The giant panda of Tibet was often cited during the 1950s and 1960s to demonstrate how a large animal could remain elusive and unknown in montane habitats not unlike some valleys of the Himalayas. Cryptozoologists note that it took sixty-seven years from the time of the giant panda's "discovery" until its live capture.

There is yet another example, especially germane to the ongoing hunt for uncatalogued large primates. Though the lowland gorilla was officially recognized in 1840, the mountain gorilla eluded detection, considerable searching notwithstanding, until the twentieth century. Indeed, not until 1860 were the first native tales collected of a monster ape said to live on the misty heights of the Virunga volcanoes of East Africa. But to Western zoologists these were no more than unconfirmed anecdotes until October 1902, when Belgian army captain Oscar von Beringe and a companion killed two gorillas on the Virungas' Mount Sabinio, thereby removing the animals from the realm of mythology and into a secure place among the world's recognized fauna. New primates have continued to turn up at an astounding pace throughout the twentieth century. Besides the mountain gorilla, two other apes, the dwarf siamang and pygmy chimpanzee, close relatives of humans and the hominoids* described in this encyclopedia, have been found.

---

* The word "hominid" refers to members of the family of humans, *Hominidae*, which consists of all species on our side of the last common ancestor of humans and living apes. Hominids are included in the superfamily of all apes, the *Hominoidea*, the members of which are called "hominoids." Members of the family of apes, *Pongidae* are also hominoids, but not hominids. Apes and humans are hominoids. The close-to-human hominids are, for example, the Marked Hominids, the classic Bigfoot, and Neandertals. Cryptids such as Napes, Skunk Apes, and more apelike animals are included in the broader term hominoids—which then, of course, encompasses the hominids. All hominids are hominoids, but all hominoids are not hominids.

As Cuvier's "rash dictum" (Heuvelmans's phrase) has been destroyed, the modern world of zoology, of which cryptozoology is a small subdiscipline, continues to be startled as "new" animals keep getting found. It is safe to say that in its essence, cryptozoology represents a throwback to the way original zoological study was conducted. In the beginning, as explorers trekked to new lands and listened to local informants, they were led to remarkable new species. These animals would then be killed or captured, shipped back to the zoological societies and parks of Europe, and formally classified. Today, with the addition of DNA testing and telebiological techniques, cryptozoology keeps alive the tradition of discovery and recognition of new species of animals.

GROUNDED IN SKEPTICAL ZOOLOGY

Though probably no zoologist today, even two centuries after Cuvier, would make so sweeping an assertion about the unlikelihood of interesting animals remaining to be documented, many zoologists, paleontologists, and physical anthropologists still view cryptozoology with suspicion. To them, cryptozoologists' willingness to consider as possible, or at least as deserving of inquiry, some especially extraordinary claims raises eyebrows and fuels the occasional charge of "pseudoscience" (however impeccably credentialed many cryptozoologists may be).

In response, Heuvelmans has called A. C. Oudemans's *The Great Sea Serpent* (1892) the "true starting point of the new discipline." It should be stressed that Oudemans was no crank; at the time his book was published, he was director of the Royal Zoological and Botanical Gardens at The Hague and was one of the best-regarded European men of science. His book received generally respectful reviews. Even though many of his colleagues were skeptical, and a scientist with less sterling credentials would have at least hesitated before expressing a positive view of so contested a subject, Oudemans was not entirely alone in arguing for the reality of what nineteenth-century observers often called the "great unknown." Decades earlier, prominent biologists Thomas Henry Huxley (a towering figure in Victorian science, if usually remembered today only as "Darwin's bulldog") and Louis Agassiz argued for the existence of Sea Serpents. In 1847, on assuming editorship of England's *Zoologist,*

Edward Newman wrote of Sea Serpent sightings, "A natural phenomenon of some kind has been witnessed; let us seek a satisfactory solution rather than terminate enquiry by the shafts of ridicule."

At the same time, however, Sea Serpents and their freshwater cousins, Lake Monsters, figured largely in all manner of hoaxes. In the Americas particularly, stories about such creatures were regularly concocted in newspaper offices when space needed filling. For example, in 1892 the *Chicago Tribune* reported that a giant serpent was menacing Wisconsin's Lake Geneva, causing "thousands of people" to flock to the shore hoping to glimpse the beast. Tellingly, not a single other contemporary source refers to this remarkable matter, but the *Tribune* yarn is only one of many hundreds to generate confusion among later cryptozoologists and to engender deep doubts about fantastic creatures generally in scientists then and now.

To figure in a hoax, the critter in question did not have to live in water. The (Victoria, British Columbia) *Daily British Colonist* for July 4, 1884, reported the capture, by a train's crew, of a beast "of the gorilla type standing about 4 feet 7 inches and weighing 127 pounds. He has long, black, strong hair and resembles a human being with one exception, his entire body, excepting his hands (or paws) and feet are covered with glossy hair about one inch long. His forearm is much longer than a man's forearm, and he possesses extraordinary strength." A young Sasquatch? Alas, no. Historically minded Bigfoot researchers have reluctantly concluded that this is just another tall tale cooked up by a local newspaper.

There were other notorious hoaxes, including an ill-conceived brontosaurus hunt in Africa in the early years of the twentieth century. No sooner had the Loch Ness Monster started to attract international attention (in 1933) than pranksters were faking photos and footprints. To many observers, the search for unknown animals was at best a tainted enterprise, at worst an exercise in folly.

Yet some serious-minded scientists, amateur naturalists, and journalists could not restrain their curiosity, and a small library of books and articles attempted to document reports and other evidence of a variety of cryptids. Among them was the Swedish scientist Gunnar Olof Hylten-Cavallius, who in the late nineteenth century investigated reports of giant snakelike creatures (known as lindorms) in the provinces of his native country. Another, Rupert T. Gould, an educated Englishman with wide-ranging interests, wrote *The Case for the Sea Serpent* (1930) and *The Loch Ness Monster and Others* (1934), the first book on that destined-to-be-much-discussed subject. When he was not writing about rockets and space travel, Willy Ley, who in 1935 fled Hitler's Germany for the United States, pursued what he called "romantic" or "exotic" zoology, even to the point of radical speculation about living dinosaurs, without notable damage to his reputation. (Years later biologist Aaron M. Bauer would praise Ley for drawing on "not only zoological information, but historical, mythological, and linguistic clues, presaging the modern, interdisciplinary approach to cryptozoology.")

In the January 3, 1948, issue of the *Saturday Evening Post,* biologist Ivan T. Sanderson—who would later play a significant role in early post-*On the Track of Unknown Animals* cryptozoology—suggested (in the words of the title) "There Could Be Dinosaurs." This and other Sanderson articles gripped a young Belgian, who found the whole question of "unknown animals" so fascinating that he vowed to devote the rest of his life to it, which is exactly what Bernard Heuvelmans did. Bernard Heuvelmans's interest in writing about what he felt was a vast neglected area of zoology led to the 1955 French publication of his book *On the Track of Unknown Animals.* This was followed by years of personal correspondence among his colleagues, and the first published use of the word "cryptozoology" in 1959. Because of Heuvelmans's important presence in the early history of the science, today he is generally referred to as the "Father of Cryptozoology."

CRYPTOZOOLOGY TODAY

Nowadays cryptozoology is all around us. Just a few years ago, only a handful of people even knew the word. Today, from the Internet to the corner newsstand, cryptozoology has become an integral part of our culture. Mainstream magazines such as *BBC Wildlife* now regularly carry articles on hidden animals, and numerous documentaries on PBS, Discovery, A&E, and other television networks treat the subject seriously.

Less seriously but still indicative of cryptozoology's influence, an episode of the popular science-fiction series *X-Files* called "Quagmire" concerned reports of a monster, "Big Blue," at a Georgia reservoir appropriately named "Heuvelmans Lake." In the course of the drama, FBI agents Fox Mulder and Dana Scully debate the pros and cons of "cryptozoology." Though other *X-Files* episodes have employed cryptozoological motifs, this was the first time the word itself passed through the characters' mouths. As the episode ends, a large alligator is destroyed and blamed for the "monster" sightings. The agents turn their backs on the lake just as Big Blue rises from the depths of Heuvelmans Lake in a kind of symbolic representation of what happens often enough in real-life cryptozoology, where many mysteries have a way of staying stubbornly unsolved.

BEGIN YOUR ADVENTURE

Before you start your trek through the following pages and into the world of cryptozoology, we wish to insert some words of caution:

If to many mainstream biologists cryptozoology has yet to make its case, there is reason for such a cautious judgment. Until or unless there is better, more conclusive evidence for the reality of the cryptids with which you will become acquainted in the pages ahead, their status as reality will remain uncertain. Cryptozoological animals are by their nature intensely controversial. Reasonable persons come down on both sides of the debate, and even the authors of this book do not entirely agree about which cryptozoological animals are most likely to coexist, however covertly, alongside us on this crowded planet.

In what follows, we accentuate the positive. For the sake of argument, we take the best available evidence—even if, by the more demanding standards of scientific proof, it may not be satisfactory in one fashion or another—and scrutinize it through the lens of what zoology does know about conventionally recognized animals, living and (allegedly) dead, and early protohumans. Seen that way, even the most exotic reports begin to make a surprising kind of sense—even as they remain unproved and problematic.

Most of the mysteries here are potentially solvable. They demand, however, real commitment, real expertise, real funding, and real open-mindedness to nature's possibilities—the last being a quality not always in evidence in scientists' confrontation of (or, on occasion, unwillingness to confront) the unknown. In the meantime, many curious and intriguing questions nag away like muffled voices just slightly outside the range of hearing. What they are saying to us, we don't know. In the pages you are about to read, we suggest one way of hearing the words.

Loren Coleman
Maine

Jerome Clark
Minnesota

February 23, 1999

A

ABOMINABLE SNOWMAN

When most people ponder on the "big three" of cryptozoology, they are thinking of the **Loch Ness Monsters, Bigfoot,** and the Abominable Snowman. Though many assume these beasts to be mythical, a body of intriguing evidence exists for each. Of the three, the Abominable Snowman is the cryptozoological animal longest known and discussed in the West.

The more proper name is **Yeti,** but most Westerners have been more familiar with the moniker "Abominable Snowman." "Abominable Snowman" is a phrase coined, accidentally, by a *Calcutta Statesman* newspaper columnist, Henry Newman, in 1921.

It happened when Newman wrote about the 1921 sighting by Lieutenant Colonel (later Sir) C. K. Howard-Bury and his party, who saw dark forms moving about on a twenty-thousand-foot-high snowfield above their location, the Lhapka-La pass on the Tibetan side of the Himalayan mountains, and viewed them through binoculars. This is the first credible Western sighting of what until then had been mostly a shadowy tale (at least to Westerners) of strange, hairy upright creatures in Tibet, Bhutan, Sikkim, Mustang, and Nepal. Howard-Bury would later, on September 22, 1921, find footprints "three times those of normal humans" at the site where the dark forms were moving about.

The Sherpas insisted that the prints were those of the *metoh-kangmi,* as Howard-Bury rendered it. *Kang-mi* loosely means "snow creature." The *metoh* part should have been written as *met-teh,* which translates as "man-sized wild creature."

Newman's mistake was caused in part by Howard-Bury's mistransliteration of the Sherpa word. Howard-Bury did not understand that the Sherpas recognized several types of creatures; on this occasion they had used a generic, not a specific, term. The error was compounded when Newman changed Howard-Bury's *metoh-kangmi* to *metch kangmi,* which he explained as a Tibetan word meaning "Abominable Snowman."

In any case, this proved to be a pivotal event in cryptozoological history. As **Ivan T. Sanderson** wrote, "The result was like the explosion of an atomic bomb." The melodramatic name "Abominable Snowman" spurred gigantic press interest. Newspaper coverage multiplied as more and more expeditions sought to climb Mount Everest.

The true origin of the phrase "Abominable Snowman" has been misrepresented over the years. For example, on a 1992 episode of the television series *Unsolved Mysteries,* a well-known Irish explorer wrongly claimed that the creature got its name because of its horrible odor.

The real animal behind the name is neither abominable nor a true creature of the snows. These beasts usually appear to live in quiet retreat in the steamy mountain valleys of the Himalayas, using the snowy passes as a way to move from one spot to another, leaving behind huge mysterious footprints. They are not—contrary to another widespread misunderstanding—white. And they are not a single creature.

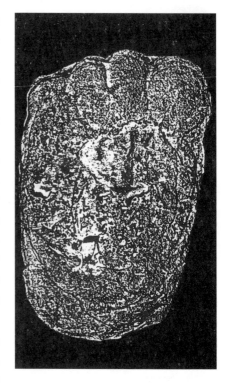

The 1957 footcast of the seven-by-ten-inch track of an Abominable Snowman found in mud, in Nepal, by Tom Slick. Five toes were originally visible, but two blurred in the casting process. (Bernard Heuvelmans)

A better generic term for Abominable Snowman is the Sherpa *yeti,* loosely meaning "that there thing." Yetis are known as huge creatures— humanoid beasts, covered with thick coats of dark fur with arms, like those of anthropoid apes, which reach down to their knees.

A description of the reportedly three types of Yeti is discussed, in depth, within that entry.

AGOGWE

The Agogwe is a little downy, woolly-haired unknown biped reported throughout East Africa. Said to have yellowish, reddish skin underneath its rust colored hair, the Agogwe allegedly inhabits the forest of this remote region.

One of the most discussed sightings occurred around 1900 when Captain William Hichens was sent on an official lion hunt to this region. While there, waiting in a forest clearing for a man-eating lion, he saw (as he would write in 1937) "two small, brown, furry creatures come from the dense forest on one side of the glade and disappear into the thickets on the other. They were like little men, about four feet high, walking upright, but clad in russet hair." The native hunter said they were *agogwe,* the little furry men. Hichens made efforts to find them, but without success, in the impenetrable forest.

In support of Hichens's story, Cuthbert Burgoyne wrote a letter to the London magazine *Discovery* in 1938, noting that he and his wife had seen something similar while coasting Portuguese East Africa in a Japanese cargo boat in 1927. Close enough to shore to see things on the beach using a "glass of twelve magnifications," they spied a troupe of feeding baboons, apparently picking up shellfish or crabs. "As we watched, two little brown men walked together out of the bush and down amongst the baboons. They were certainly not any known monkey and yet they must have been akin or they would have disturbed the baboons. They were too far away to see in detail, but these small human-like animals were probably between four and five feet tall, quite upright and graceful in figure. At the time I was thrilled as they were quite evidently no beast of which I had heard or read. Later a friend and big game hunter told me he was in Portuguese East Africa with his wife and three hunters, and saw a mother, father and child, of apparently a similar animal species, walk across the further side of a bush clearing. The natives loudly forbade him to shoot."

These primitive, hairy, long-haired beings of small size are known by a variety of names throughout Africa. The Agogwe of East Africa match exactly the descriptions of little reddish-haired *sehite* of the Ivory Coast, where, in the 1940s, numerous reports were heard, even though no known pygmies at all live there. The cryptozoologist **Bernard Heuvelmans** believes these small African creatures may be **Proto-Pygmies,** proto-bushmen, or australopithecine (gracile species). In *On the Track of Unknown Animals,* Heuvelmans comments: "Now there is no known ape, even among the anthropoids, which normally walks upright on its hind legs. . . . Perhaps the *agogwe* are therefore really little men."

AHOOL

In 1925 Dr. Ernest Bartels, son of the noted ornithologist M. E. G. Bartels, who discovered many new bird species in Java, was exploring a waterfall on the slopes of the Salek Mountains when a giant unknown bat, the Ahool, flew over his head. Named after its call—a long "ahOOOooool"—this as-yet uncatalogued bat was, according to cryptozoologist **Ivan T. Sanderson,** still reported from time to time. Bartels's account had been passed on to Sanderson by **Bernard Heuvelmans**. In an article about the Ahool written in 1966, Bartels and Sanderson noted that sightings of this giant bat have been reported throughout western Java. According to the locals, the Ahool is quite real and known in several areas; it is not merely a folkloric beast.

The Ahool looks like a huge bat in flight, larger than any known flying fox (a fruit-eating bat). The Ahool, however, is a fish-eater. It allegedly uses its enormous claws—situated at the tops of the forearms, which are part of the wings—to capture large fish from the rivers it lives near. An Ahool is said to be the size of a one-year-old child, dark gray in color, with a head like a macaque or gibbon.

Sanderson thought the Ahool was an Oriental form of the giant unknown bat he had seen in Africa, known most popularly as the **Kongamato,** although he knew the Kongamato as the Olitiau. Sanderson felt the Ahool, like the Olitiau or Kongamato, was an unknown giant bat related to the species *Microchiroptera*.

ALMAS

In the 1420s Hans Schiltberger, a Bavarian nobleman held prisoner by Mongols, took note of the presence, in the Tien Shan mountain range of present-day China, of "wild people who have nothing in common with other human beings." Except for hands and face, they were covered with hair. Subsisting on grass and wild vegetables, they lived like animals. Schiltberger himself saw two of them, a male and a female, whom a warlord had given as a gift to his own captors.

A second early printed reference to a Mongolian "man-animal," as the text calls it, appears in a drawing in a natural history manuscript prepared in China in the late eighteenth century. The serious context, an exposition on local flora and fauna, makes it clear that the creature was not thought to be supernatural or fantastic.

Though unrecognized by science, *almas*—Mongolian for "wildmen"—allegedly dwell in the Altai Mountains in the west of Mongolia and in Tien Shan in the neighboring Chinese province of Sinkiang. They have been the object of periodic attention by individual scientists. In 1913 one of them, V. A. Khakhlov, sent a report of his investigations to the Russian Imperial Academy of Sciences, but it has not survived.

From the 1890s until 1928, another investigator, the ill-fated Leningrad-based professor Tsyben Zhamtsarano, conducted considerable field research into the Almas question, interviewing numerous witnesses. For the crime of being interested in Mongolian culture and folklore, the Soviet regime under Stalin declared him a "bourgeois nationalist" and sent him to the gulag, where he perished around 1940. His field notes, including illustrations (a professional artist had accompanied him to provide sketches based on eyewitness accounts), were lost or destroyed.

Most of what we know about Zhamtsarano's research comes from Dordji Meiren, who participated in some of the work. According to Meiren, sightings began to decline in the nineteenth century, perhaps suggesting that the creatures were retreating into more remote locations in response to population pressures (a view endorsed by a later Mongolian researcher, Y. Rinchen). Meiren also claimed to have seen an Almas skin in a Buddhist monastery in the southern Gobi region of Mongolia. Because the cut was straight down the spine, the features had remained intact. The body was covered with curly red hair except for the face, Meiren said, and its fingernails and toenails resembled those of a human being.

Both adult and young Almas have been reported, according to researcher **Marie-Jeanne Koffmann**. The adults are said to stand approximately five feet tall, with prominent eyebrow ridges and jutting jaws. Almas use simple tools but are without language. Anthropologist Myra Shackley, one of the few Western scientists to pay attention to the question, has proposed the radical hypothesis that the creatures are relict **Neandertals.** Critics of her work, however, point out that she used outdated models of Neandertals, instead of the very different and intelligent, physically human-like Neandertals we are now aware of, to compare to the subhuman Almas. **Mark A. Hall, Loren Coleman, Patrick Huyghe,** and others suggest the answer may lie with the unlikely but possible survival of *Homo erectus* relict populations.

B

BARLOY, JEAN-JACQUES (1939–)

With a doctorate in zoology, specializing in ornithology, Jean-Jacques Barloy is a natural history journalist and the author of hundreds of French articles and a few books dealing with cryptozoology, including *Serpent de mer et monstres aquatiques* (1978), about the **Sea Serpent,** and *Les survivants de l'ombre* (1985), about relict populations of hominids. In the 1980s, in one especially important contribution, he used a computer to analyze data related to the **Beast of Gevaudan.** In France, Barloy often appears on television programs and radio shows to discuss cryptozoology.

BARMANU

During the early 1990s several French expeditions to the Shishi Kuh Valley, in the Chitral region of northern Pakistan, learned of sightings of the *barmanu* ("Big Hairy One"). They also found Barmanu footprints. Zoologist Jordi Magraner, medical doctor Anne Mallasse, and another team member, all Europeans, also heard unusual guttural sounds that they thought could have been uttered by a primitive voice box. Local witnesses claimed they had seen and smelled the animal that made the noises. The expedition leaders later told reporters, "Eyewitnesses shown pictures of a selection of human and humanlike creatures consistently selected the image of a primitive man found preserved in ice some twenty years ago by a Belgian team." This is a confused reference to the allegedly unknown hominoid (or, in skeptics' view, model) that **Bernard Heuvelmans** and **Ivan T. Sanderson** described frozen in a block of ice, known universally as the **Minnesota Iceman.** Further expeditions are planned.

In 1995, after an *Unsolved Mysteries* segment on the Minnesota Iceman, **Loren Coleman,** who consulted for that show, was contacted by Pakistanis who claimed to know where a body just like the one in the program was buried. The informants did not respond to follow-up queries. The link to Pakistan and the Barmanu, not mentioned in the television program, is nonetheless intriguing.

BATUTUT

While in the Malaysian state of Sabah in 1970, the British zoologist **John MacKinnon,** who would become world-renowned for his discoveries of new mammals in Vietnam during the 1990s, found short, broad, human-like but definitely nonhuman footprints of a shy, nocturnal **Proto-Pygmy** similar to Nepal's **Teh-lma.** They were the footprints of what the locals called the *batutut.*

MacKinnon's initial reaction tells us much about how mainstream scientists often deal with evidence of cryptids. "I stopped dead," he would later write in his book *In the Search of the Red Ape.* "My skin crept and I felt a strong desire to head home." But MacKinnon pressed on, noting that "farther ahead I saw tracks and went to examine them. . . . I found two dozen footprints in all [but] was quite happy to abandon my quest and shelter under a leaning tree-trunk waiting out a sudden rainstorm."

MacKinnon later related the Batutut footprints' lasting impact: "I was uneasy when I found them, and I didn't want to follow them and find out what was at the end of the trail. I knew that no animal we know about could make those tracks. Without deliberately avoiding the area I realize I never went back to that place in the following months of my studies."

The Malaysian Batutut appears to demonstrate an extension of the geographic range of the kind of unknown primate also known as the Teh-lma, the tiny frog-eating **Yeti** that lives in the tropical valleys of Nepal.

BAYANOV, DMITRI (1932–)

Born in Moscow, Dmitri Bayanov has emerged as the foremost living Russian cryptozoologist and hominologist. He majored in humanities at

Dmitri Bayanov (left) is shown in 1972, meeting with other researchers (Karapetian, René Dahinden, and Marie-Jeanne Koffmann) discussing the Patterson Film. (FPL)

a teachers college, graduating in 1955. He worked first as a teacher and later as a Russian-English translator. He studied under such individuals as Professor **B. F. Porshnev** and P. P. Smolin, chief curator of the Darwin Museum in Moscow. He took part in **Marie-Jeanne Koffmann**'s expeditions in search of **Almas** in the Caucasus and made reconnaissance trips in the same region on his own. An active member of the Relict Hominoid Research Seminar at the Darwin Museum since 1964, he became the chairman of the seminar in 1975. Bayanov was a founding board member of the **International Society of Cryptozoology** and served on the ISC Board of Directors through 1992.

Through a series of exchanges with his colleagues, Bayanov coined the words **"hominology"** and "hominologists" in the early 1970s to describe the specific study of unknown hominoids and those who study them. Bayanov has recently published *In the Footsteps of the Russian Snowman* (1996) and *America's Bigfoot: Fact, Not Fiction—U.S. Evidence Verified in Russia* (1997).

BEAST OF BODMIN MOOR

One of the most popular subcategories of current cryptozoology, particularly in Britain, is the investigation of what are known as Alien Big Cats, or ABCs. The word "Alien" here is meant to denote large felines that are "out of place," rather than "extraterrestrial"—for instance, a common panther or leopard found somewhere that conventional zoology says it should not be. *Fortean Times* coeditor Paul Sieveking reported that ABC sightings have recently become the hottest topic of interest among the magazine's British readers. Perhaps ABCs are popular because they are a more tangible quarry for British monster-hunters than American creatures like **Bigfoot.** And there are sightings aplenty. Around three hundred occurred in 1996 alone.

In the early 1990s reports started to circulate of ABCs in and around Cornwall, in southwestern England. Bodmin Moor became a kind of nerve center of these sightings and reports of inexplicably slain livestock, and the alleged leopard-like felines of the region became known as the Beast of Bodmin Moor. Talk of dangerous wild cats led Great Britain's Ministry of Agriculture, Fisheries and Food to conduct an official investigation in 1995. The study's findings, released on July 19, concluded that there was "no verifiable evidence" of exotic felines loose in Britain and that the mauled farm animals could have been attacked by common indigenous species. The report did concede, though, that "the investigation could not prove that a 'big cat' is not present."

On July 24, less than a week after the government report, a boy uncovered a startling piece of evidence in Bodmin Moor. Fourteen-year-old Barney Lanyon-Jones, walking with his brothers by the River Fowey at the southern edge of the Moor, saw a strange-looking object bobbing in the river's current. Barney thought it was an oddly shaped rock until he pulled it out of the water and discovered that it was a large cat skull. Measuring about four inches wide and seven inches long, the skull was missing its lower jaw but possessed two sharp, prominent teeth that suggested a leopard. The story hit the national press on July 31, a well-timed counterpoint to the official denial of ABC evidence in Bodmin Moor.

The Lanyon-Jones family turned the skull over to London's British Museum of Natural History for verification. Dr. Ian Bishop, the museum's assistant keeper of zoology, examined it and determined that it was a genuine skull from a young male leopard. But he also found that the cat had not died in Britain. Bishop concluded that the skull had been imported as part of a leopard-skin rug.

The back of the skull had been cleanly cut off in a way that is commonly used to mount the head on a rug, and there was an egg case inside the skull that had been laid by a tropical cockroach that could not possibly be found in Britain's climate. There were also fine cut marks on the skull, indicating that the flesh had been removed with a knife, and the skull had begun to decompose slightly only after a recent submersion in water.

This was not the first time the skull from a mounted trophy had stirred confusion in the search for ABCs. In 1988, two teenage boys found a skull on Dartmoor that was never turned over for official study, but the witness testimony that the back of its skull was missing caused experts to suspect a rug-based origin. In 1993, the Natural History Museum identified a large cat skull found in Exmoor as part of a work of taxidermy. Doug Richardson, assistant curator of mammals at London Zoo, has suggested that a prankster may be planting these skulls on the moors intending to mislead their discoverers.

Sightings of the Beast of Bodmin Moor still continue. In October 1997, officials from Newquay Zoo claimed to identify pawprints left in mud to the south of Bodmin Moor as the fresh tracks of a puma. Soon after that discovery, a photograph allegedly of the Bodmin Beast materialized, which seemed to show an adult female—and apparently pregnant—puma. The photograph, never authenticated or conclusively debunked, remains controversial.

BEAST OF 'BUSCO

Churubusco (near Fort Wayne), Indiana, has been the home for almost sixty years of a legendary **Giant Turtle** with the affectionate nickname Beast of 'Busco, or Oscar. The turtle allegedly lives in Falk Lake. Over the years many hunters have tried to catch it without success. 'Busco is said to have measured about four feet across the shell, and to weigh between one hundred and five hundred pounds. A spate of sightings in 1949 attracted national press attention.

In his *Natural Mysteries,* **Mark A. Hall** takes note of reports of another Giant Turtle in Indiana. In July 1950, a surveyor for Lake County,

Samuel E. Brownsten, and farmer Henry "Potato King" Ewen were draining one of four swamps at Black Oak, near Hammond, to convert them to farmland. The two men made an opening into a culvert (thirty inches wide) into the Little Calumet River. Soon the drain was clogged with frogs and fish, and as the men tried to unplug it, they noticed something bigger. It was approaching them, and when it got close enough, Brownsten reported, "We saw a turtle. Its head was as big as a human's."

Ewen added: "It was too big to even get into the thirty-inch drain. I tried to help it. I pushed on its shell, but man, when I saw the size of that thing, I knew I didn't want to tangle with it. It was as big as a beer barrel."

Hall speculates that the draining of swamps across the South and Midwest destroyed the habitat of many old, large turtles, forcing them to move closer and closer to human communities. While the reported sizes of the American mystery turtles sound extraordinary, they are well within the range of those associated with the alligator snapping turtle (*Macrochelys temminicki*). These giant turtles can measure up to two hundred pounds routinely, and one individual found in 1937, in Kansas in the Neosho River, weighed 403 pounds.

BEAST OF GEVAUDAN

In the mid-1760s the ravages of a large, ferocious animal sent panic through a mountainous area of south-central France known as Le Gevaudan. The creature was described in a contemporary account as "much higher than a wolf, low before, and his feet are armed with talons. His hair is reddish, his head large, and the muzzle of it is shaped like that of a greyhound; his ears are small and straight; his breast is wide and gray; his back streaked with black; his large mouth is provided with sharp teeth." Thought by many terrified peasants to be a *loup-garou* ("werewolf"), it left the bloody remains of many men, women, and children in its wake.

The panic began in June 1764 with the killings following in July. As the slaughter went on, the story spread that the creature could not be brought down by knife, lance, or bullet. Hunters reported shooting it at close range, only to watch it run away to reappear elsewhere soon afterward.

Eventually, King Louis XV sent a cavalry troop to the region. The

The Beast of Gevaudan is shown in an illustration made during the time of the mystery attacks. (FPL)

soldiers observed the "beast of Gevaudan" on several occasions and managed to fire on it. Though it escaped each time, the depredations gradually stopped, and the soldiers, concluding that the animal had died of its wounds, departed. Soon, however, it was back.

Lured by a big reward posted for the killing of the beast, hunters scoured the countryside. Some saw the creature and swore they had wounded it. Others killed any wolf that crossed their paths. Nothing seemed to work. As the panic spread, entire villages were abandoned. By now the episode had become an international sensation. The English periodical *St. James's Chronicle* was not alone in speculating that some "new Species" neither wolf nor tiger nor hyena had been set loose in the French provinces.

By the time it was brought down, on the evening of June 19, 1767, the beast of Gevaudan had slain some sixty persons, many of them children who had been guarding their parents' sheep flocks. The man who killed it, Jean Chastel, a member of a hunting party organized by the

Marquis d'Apcher, used silver bullets in the belief that the creature was a *loup-garou*. When the animal's stomach was opened, it was found to contain a small child's collar bone.

The creature's death caused understandable jubilation in the afflicted peasant communities. The hunters who had run it down paraded its putrefying remains through the region for the next two weeks before delivering it to the royal court in Versailles. By this time it stank so badly that the king ordered it to be disposed of immediately. Buried in an unknown location, the remains have never been recovered, sparking more than two centuries of speculation about the creature's identity.

In 1960, after studying a notary report prepared by two surgeons who had examined the carcass in the 1700s, one authority determined that the creature's teeth were purely wolflike. But during the summer of 1997, discussion of the fur of the Beast of Gevaudan resurfaced. Franz Jullien, a taxidermist at the National Museum of Natural History in Paris, discovered that a stuffed specimen similar to the Beast of Gevaudan that had been shot by Jean Chastel had been kept in the collections of the museum from 1766 to 1819. It had been definitely identified, a fact that all researchers had overlooked. It was a striped hyena (*Hyaena hyaena*).

Novelist Henri Pourrat and naturalist Gerard Menatory had already proposed the hyena hypothesis, based on historical accounts, since Antoine Chastel (Jean Chastel's son) reportedly possessed such an animal in his menagerie, a hypothesis now supported by a zoologist's identification. While Jullien's rediscovery must be congratulated, questions remain about the role of the Chastels as creators of a false story involving an escaped hyena in order to cover the rumors of one of the Chastels being a serial killer.

BERGMAN'S BEAR

Reports of a giant bear of Kamchatka, a "God Bear" in Russian folk traditions, have circulated for centuries. In recent years, indeed, some scientific evidence has emerged to validate reports of a cryptid known as Bergman's Bear.

In 1920 the Swedish zoologist Sten Bergman examined the skin of a giant, black-furred variety of the Kamchatka bear. Bergman, who spent two years studying Kamchatkan wildlife, wrote that the pelt "far surpassed" the size of any bearskin he had ever seen. Most notably, the black bear's pelt was shorthaired, unlike the long coat of the normal Kamchatka bear. Bergman's 1936 paper also described a huge pawprint, 14.5 inches by 10 inches and a report of an equally outsized skull. David Day, in his book *Vanished Species,* lists this animal, *Ursus arctos piscator,* as "Extinct, ca. 1920." No specimens have been collected since Bergman wrote in 1936. The animal may well be extinct.

On the other hand, it may not be. In *Bears of the World* (1988), Terry Domico observes that much of the Kamchatka Peninsula has long been closed off for military reasons. A former Soviet official who did have access to the area told Domico that the black giants were still reported. Domico also suggests the giants are a variant of the brown bear. Unfortunately, without a specimen this can be only conjecture.

BESSIE

For some time people have been reporting an unknown creature—later nicknamed South Bay Bessie or just plain Bessie—in Lake Erie. It is described as gray, snakelike, and thirty to forty feet long. Though sightings have been logged in recent years, the monster is known mostly from historical accounts.

"For a number of years, vague stories about huge serpents have come with each recurring season from Dominion [Canadian] shores, and now, at last, the existence of these fierce monsters is verified and the fact so well established that it can no longer be questioned," wrote a reporter in the July 8, 1898, edition of the *Daily Register* of Sandusky, Ohio.

The **Lake Monster** reported that year was able to live both on land and in water. It was a "fierce, ugly, coiling thing, call it a snake or what you will." It was said to be twenty-five to thirty feet long and at least a foot in diameter.

By 1912 the monster had become the source of local practical jokes. A *Daily Register* article published in the spring of that year recounts an encounter between Kelleys Island residents and a large "sea" monster that broke through a sheet of lake ice and headed for shore. Witnesses described a black object with a huge head, gaping mouth, and a row of teeth. The story's last line read "April first," its date of publication and the reason for the tale.

At other times the newspaper was at the receiving end of a hoax. The July 22, 1931, edition of the *Register* stated: "Sandusky was all agog Tuesday night because it was reported that the sea serpent, supposed to be in the waters of Sandusky Bay, had been captured." A *New York Times* reporter who happened to be visiting the town that day picked up the story. As the story portrayed it, two vacationing men from Cincinnati saw the **Sea Serpent** while on a boat on Lake Erie. The two frightened men clubbed the animal into submission, brought it aboard, and placed it in a crate.

Harold Madison, curator of the Cleveland Museum of Natural History, journeyed to Sandusky and pronounced the "sea serpent" an Indian python. The two men quickly left town. Further investigation revealed that the men, one of whom had family ties in Sandusky, worked for a touring carnival.

Still, stories of the monster persisted, either in spite or because of the hoaxes perpetrated in its name. Sightings were reported in 1960, 1969, 1981, 1983, 1985, and 1989. A flurry of reports occurred in 1990, including a sighting by two Huron firefighters.

By 1993 monster mania was in full swing. National media grabbed hold of the story. The *Wall Street Journal* took a cynical approach to the sightings. It ran an article, published on July 29, characterizing the excitement as a clever marketing ploy to draw tourists into the small town of Huron as they sped toward Cedar Point.

Huron did take a particular interest in the beast, and the city soon produced a crop of pseudocryptozoologists and declared itself the National Live Capture and Control Center for the Lake Erie Monster. Tom Solberg of the Huron Lagoons Marina offered a $100,000 reward for the safe and unharmed capture of the beast. The reward has never been claimed.

David Davies, a fisheries biologist for the Ohio Division of Wildlife, spends much of his time on the lake. "It's probably something closely related to a dinosaur. It looks like a brontosaurus, don't you think?" he joked when a reporter asked him what the Lake Erie Monster could be.

More seriously, Davies thinks the animal is a large specimen of the lake sturgeon. Lake sturgeon can grow to be 150 years old, exceed seven feet in length, and weigh more than three hundred pounds.

Caviar comes from the eggs of sturgeon. The Sandusky lakeshore was home to so many lake sturgeon in the 1800s that it was known as the caviar capital of North America. The sturgeon was fished nearly out of existence on Erie, but it is now making a comeback. In the summer of 1998, a fisherman off New York's Lake Erie coast caught a seven-foot, four-inch, 250-pound sturgeon.

"They do look prehistoric," Davies said. "In fact, they very much resemble their prehistoric ancestors." Where other fish have scales, the lake sturgeon has boney plates. The plates give the fish a reptilian, leathery look. The sturgeon is a bottom feeder, though it rises occasionally to the surface of the water. Its tail could conceivably be interpreted as the neck of a great sea monster when it rises over the water's surface. Its fins could be imagined as its undulating body.

Few reports of Bessie have been made since 1993.

BIG BIRD

The "Big Bird" that overflew the Rio Grande Valley in January 1976 got its name from the *Sesame Street* character. Witnesses described it as, however, less amiable than its television counterpart. Some called it "horrible looking." It was at least five feet tall, with wings folded around its body and large red eyes on a "gorilla-like" face. While it may have been big, it hardly seemed a bird.

When Alverico Guajardo of Brownsville, Texas, encountered it on the evening of January 7, 1976, he thought it looked something like a giant bat. A week later, at Raymondville, Armando Grimaldo heard a "sound like the flapping of batlike wings and a funny kind of whistling." Suddenly big claws gripped his back and ripped his shirt. The assailant was a flying creature with leathery skin. It had a monkey-like face, but unlike the creature reported by Guajardo, it had no beak. Grimaldo fled under a tree, and the creature flew away.

Sightings like these arose out of murky folk traditions about a large evil bird that sometimes attacks people. During the Big Bird scare theorists ascribed the sightings to various conventional causes, such as great blue herons and pelicans. There is good reason to believe that at least some reports can be so explained, though they do not fit the profile for the more exotic sightings, like Guajardo's or Grimaldo's.

BIGFOOT

Bigfoot is unquestionably North America's biggest cryptozoological mystery. But we have had to learn to share it with the world; the name Bigfoot is applied to any hairy unknown hominoid reported today anywhere around the globe. For our purposes, however, "Bigfoot" denotes those unknown hairy hominids reported in the Pacific Northwest of the United States and believed to leave large human-like footprints and to walk upright.

But it was not always so, even in North America. The Canadian version of Bigfoot, called **"Sasquatch,"** has an even longer history. According to researchers **John Green** and **Ivan T. Sanderson,** this

One contemporary interpretation of Bigfoot's likely appearance. (William M. Rebsamen)

Indian-sounding word was coined in the 1920s by J. W. Burns, a teacher who for years collected stories about wild, hairy giants from his Chehalis Indian friends. Burns combined several similar Native Canadians' names for these creatures and created the word "Sasquatch." In recent years, scientists and folklorists looking to bring respectability to the subject have been using that more sober-sounding name. But most North Americans still call these creatures "Bigfoot."

The first use of the now widely used label did not occur until a quiet, churchgoing construction worker named Jerry Crew appeared at a northern California newspaper office with the plaster cast of one of many large hominid footprints he had found in the mud in Bluff Creek Valley. His widely reprinted account—and photograph holding the massive footcast, which stretched across his upper torso—first appeared in the *Humboldt Times,* along with the word "Bigfoot," on October 5, 1958. The story was written by the paper's "RFD" columnist and editor Andrew Genzoli, who introduced the word "Bigfoot," as the road construction workers were calling this big-footed creature, to the outside world.

The naming of Bigfoot was a significant cultural event. To deny this would be to ignore how intrinsic Bigfoot has become in global day-to-day living, as evidenced in scores of examples. Today Bigfoot can be seen used as a name for skateboards, pizza, big trucks, and other commercial products. Since the advent of Bigfoot, the word has made it easier for law-enforcement officers, media reporters, and the general public to accept sightings of all kinds of unknown hairy hominoids.

The classic Bigfoot of the Pacific Northwest is reported, in the most concentrated fashion, in the northern corner of the United States (northern California, Oregon, Washington, and Idaho) and far western Canada (British Columbia and Alberta), with lesser activity up through Canada into Alaska. In the vastness of these montane forests, the idea that an undiscovered, extraordinary primate could survive, albeit fantastic, is at least imaginable.

Bigfoot is bulky and stocky, with an enormous barrel torso and a height, when mature, of six to nine feet. The creature has a small, pointed head, with no neck or forehead. Its eyes are small, round, and dark, and stare forward. The face is light in young, dark in older individuals, with a heavy brow ridge and a continuous upcurled fringe of hair on the brow ridge. The hair covering is shaggy. There is no difference between body and head hair. All of it is relatively short, with darker colored hair at younger ages, moving into red-browns with some evidence of silver at extreme maturity. The distinctive footprint, as the name implies, shows a track as left by a giant five-toed human foot. The average length is fourteen to sixteen inches long. When the first Bigfoot incidents, noted above, occurred in October 1958, the massive tracks in the mud near Bluff Creek, California, all measured sixteen inches long and were seven inches wide.

Bigfoot is generally nocturnal and mostly solitary, although some sightings have reported family groups. From their calls it appears that they have no language. They emit high-pitched whistles, calls, animal-like screams, howls, *"eeek-eeek-eeek," "sooka-sooka-sooka," "ugh-ugh-ugh,"* or *"uhu-uhu-uhu."* According to Sanderson and other chroniclers, the creatures may on occasion kidnap human females (and, at least according to some folk traditions, males).

Californian and Canadian Indians have many folktales that arguably refer to the Bigfoot and Sasquatch. Sanderson believed that the description of the California hairy big man, *oh-mah,* closely matched those of Bigfoot.

One of the most often told, most spectacular accounts is Albert Ostman's. Ostman, a British Columbia man, came forward in 1957 to recount an incident that he said had taken place in 1924. While on a prospecting trip at the head of Toba Inlet, opposite Vancouver Island, he was gathered up one night inside his sleeping bag and after many miles dumped out, to discover that he was the captive of a family—adult male and female, juvenile male and female—of giant apelike creatures. Though they were friendly, they clearly did not want him to escape from their canyon home, and he managed to do so only after six days when the older male choked on Ostman's snuff tobacco. Those who interviewed Ostman did not doubt his sincerity or sanity, and Sasquatch investigator Green, biologist Sanderson, and Smithsonian anthropologist John Napier all separately wrote that his account was convincing and did not sound false.

Late in the 1950s, Sanderson wrote two articles for *Argosy,* a men's adventure magazine, calling Bigfoot "America's Abominable Snowman." He caught the American imagination, and hundreds of people wrote him for more details. Sanderson followed up with his *Abominable Snowmen: Legend Come to Life* (1961), the first book to discuss Bigfoot/Sasquatch in any comprehensive manner, and linked the North American reports with worldwide traditions of other hairy hominoids such as **Almas** and **Yeti.**

Among those who went looking for Bigfoot after they read the first *Argosy* article was Roger Patterson, a rodeo rider and author of *Do Abominable Snowmen of America Really Exist?* (1966). Patterson's searching paid off and he, along with companion Bob Gimlin, filmed the now famous **Patterson Film** of a large female Bigfoot on October 20, 1967.

Patterson died in 1972, swearing to the authenticity of both sighting and film. Gimlin, still alive, also sticks by the story. The first investigator

Bob Titmus (center) with Bruce Berryman (left) and Syl McCoy (right) examine a collection of the unknown hairy primate's footcasts. (John Green)

on the site, **Bob Titmus,** found tracks corresponding exactly to the creature's route as depicted in the film and made casts of ten of them.

Intriguingly, the two most historically significant Bigfoot incidents—Crew's first finds in 1958 and the Patterson Film of 1967—took place near each other at Bluff Creek, California. The sets of footprints from both events show similar but not identical creatures were involved. Unfortunately, as the years have seen copies of these two sets of prints mass-copied, hoaxers have employed plaster casts of these genuine tracks to create some confusing hoaxes throughout the United States and Canada.

Most tracks of Pacific Northwest Bigfoot, however, show distinctive forensic features that to investigators indicate they are not fakes. The occurrence of tracks in remote, seldom-traveled areas also argues against the hoax hypothesis.

Other evidence consists of feces and hair samples associated either with sightings or with other indications of a Bigfoot's recent passage. Some of these have been identified and linked with human beings or known animals. In a few cases the samples seemed to resist such identification. In one analysis by a **Tom Slick**–sponsored Bigfoot expedition, fecal matter was found to contain parasites that were unknown, thus indicating they were from an unknown animal.

If Bigfoot is out there, it is almost certainly a relative of ours.

Sanderson classified these creatures as Neo-Giants, giant unknown primates, an analysis echoed by **Loren Coleman, Mark A. Hall,** and **Patrick Huyghe.** (The truly huge Bigfoot is what researcher Hall calls **True Giant.**) **Grover Krantz** theorizes that Bigfoot is an example of a relict population of the long-extinct Ice Age giant apelike creature, *Gigantopithecus*. In *Big Footprints* (1992), Krantz argues that no new name is needed for Bigfoot, since the animal responsible for Bigfoot sightings is already known, though thought extinct. Krantz holds that "we in fact have footprints of *Gigantopithecus blacki* here in North America." Bigfooters, those currently hunting Bigfoot with guns and cameras, accept the *Gigantopithecus* argument because Krantz's thoughts on the matter were widely disseminated in the 1980s and early 1990s.

However, with the publication of a new field guide to Bigfoot and similar creatures by Loren Coleman and Patrick Huyghe, the idea that Bigfoot may be a man-sized hominid named *Paranthropus* is gaining new attention. The notion was first proposed in scientific journals in 1971, when anthropologically oriented cryptozoologist Gordon Strasenburgh wrote that Bigfoot would be found to be related to *Paranthropus robustus*. He proposed the name *Paranthropus eldurrelli* to be specifically used for the Pacific Northwest Bigfoot. Because of the apparent sagittal crest of the Bigfoot in the Patterson film, this candidate is getting a new look. If its existence is ever proven—and nothing short of an actual specimen will satisfy most scientists—it would, at the very least, provide revolutionary insights into human evolution.

All of these prehistoric fossil primates may have affinities to Bigfoot because of certain features, such as the overall size of *Gigantopithecus* and the body size and crests on the heads of *Paranthropus*. But until a body is scientifically examined, the riddle of Bigfoot will continue as one of cryptozoology's biggest and most famous enigmas.

BILLE, MATTHEW A. (1959–)

Editor of *Exotic Zoology,* Matthew A. Bille is also the author of *Rumors of Existence* (1995), on recent zoological discoveries (like the **megamouth** and the **coelacanth**) as well as various **cryptids** still unknown to science (such as mysterious whales, one of his specialties). *Rumors of Existence* was his first book. He is working on a second book, on cryptocetology, the study of hidden or undiscovered whales. Most of his previous

Matthew A. Bille with a rare Cuban ground iguana. (Tricia Childers)

publications have been articles and professional papers on space technology.

BLACK PANTHERS

Animals called "Black Panthers" are reported throughout the world, as mystery felids, when they are seen in locations which they are not normally said to inhabit. Technically, the known cats labeled black panthers that are seen in zoos, wildlife documentaries, and in their native habitat are actually black or melanistic leopards, or less frequently, black or melanistic jaguars.

To confuse matters even further, "panther" is a term synonymous with mountain lion, puma, cougar, or painter; all denote the same animal, a tawny (not a black) felid. No scientifically verified specimen of a black mountain lion is known to exist or is accepted by zoology.

Melanistic mystery cats seen in the wilds of North America, however, are often called, popularly, Black Panthers and have been sighted for decades. These big black cats may be an undiscovered group of felids, the Pleistocene's *Panthera atrox,* which are intelligent, behave aggressively, have a taste for livestock, and avoid human beings when possible.

Seen in places they should not be, mysterious Black Panthers have been reported throughout eastern North America. (Loren Coleman)

The *atrox* males may have manes, and the females sometimes, perhaps often, are black.

BLUE TIGER

Harry R. Caldwell's *Blue Tiger* caused a sensation when it was published in 1925, and seventy-five years later it has not entirely gone away. Caldwell, a big-game hunter and Methodist missionary to China, wrote of his close encounter with one of the blue cats mentioned in the title. The incident occurred in September 1910, in the Futsing region of Fujian Province, when his attention was directed to a blue object, which he at first took to be the blue in a man's clothes. On second look he found that the blue was the body of the tiger.

Caldwell described it this way: "The markings of the animal were marvelously beautiful. The ground color seemed a deep shade of maltese, changing into almost deep blue on the under parts. The stripes were well defined, and so far as I was able to make out similar to those of a tiger of the regular type."

He tried to get a shot off, but two boys were in the line of fire. By the time he changed position, the tiger had slipped away. Caldwell said other sightings of the Blue Tiger were reported from the same region, but that was to be his only sighting of it.

According to **Bernard Heuvelmans,** these large Blue Tigers have been "persistently" reported from China since the 1920s. Similar accounts of Black Tigers, which are also known only from sightings and not from any physical evidence, have been recorded from India, Java, Burma, and China since the 1800s. For example, in an 1889 issue of the *Journal of the Bombay Natural History Society,* the famous naturalist C. T. Buckland reported that in March 1846, in the region around Chittagong, India, a Black Tiger killed a local man. It—or one very much like it—was killed with a poison arrow. When he went to examine the body, Buckland found it, bloated and fly-infested, along the road near Tipperah, two miles from Chittagong. He took no skin or photographs, so all that is known of the matter is what he wrote about it.

As recently as 1998, unknown black mystery cats were being reported in China. News accounts in late November related that black felines were killing livestock in the Qinling Mountains in northwest China's Shaanxi Province. Liu Shifeng, a professor of biology from Northwest China University, on his way to the Qinling Mountains to investigate, said that if the mystery felids are proved real, they will constitute a major zoological discovery. In 1984, he told a reporter, a hunter informed him that he had killed a black-panther–like animal on the hillside near his house in Taibai.

Heuvelmans suggests that the color in Blue or Black Tigers may be caused by melanism. Because no official verdict exists and we know relatively little about the animals, these large cats remain cryptids.

BONDEGEZOU

For Western scientists this former **cryptid**'s story begins in the late 1980s, when Tim Flannery, a senior research scientist with the Australia Museum in Sydney, received a photograph showing an unknown creature known locally as the *bondegezou* ("man of the forests"), from the Mauke Mountain Range of Irian Jaya, the Indonesian province of New Guinea. Flannery immediately recognized it as a young tree kangaroo. But it was not until May 1994, when he conducted a sponsored survey of the wildlife of the region, that he realized the animal in the picture was new to zoology.

Located in dense, mossy pine forest about ten thousand to eleven thousand feet up on the southern slopes of the Moni people's homeland, the bondegezou is a boldly colored marsupial with a white star in the middle of its forehead, two white blazes across its black muzzle, a striking white underbelly, and long black fur over its back and head. Males are around thirty inches tall and weigh about thirty pounds. The tail is the shortest for any kangaroo relative to body size, at twenty inches, and though adapted well for tree life, the bondegezou lives mostly on the ground. It descends from trees like a human being with hind legs first. When threatened, it puts its arms over its head, showing its white belly and sounding off at the same time with a whistle.

While the Moni tribe, who revere it, do not kill it, apparently the neighboring Dani do. And it is from the Dani that Flannery received his first real evidence of the bondegezou, in the form of skins and assorted trophies. In June 1994, Flannery returned to the Australian Museum with "remnants" of five of the tree kangaroos, thus moving this cryptid known only to the local natives to the status of an accepted animal within Western zoology. Although a formal scientific journal description has yet to be submitted, Flannery and a group of Indonesian zoological museum researchers decided to release the announcement of the discovery to the press in July 1994. To date no bondegezou exists in captivity.

BRITISH COLUMBIA SCIENTIFIC CRYPTOZOOLOGY CLUB

Founded in 1989 by writer **James A. Clark,** marine biologist **Paul LeBlond,** and television documentarian **John Kirk,** the British Columbia Scientific Cryptozoology Club (BCSCC) is a broadly based membership of enthusiasts interested in the investigation of various animals as yet unidentified by science. It publishes a quarterly, *CryptoNews*. Kirk is its current president.

The group holds that British Columbia produces more sightings and reports of unknown terrestrial and aquatic animals per capita than any other locale in the world. Unidentified animals have been reported in more than thirty lakes around the province, and sightings of **Bigfoot/Sasquatch** and a marine **cryptid** dubbed **Caddy** or Cadborosaurus are legion.

Regular meetings are held in a variety of British Columbia cities, with special guest speakers well-versed in cryptozoology or allied fields holding the floor. The BCSCC is the annual joint-organizer, along with the Vancouver Sasquatch Society, Columbia Brewery, and the North American Science Institute, of the International Sasquatch Symposium held in various venues around the city of Vancouver, most recently on the University of British Columbia campus.

Club members have participated in four expeditions to Okanagan Lake to obtain evidence for the existence of **Ogopogo,** a large aquatic animal said to resemble the **Sea Serpent** reported for centuries. Seven club members have sighted the creature on several occasions, and some interesting footage of the animal has been recorded on videotape. BCSCC Sasquatch investigation director Anthony Vanzuilekom has found a footprint as well as hairs that may belong to the enigmatic hominid.

Postal Address: BCSCC
c/o Suite 89, 6141 Willingdon Avenue
Burnaby, British Columbia V5H 2T9
Canada

BROSNIE

According to news reports that circulated in late 1996, residents of Benyok, 250 miles northwest of Moscow, had reported a **Lake Monster** for almost 150 years. It was, they claimed, a huge aquatic beast, Brosnie, which lived at the bottom of Lake Brosno and occasionally rose to the surface.

In one incident in 1996, a family of tourists camping near the lake took a photograph after the seven-year-old son shouted that he had seen a dragon monster. *Caravan-1,* a newspaper in Tver, the nearest large community, published the picture—a panoramic view of the lake with an indistinct object floating in the foreground—and the story flourished in the Russian media. "It was big like this," said a resident, identified as Tanya, as she sketched a snakelike head rising from the water with a large eye on its side. Curiosity-seekers flocked to the lake in hopes of catching a glimpse of the serpentine creature, estimated to be thirteen to sixteen feet long.

Local people say that written reports attest to Lake Monster sightings at Brosno dating back to 1854. Oral traditions suggest a monster in the lake even earlier than that. Russian zoologists, however, asserted that the photograph showed nothing more than a log. Brosnie, they stated, is a mere "fairy tale."

BUNYIP

The Bunyip, a legendary, elusive, creature, figures in reports that range back in time into the oral folklore of the Aboriginal people of Australia and continue into the present day. Particularly intriguing reports have come from around Lake George and Lake Bathurst, both near the Australian Capital Territory, a place notorious for sightings of other cryptids such as Alien Big Cats, **Yowie,** and even the **Queensland Tiger.** Interestingly, Lake George and Lake Bathurst are sacred places to Aboriginal people of the area.

What is a Bunyip? "Not an easy question to answer," remarked cryptozoologist **Bernard Heuvelmans** in 1955 in *On the Track of Unknown Animals*. It is no simpler to find a solution almost half a century later. The word itself means "bogey" in Australia today and seems to have an

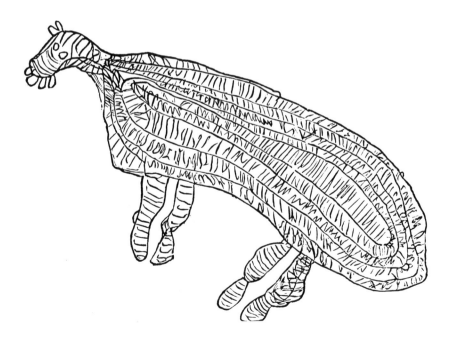

An Australian aboriginal drawing of a Bunyip made in 1848. (FPL)

Aborigine origin meaning something like "devil" or "spirit." Heuvelmans thought it came from the word *buynil,* which Victorian-era Aborigines used for their Supreme Being. Over time, European colonists used Bunyip to refer to any mysterious animal. But down through the years, the word "Bunyip" has mostly been employed to describe one cryptid that has been reported for more than two hundred years in Australia. Generally it has been described as a large, hairy, semi-aquatic creature with the head of a horse. The body of the creature is generally not reported because sightings occur within rivers or lakes. Nevertheless, in some eyewitness encounters, a few good views of the creature have occurred, reports Charles Barrett, in his classic, *The Bunyip* (1946).

During the 1800s, several close-up sightings of the Bunyip occurred in New South Wales. Lake George was the frequent location for many sightings of the Bunyip, especially in the 1830s. Nearby, early in April 1872, a shepherd camped at Midgeon Lagoon saw a strange, fast-swimming beast, much larger than a retriever dog, covered with shining, long jet-black hair. It was tailless but had large ears. A Melbourne Zoo expedition of 1890 failed to capture a Bunyip frequently seen in the Euroa district near Victoria. Similar water monsters have been reported from Tasmania, and Heuvelmans mentions Bunyip sightings as recently as 1932, near the large hydroelectric dams there.

The *Oxford Companion to Australian Literature* defines the Bunyip rather nicely as "a monster of Aboriginal mythology with a huge body covered with fur . . . said to live in swamps, lagoons and billabongs from which it emerges on moonlit nights to prey on humans, especially women and children." Cryptozoologists find no basis in fact for the aggressive behavior traits the dictionary attributes to the Bunyip.

BURU

The Buru is a large, unknown monitor lizard thought by some to have lived in remote valleys of the Himalayas of Assam, a province in the northeastern corner of India. Reported routinely during the 1940s, Burus allegedly looked, in most descriptions, something like twenty-foot aquatic versions of the **Komodo dragon.** Witnesses who heard them said they emitted hoarse, bellowing calls.

In 1948 London's *Daily Mail* dispatched the Buru Expedition to the Himalayas with the hope that it would return with physical evidence of the animals. The expedition's members included such notables as Charles Stonor, a professional zoologist, and Ralph Izzard, a journalist who would later write *The Hunt for the Buru* (1951). Though they failed to uncover any solid evidence for the creatures, they did hear enough testimony of earlier encounters to persuade **Bernard Heuvelmans** that these unidentified monitors may be only recently extinct.

Heuvelmans points out that current sightings describe a similar regional beast, what the natives call a *jhoor,* from the Gir region of India. Other sightings of large, unknown monitor lizards are known in Bhutan, whose king claims to have seen one, as well as in Burma.

C

CADDY

The waters off the Pacific Northwest coast of North America are said to be the home of a specific form of **Sea Serpent,** dubbed Cadborosaurus by Victoria, British Columbia, newspaper editor Archie Willis in the early 1930s. The large snakelike creature, now known more popularly as Caddy, has been seen from Alaska to Oregon, with most of the reported sightings occurring in the inland waters around Vancouver Island and

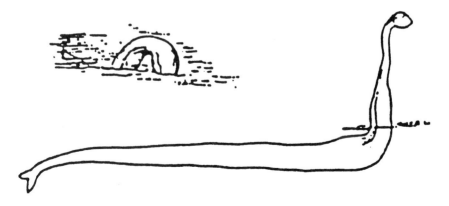

An 1897 drawing of Caddy sketched by witnesses Osmond Fergusson and D. Mattison. (FPL)

the northern Olympic Peninsula, especially in Cadboro Bay, near British Columbia's capital city of Victoria. Sighted many times over the centuries, Caddy also figures in Aboriginal legend. In addition, some suggestive petroglyphs from Aboriginal sources seem to depict the animal.

After years of study, Vancouver biologist Edward L. Bousfield and **Paul H. LeBlond,** a professor of oceanography at the University of British Columbia, put together a composite description of the creature based on numerous sightings. They found Caddy is basically fifteen to forty-five feet in length, serpentine, with flexibility in the vertical plane, having a horselike or camel-like head, a long neck, vertical humps or loops in the body, a pair of side flippers, spikes on a flukelike tail, and an ability to swim at speeds of forty knots.

What is Caddy? Theories range from a descendant of the Jurassic giant sea reptiles to a type of the prehistoric, now supposedly extinct, ancient serpentine-shaped whale, the **zeuglodon,** to tourists drinking too much. The Pacific Northwest borders one of the deepest undersea trenches in the world, and the region has a rugged coastline, with infrequently visited inlets and bays.

Bousfield speculates that Caddy can breathe underwater like a turtle. Perhaps, he suspects, the females come to the shores of shallow estuaries to bear live young. More than three hundred sightings are known. There is also an apparently authentic report of a capture (and release) of an immature specimen.

No evidence for Caddy, however, is as compelling as the so-called Naden Harbor carcass, named thusly after the location in British Columbia where it was examined. Photographs survive of a unique specimen that was pulled from the stomach of a whale in 1937. Records at the time tell of the "creature of reptilian appearance" being ten and a half feet long with a head like that of "a large dog with features of a horse and the turn-down nose of a camel." In 1937, the matter of the Naden Harbor "sea serpent carcass" was quickly quieted when a museum said it was nothing more than material from a premature baleen whale. Later scientists would question this suggestion, but by then the carcass had been thrown out. During the 1990s, Bousfield and LeBlond would point to this apparently misidentified sample from the stomach of a sperm whale as physical proof of Caddy's existence. From their analysis of this evidence, Bousfield and LeBlond have classified the specimen as *Cad-*

borosaurus willsi. But since the discovery of the Naden Harbor carcass, no one has brought a dead Caddy in for further scientific examination.

Nevertheless, sightings of Caddy do continue to occur almost every summer. One of the most recent took place on July 17, 1998, when Hugh and Sally Campbell saw a sea monster in Saanich Inlet.

"I'm a believer now," Campbell told the Victoria, British Columbia, *Times Colonist.* He was boating with his wife and daughters as Cadborosaurus rose from the calm waters at 5:30 P.M. "My wife saw the water moving and then saw this thing round and black. It was quite fat, more than a foot across. It has stepped fins on its back." The Campbells were about halfway between the cement plant and Senanus Island, en route to spread their dead son's ashes.

The monster quickly disappeared, but five minutes later his daughter pointed to "two heads." When Campbell looked, he saw two dark objects like coils and then they disappeared. Farther up the inlet the witnesses heard a commotion on shore and a swooshing sound.

"My wife is 100 percent sure of what she saw," he said. "We have all seen other sea life and it was none of that. It wasn't a seal or otter."

Bousfield links Caddy to **Ogopogo,** the frequently encountered cryptid of Lake Okanagan, British Columbia. Both animals are supposed to have a serpentine body with humps or coils, horselike head, flippers, and split tail—indications that they are related, in Bousfield's view. The animal "has also been seen in nine different British Columbia lakes. The connection with Ogopogo is that where you find these sightings, you find sea-run salmon. If there are not as many sightings now, it could be that it is going into a low-ebb [population density] cycle the same as the salmon are.

"It's real, but it's extremely rare and difficult to study," says Bousfield. "The problem is all our information is from amateurs. We need the scientists to get involved."

CASSIE

Just as an assortment of lake monsters have taken on the names **Tessie, Bessie,** and such to echo Nessie (the **Loch Ness Monster**), so, too, have a few members of the ocean-dwelling **Sea Serpent** tribe. **Caddy** off the coast of British Columbia and Chessie from the Chesapeake Bay are two of the more famous ones. A lesser-known sea monster is Cassie, the

Casco Bay Sea Serpent of Maine. Cassie is known from a growing body of reports dating back to the eighteenth century in the Northeast.

As **Bernard Heuvelmans** remarks, most of the sightings for the hundred years between 1777 and 1877 were in New England, with two-thirds of those off Maine (though it was the Massachusetts reports that attracted the most attention). Off Maine, in Broad Bay in 1751 and in Penobscot Bay in 1779, men fishing the Atlantic coastal shelf sighted sea serpents. During June and July 1818 others claimed to have seen a sea serpent in Portland Bay. Many sightings occurred off Woods Island, Maine, in the early 1900s. Eastport, Maine, hosted encounters in the late 1930s and in 1940.

Loren Coleman wrote the first article published about Cassie in *Portland Monthly* (May 1986). In it he related the experience of Commander Edward Preble, among others. After seeing the creature near Penobscot Bay in 1779, he rowed out toward the sea monster, ten feet of which was visible above the waterline. When he got close enough, Preble would state, he fired the bullets of his swivel gun at the monster. The only apparent effect was to cause Cassie to swim away even more rapidly.

Coleman has interviewed Maine residents who saw Cassie as late as the 1950s. Few sightings have been reported in recent years. Possibly the noisy sea traffic has moved Cassie—as well as other animals, such as seals and dolphins—away from their former haunts, which were closer to the Maine shore, in Casco Bay.

CHACOAN PECCARY

This "rangy big pig," as University of Connecticut biology professor Ralph M. Wetzel characterized his 1974 discovery, was a big surprise—a Pleistocene Epoch survivor of a species thought to have died out ten thousand years ago. The Chacoan peccary, a relative of pigs, boars, and warthogs, weighed in at more than one hundred pounds, the largest and most unusual of the three known peccaries. Wetzel found it in the wilds of Paraguay after interviewing the natives about a mysterious pig variously called *tagua, pagua,* or *cure'-buro* ("donkey-pig"). Wetzel stated that it differed from other known peccaries by its larger size; longer ears, snout, and legs; and proportionately shorter tail. In 1975, Wetzel formally named the species *Catagonus wagneri,* the Chacoan peccary or tagua.

Karl Shuker, in his book *The Lost Ark,* adds an ironic twist to the story: "Following its 'official' return to the land of the living, news emerged that for a number of years prior to this, and wholly unbeknownst to science, its hide had routinely been used by New York furriers to trim hats and coats."

Today, the Chacoan peccary is known to exist in Paraguay, Argentina, and Bolivia. Unfortunately, it has also become an endangered species. As often happens when species long thought to be extinct are rediscovered, this peccary may have been found only to be lost in the near future to habitat destruction and overhunting.

CHAMBERS AFFAIR

For years, a rumor has circulated that John Chambers, famed Academy Award–winning Hollywood special effects man, manufactured the suit

Film director John Landis, who is in the Sasquatch suit, and John Chambers (right) discuss their 1972 Bigfoot movie, Schlock. (Bob Rickard)

allegedly worn by the ostensible **Bigfoot** pictured in the famed **Patterson Film** that spawned renewed interest in the creature.

The controversy peaked in 1997, on the thirtieth anniversary of the filming, when press accounts from around the world recycled this rumor without benefit of a personal interview with Chambers. Typical of the headlines is one that appeared in London's *Sunday Telegraph* for October 19, 1997: "Hollywood admits to Bigfoot hoax." The article reads in part:

A piece of film, which for thirty years has been regarded as the most compelling evidence for the existence of Bigfoot, the North American "abominable snowman," is a hoax, according to new claims. John Chambers, the man behind the *Planet of the Apes* films and the elder statesman of Hollywood's "monster-makers," has been named by a group of Hollywood makeup artists as the person who faked Bigfoot.

In an interview with Scott Essman, an American journalist, the veteran Hollywood director John Landis . . . said: "That famous piece of film of Bigfoot walking in the woods that was touted as the real thing was just a suit made by John Chambers." He said he learned the information while working alongside Mr. Chambers on *Beneath the Planet of the Apes* in 1970.

On October 26, 1997, California Bigfoot researcher **Bobbie Short** interviewed Chambers, living in seclusion in a Los Angeles nursing home. The makeup artist insisted he had no prior knowledge of Roger Patterson or Bob Gimlin before their claimed Bigfoot encounter on October 20, 1967. He also denied having anything to do with creating the suit, and blamed the Hollywood rumor mill. Chambers went on to say that he was "good" but he "was not that good" to have fashioned anything nearly so convincing as the Bluff Creek Bigfoot.

As stated in the article, the well-known movie director John Landis has claimed that Chambers not only made the Patterson suit but helped make the film. For just as long people have pointed to Landis as the one from whom they heard the story, not Chambers. But Chambers himself says the only Bigfoot he made was the "Burbank Bigfoot," a large stone prop intended to imitate a real Bigfoot-like creature and used for a carnival tour.

CHAMP

The Lake Champlain monster, or "Champ," is credited with a long history, which it may or may not deserve.

In older articles about Champ, the claim is made that the first white man to see the Lake Champlain monster was the lake's namesake, explorer Samuel de Champlain, who in his journal entry for July 1609 records an observation of a serpentine creature about twenty feet long, as thick as a barrel, and with a horselike head. Champlain wrote that the Indians called the animal a *chaousarou*. Today, most cryptozoologists think that what Champlain saw was a sturgeon.

Between the time of Champlain's sighting and the 1800s, there were no known reports of Champ sightings, perhaps because the area was sparsely settled until just before the War of 1812. Previously, the only Europeans in the Champlain Valley were mostly Jesuits and soldiers, and they left no stories of any missionary or military encounters with the creature. By 1810, however, Champ reports began to come into the record, as 150,000 settlers looking for inexpensive land found their way to the lake.

Lake Champlain is the largest body of water in the U.S. other than the Great Lakes, occupying portions of what is now Vermont and New York as well as the province of Quebec in Canada. It is almost 110 miles long and 13 miles wide, with a maximum depth of 400 feet. The surface area is 436 square miles. The action of ancient glaciers carved out the lake, and as the ice sheets retreated, they left behind a finger of inland sea that at different times was connected to the ocean. Like Loch Ness in Scotland, Okanagan Lake in British Columbia, and scores of other deep, cold-water lakes in the northern temperate zone, Lake Champlain appears to be an ideal home for monsters.

Sandy Mansi at Lake Champlain, the home of Champ. (Loren Coleman)

The early inhabitants came to believe that the lake was the residence of a monster of its very own. Accounts of the time, published in the *Plattsburgh* (N.Y.) *Republican,* tell of how, in 1819, pioneers were alarmed by a beast as it stuck its head above the surface of Bulwagga Bay, near what is now Port Henry, New York. Between the arrival of the steamboat, around 1870, and 1900, according to one historian, the lake's creature was reported on at least twenty occasions. In all but two instances the monster was seen by a number of people of "unimpeachable character," according to news accounts.

On August 30, 1878, for example, as the yacht *Rob Roy* lay becalmed off Button Bay Island, the boat's party of six saw a large monster swimming rapidly by, its head occasionally projecting through the "smooth as glass" surface of the water. On November 5, 1879, three University of Burlington students saw the monster—fifteen feet of it visible above the water—travel gracefully from Appletree Point, near Burlington, around Rock Dunder, and head for Essex. On July 9, 1887, the creature made a spectacular appearance as a group of East Charlotte, Vermont, picnick-ers saw it come around a bend, its flat snakelike head poking above the water, and make straight toward them. As it grew closer at a terrific speed, some witnesses screamed, and the monster whirled to the right and disappeared under the waves. On August 4, 1892, the American Canoe Association's annual outing, at Willsborough, New York, was abruptly ended when the monster surfaced near their gathering, and ca-noeists scattered in panic. During this "monster scare" of 1870 to 1900, P. T. Barnum offered $50,000 for the "Champlain Sea Serpent" carcass, which no one was able to produce.

In 1915, according to a *New York Times* account, observers viewed the monster as it was stranded in the shallows at the entrance of Bul-wagga Bay near the Crown Point fortifications. The animal, said to be forty feet long, lashed the waters trying to escape, eventually releasing it-self. It swam for the Vermont side, to sink "submarine fashion, leaving a wake which was well defined on the glassy surface of the lake."

The next series of monster sightings occurred in the 1930s and 1940s. One especially close encounter was experienced by a Mr. and Mrs. Langlois, while fishing in their motorboat off Rouses Point, New York, in August 1939, when the monster headed for them and the cou-ple hastily veered to avoid being hit. As they fled for shore, the monster disappeared below the lake's surface. In 1943, Charles Weston watched through binoculars as a large animal churned up the water off Rouses Point. In 1945, a Winooski, Vermont, woman aboard the S.S. *Ticon-deroga* related how she and other passengers witnessing a bridge dedica-tion saw the beast raise its head from the water nearby.

Through the 1950s, 1960s, and early 1970s, sightings of the Lake Champlain monster were either infrequent or infrequently reported. But all that changed with the arrival in the early 1970s of Joseph Zarzynski, a dynamic investigator, lecturer, and social science instructor at a junior high school in Saratoga Springs, New York. He organized the Lake Champlain Phenomena Investigation and made the search for Champ his life's passion. Zarzynski's no-nonsense approach to monster hunting meant that those who for years had been ridiculed because they saw something "strange" in the lake now had a sympathetic ear.

The towering, six-foot-six Zarzynski's friendly manner and confident style made him one of the most trusted cryptozoologists of the 1970s and

1980s. Zarzynski also talked with the scores of witnesses who have seen Champ. Among them was Sandra Mansi, a thirty-four-year-old tinsmith and amateur photographer with no previous exposure to cryptozoological controversies. She produced what Zarzynski calls "the single most impressive piece of evidence" for Champ. Without Zarzynski, Mansi's incredible photo of Champ might have never been made public.

Mansi's adventure began on July 5, 1977, as she, her husband-to-be, and her two children were picnicking and sightseeing along the Vermont side of Lake Champlain, north of St. Albans. The group decided to get a closer look at the lake and cut across a farm field. The day was bright and sunny.

As she sat there, watching her children play in the water, Mansi noticed an object near the middle of the lake. At first, she took it to be a large fish, then the hand of a diver surfacing, but eventually she realized it was the grayish-brown head and long snakelike neck of a creature breaking the lake's surface. The thing's head seemed to be twisting around, scanning the countryside. Though frightened, she rushed to get her Kodak Instamatic camera from her car, and snapped one shot of the beast. Once the photograph was taken, she grabbed the children and fled the scene.

Fearful of the jokes and ridicule she might be subjected to, Mansi hid the picture for three years. Finally, encouraged by friends and the growing interest in Champ promoted by Zarzynski and his investigation, Mansi, now living in Winchester, New Hampshire, produced the photograph for scrutiny by some academic types allegedly interested in the monster who had approached her. The fact that Mansi had lost the negative, and had never known the exact location of the sighting, led to some difficult moments, until Mansi was introduced to Zarzynski.

After interviewing Mansi, Zarzynski contacted other figures in the field of cryptozoology to help him evaluate her evidence. **Roy Mackal,** a University of Chicago zoologist famed for his **Loch Ness Monster** work, and **J. Richard Greenwell** and B. Roy Frieden, both of the University of Arizona, examined Mansi's photograph and subjected it to computer tests. According to Frieden, a professor of optical sciences, no evidence of a montage or superimposition could be found. Greenwell and Mackal were similarly convinced that Mansi had a picture of an unknown animate object in the lake. Greenwell was convinced that the object in

Mansi's photo was a plesiosaur, an extinct marine reptile, like the ones he believes to be responsible for Loch Ness Monsters. Mackal, on the other hand, speculated that the creature—in common with other **Lake Monsters**—was a **zeuglodon,** a primitive whale generally thought to have become extinct 20 million years ago.

Zarzynski has ceased active involvement in the investigation of what he used to call "the Champ animals." Today he devotes his spare moments to the search for shipwrecks. The work at Lake Champlain during the 1990s is largely in the hands of **Dennis Jay Hall,** the director of Champ Quest.

CHUCHUNAA

Chuchunaa ("Wildmen") is a western Siberian name for a specific type of unknown hairy hominid which may now be extinct. Anthropologist Myra Shackley, who calls the creature the "Siberian Snowman," writes that they are most frequently reported by the Tungus and Yakuts, the local nomadic peoples. The Chuchunaa are shy but not entirely retiring; they have been known to throw dogs about when bothered. The Chuchunaa are notable for being among the few unknown hairy hominids said to wear clothing, perhaps as an adaptation to the severe temperatures where they live. Reported to be seven feet tall and neckless, they are restricted regionally to Siberia.

As with any unknown hairy hominid, regionalized names are given to these creatures. One local Chuchunaa was given the pet name "Mecheny" ("The Marked One") because it appeared at the edge of a forest often enough for the locals to see that it had a distinctive white forearm on a body of darker hair. Another name for the Chuchunaa is Mirygdy ("Broad-Shoulders") because the Chuchunaa have wide shoulders on a relatively narrow body. They allegedly raid barns and other dwellings. Significantly, another name for the Chuchunaa of southeastern Siberia is "Mulen" (a Tungus word for "Bandit").

The Chuchunaa issue was taken seriously in the Soviet Union as early as 1928, when search parties were dispatched to gather information on them. The following year, a formal report on the Chuchunaa was presented to the Commission for the Discovery and Study of Antiquarian Curiosities attached to the Western Siberian section of the Russian Geographical Society. The report recommended that detailed investigations and systematic studies occur before the Chuchunaa became extinct. In 1933, Professor P. Dravert called upon the government to abolish the hunting of these "people" on the grounds that all people of the U.S.S.R. deserved equal protection. But little was done. Surveys were conducted in the 1950s, but by the time geologist Vladimir Pushkarev conducted research in Siberia in the 1970s, the Chuchunaa appeared to have become extinct, or nearly so.

Mark A. Hall has pointed out that in their habits and body type the Chuchunaa resemble other localized unknown hominids in Canada and elsewhere. **Loren Coleman** theorizes that the Chuchunaa-Mecheny-Mirygdy-Mulen are one form of what he calls the **Marked Hominids,** a class of unknown hairy bipeds exhibiting body hair colors that are piebald, two-tone, or albino in high numbers. According to Coleman's analysis, these large creatures live mostly in the northern wilderness and near subpolar areas. Shackley holds that the Chuchunaa are recently extinct or surviving **Neandertals.** In separate writings Hall and Coleman dispute this view, arguing that in addition to having vastly different behavioral traits, Neandertals were never more than five and a half feet tall, while the shortest mature Chuchunaa are reported to be a foot taller.

CHUPACABRAS

The single most notable cryptozoological phenomenon of the past decade is undoubtedly the *chupacabras* ("Goatsucker") of Hispanic America. The legend of this livestock-slaughtering monster was born in small villages in Puerto Rico in 1995 and quickly spread to Mexico and Hispanic communities in the United States, on its way to becoming a worldwide sensation like no unexplained creature since the **Bigfoot** of the late 1950s and 1960s.

In March 1995, carcasses of goats, chickens, and other small farm animals, seemingly devoid of blood, began to be found near the Puerto Rican towns of Morovis and Orocovis. In September came the first sightings of an animal said to combine the features of a kangaroo, a gargoyle, and the gray alien of abduction lore. It was said to be hairy, about four feet tall, with a large, round head, a lipless mouth, sharp fangs, and huge, lidless red eyes. Its body was small, with thin, clawed, seemingly webbed arms with muscular hind legs. The hairy creature also had a series of pointy spikes running from the top of its head down its backbone. Investigator Jorge Martin drew a widely circulated sketch based on these descriptions. Local media repeated its widely popular name, "Chupacabras," in many stories.

Sightings and slain livestock continued to be reported in parts of Puerto Rico throughout the fall of 1995. In March 1996, a segment on the Chupacabras appeared on the TV talk show *Christina,* the Spanish-language Univision network's popular counterpart to Oprah Winfrey. The media attention from this exposure appears to have caused the migration of Chupamania into Mexico and the United States.

As media observer Donald Trull has noted, whatever else it may or may not be, Chupacabras represents folklore in the modern age of electronic telecommunications. Once it took centuries for a legend like the **Abominable Snowman** to be disseminated through generations. The stories told now are similar; what has changed is the speed at which word of mouth travels.

This drawing of the Chupacabras represents features described by most witnesses. (Scott Corrales)

Hispanic television and radio reports ignited the Chupacabras phenomenon, but more significantly, the Chupacabras is the first monster, as Trull points out, that the Internet can call its own. In 1995, the Internet was gaining a powerful foothold, and the Chupacabras was ideal for the medium. Martin's celebrated Chupacabras sketch was flashed instantly to a "global network of weirdness-watchers," Trull discovered. Meantime, Hispanic-oriented information sources eagerly spread Chupacabras tales. This generated a one-two punch of underground publicity, bridging two cultures, and the Chupacabras phenomenon was in full flower before the mass media even knew what it was.

As Trull notes on his Parascope website:

At the height of the craze, there were probably a couple dozen Chupacabras or "Goatsucker Home Pages" on the Internet. Some of them are still around today, including one at Princeton University that may legitimately be the original Goatsucker site. The web site of sensational radio host Art Bell posted an alleged photograph of a living Chupacabras, depicting a ridiculous creature later exposed as a statue from a museum exhibit. The photo nonetheless became a major touchstone of Chupa lore, fueling American interest in the creature.

North American–based Hispanic cryptozoologist **Scott Corrales,** nevertheless, gathered and investigated Chupacabras reports in a level-headed fashion, despite the media and Internet hysteria. Corrales points out that the modern reports really began in 1974, and Chupacabras folklore dates back to Taino Indian tales of the *Maboya.* The first major American sighting of the Chupacabras took place in March 1996 in Miami, followed by others in Texas, Arizona, and other North American locations. Chupacabras "sightings" have decreased in frequency since 1996, though the occasional report still surfaces from time to time.

International Society of Cryptozoology's **Richard Greenwell** feels that the Chupacabras folklore may comprise mixed traditions about several cryptids. Other cryptozoologists sense there may be one underlying unknown cryptid linked to some of the original Puerto Rican reports on Chupacabras and related **Merbeing** traditions.

CLARK, EUGENIE (1930–)

Eugenie Clark serves on the board of directors of the **International Society of Cryptozoology.** A famous diver and scientist, she has explored the underwater world of many seas and has been popularized through a series of Scholastic paperback young-adult books, including *Shark Lady: The True Story of Eugenie Clark; Further Adventures of Shark Lady Eugenie Clark;* and *The Desert Beneath the Sea,* written with her frequent diving companion Ann McGovern. Clark's life is an interesting one: she has been married six times and is a seasoned world traveler. Clark's many adventures include diving into caves in Mexico to study "sleeping" sharks, discovering a Red Sea fish that keeps big sharks away, and proving that sharks have intelligence and good memory.

Clark is a professor emerita and senior research scientist in the Department of Zoology at the University of Maryland. An ichthyologist who began her studies on the behavior and reproductive isolating mechanisms of freshwater aquarium fish, Clark later combined her love for diving with the study of marine fish: first hard-hat diving and snorkeling, now using scuba and submersibles. Clark has studied shark behavior in the deep sea from submersibles at depths of one thousand to twelve thousand feet. Throughout the 1990s, she conducted seventy-one dives off Grand Cayman, Bermuda, the Bahamas, California, and Japan to study the behavior, movements, and population density of large deep-sea fish.

Clark has a decades-long involvement with cryptozoology. She maintains a passionate interest in discoveries of new species of fish. As recently as 1993, she published her discovery of *Helcogramma vulcana,* a new triple-fin fish from the Banda Sea, Indonesia. In 1996, according to cryptozoologist **Ben Roesch,** Clark gave an excellent slide lecture throughout Canada, entitled "Sea Monsters and Other Mysteries of the Deep," in which she discussed a New Zealand 1977 "sea monster" carcass (found to be a rotten basking shark), weird octopuses from the depths, whale sharks, and reports of possible new "cookie-cutter" sharks from subarctic waters. For many years through 1997, Clark taught a course on "Sea Monsters and Deep-Sea Sharks" at the University of Maryland. Margery Facklam has written a biography, *Eugenie Clark and the Sleeping Sharks.*

CLARK, JAMES ALEXANDER (1960-1989)

Jim Clark, one of British Columbia's foremost cryptozoological researchers, amassed perhaps the largest collection of sighting reports and papers on a variety of cryptids in that province. Along with **Paul LeBlond** and later **John Kirk,** Clark founded the **British Columbia Scientific Cryptozoology Club** (BCSCC) in May 1989. Thanks to Clark's vision, the BCSCC is today the second-largest and most active cryptozoological organization in the world.

Clark proved he was particularly adept at finding long-forgotten sighting accounts in a variety of newspaper archives in British Columbia as well as in other provinces. Although he was primarily involved in deskbound research, he also ventured into fieldwork in search of cryptids.

It was on such a fieldwork exercise in July 1989 that Clark fulfilled a long-standing dream: he saw an unknown animal. On an expedition with other members of the BCSCC, Clark and his colleagues sighted **Ogopogo,** the monster of Okanagan Lake, just a few hundred feet offshore from the beach at Peach Orchard, Summerland, British Columbia. The thirty-five-foot multihumped animal remained in the view of Clark and his team for approximately one minute before submerging to avoid two oncoming motorboats.

Several weeks after this sighting, Clark and his wife, Barbara, resolved to relocate from their home in Coquitlam to Kelowna on the shores of Okanagan Lake, in a bid to spend more time researching and, if they were lucky, observing Ogopogo. Unfortunately, just two weeks after settling into their new locale, Jim Clark suffered a heart attack brought on by a liver problem. He died in September 1989.

Since then, the Jim Clark Memorial Prize commemorating his dedication and achievements has been instituted by the BCSCC for elementary schoolchildren in British Columbia. Students are invited to submit projects dealing with cryptozoological animals for assessment by a BCSCC panel, and the winner receives a cash prize for his or her efforts. Since the prize was created in 1989, there have been winners every year.

CLARK, RAMONA (1932–1997)

Ramona Clark was one of the earliest investigators of accounts in the southern U.S. of unknown hairy anthropoids called the **Skunk Ape.** Working from her home in Brooksville, Florida, she participated in a number of research projects focused on the chimpanzee-sized, apelike primates, which were reported in central and south Florida in especially high numbers during the 1970s.

Clark was an early member of L. Frank Hudson and Gordon R. Prescott's **Yeti** Research Society, which—its name notwithstanding—was centered in her home state and concerned only with Skunk Ape reports. She later broke with the group. Even so, her work continued through fieldwork and newsletter articles. When the noted **Bigfoot/Sasquatch** researcher **John Green** interviewed Clark in Florida, he found her to be a knowledgeable investigator who had seen the creatures on a few occasions. She had also examined their tracks from time to time.

She eventually married her longtime "Yeti"-hunting partner, Duane

Hibner, and moved as near as they could to the concentrated sightings taking place in Brooksville in the 1970s.

Clark died on December 19, 1997.

COELACANTH

The coelacanth (*Latimeria chalumnae*) is the darling of cryptozoology. Its story demonstrates that unknown, undiscovered, or at least long-thought-extinct animals can still be found.

The coelacanth, a lobe-finned fish, first appeared during the Devonian period, some 350 million years ago. Its body varies from bright blue to brownish in color and produces large amounts of oil and slime. Fossils found in many parts of the world indicate that during the coelacanth's long history, various types inhabited lakes, swamps, inland seas, and oceans. Before 1938 paleontologists thought that the coelacanth had become extinct about 65 million years ago, when the dinosaurs disappeared.

The first "modern" coelacanth was a five-foot-long, 127-pound, large-scaled blue fish brought up in a net off South Africa by Captain

A few coelacanths are displayed in natural history museums around the world, like this one in Chicago's Field Museum. (Loren Coleman)

Hendrick Goosen, of the trawler *Nerine,* who was fishing the coastal waters of the Indian Ocean, near Cape Town, South Africa. On December 23, 1938, Goosen took his catch to a local fish market, and called Marjorie Courtenay-Latimer, curator and taxidermist at the East London Museum, northeast of Cape Town, to examine his haul, as she often did, looking for any unusual specimens for her collection. Courtenay-Latimer wished the crew a happy holiday and was about to leave when she saw a blue fin, and she revealed from under a pile "the most beautiful fish I had ever seen, five feet long, and a pale mauve blue with iridescent silver markings." She talked a taxi driver into taking the smelly fish back with her to the museum, and there identified it as a coelacanth, later confirming her find with the leading South African ichthyologist Professor J. L. B. Smith of Rhodes University, Grahamstown, some fifty miles south of East London. Meanwhile, Courtenay-Latimer's museum director in East London was less impressed with the find. He rejected the fish as a common grouper. Smith, who was on Christmas holiday, was not able to confirm it was a coelacanth until after a taxidermist had thrown away all of the important internal organs to mount what would turn out to be the "catch of the century."

But the story of the coelacanth's "discovery" does not end there. With no internal organs left from the East London specimen, many questions remained unanswered. Smith was obsessed with finding a second intact specimen. Finally, on December 21, 1952, fourteen years after the discovery of the first living coelacanth, lightning would strike again while Smith was on another Christmas holiday. Captain Eric Hunt, a relocated British fisherman who had attended one of Smith's coelacanth lectures and had also become obsessed with locating another coelacanth, was returning to the port of Mutsamudu on the Comoros island of Anjouan, off the coast of Mozambique, when he was approached by Ahamadi Abdallah, a Comorian who was carrying a hefty bundle. Abdallah had pulled in by hand what the locals called a *gombessa,* a large fish that turned up on the Comorian lines now and then. The second coelacanth had finally been found.

Years later, ichthyologists were shocked to learn that the local islanders had been catching and eating these **"living fossils"** for generations. Since then more than two hundred individual fish from the Comoros have been caught and studied. Most natural history museums have a mounted specimen on exhibit. Up-to-date news on this now en-dangered fish species can be found at coelacanth researcher Jerome F. Hamlin's website: http://www.dinofish.com

Four years after the "discovery" of the second coelacanth, Hunt dis-appeared at sea after his schooner ran aground on the reefs of the Geyser Bank between the Comoros and Madagascar. He was never found. Smith wrote his account of the coelacanth story in the now classic *Old Fourlegs,* first published in 1956. Smith died in 1968. Captain Hendrick Goosen passed away in 1988, just after the fiftieth anniversary of the "discovery" of the coelacanth. And Marjorie Courtenay-Latimer was alive and well and still living in East London as of 1998, the lone survivor of the coelacanth story.

Intriguingly, this fossil fish is back in the news with a "second" re-discovery in Indonesia, by marine biologist Mark Erdmann and his wife, Arnaz Mehta, a nature guide, in 1997–98 (see **Indonesian coelacanths**).

French coelacanth chronicler **Michel Raynal,** who had predicted that the fish would be found in Indonesian waters, thinks more discov-eries of the fish in unexpected locales will occur in the future. He writes that "there is a tantalizing possibility that an unknown coelacanth is lurk-ing off the coasts of Australia." There are also reports of other coela-canth populations from around the world, reportedly as far away from the Comoros as the Gulf of Mexico.

COLEMAN, LOREN (1947–)

Loren Coleman was born in Norfolk, Virginia, but moved when he was three months old to Decatur, Illinois, where he spent most of his youth, the son of a professional firefighter. Coleman grew up interested in ani-mals, nature mysteries, zoological parks, and the exploration of wild places. As a boy, he kept a large home zoo of native species of reptiles and mammals.

In March 1960, after watching a television broadcast of a film (*Half Human*) about **Yeti,** Coleman got passionately interested in researching the reality of the **Abominable Snowman.** He soon began to investigate midwestern anthropoid reports in the field. He commenced what would be a series of correspondence with **Ivan T. Sanderson** and **Bernard Heuvelmans,** who would become his researcher mentors. In 1962 Cole-

The author holds a Bigfoot footcast taken during the 1959 Tom Slick–sponsored investigative trip to Bluff Creek, California. (David Parnes)

man found a series of apelike footprints in south-central Illinois and heard a remarkable primate screech in another part of the state.

He researched, through newspaper archives, many forgotten accounts of American **Thunderbirds, Black Panthers,** and **Napes** (North American Apes). Before his twentieth birthday he was interviewing eyewitnesses and participating in expeditions throughout North America.

Coleman's undergraduate educational choice of Southern Illinois University–Carbondale was based on his wish to be closer to the swampy bottomlands' folklore and reports of unknown apes. Working his way through school, he obtained his degree in anthropology with a minor in zoology and years later would fine-tune his interviewing and psychological analytic skills with a postgraduate degree in psychiatric social work and doctoral-level work in social anthropology, sociology, and family violence.

Since the Yeti caught his interest in 1960, Coleman has been investigating cryptozoological evidence and folklore, leading him to research mysterious panther sightings and reports of unknown apes and **Bigfoot** throughout North America. He has traveled to forty-five states and throughout Canada, Mexico, and the Virgin Islands speaking with witnesses and joining other researchers in the search for everything from **Lake Monsters** to **Skunk Apes.** Coleman has been picked to be the cryptozoologist for the 1999 Nessa Project's submarine search for Scotland's **Loch Ness Monsters.** He has worked with four generations of cryptozoologists, creating strong intellectual bonds with several researchers and writers, including especially **Mark A. Hall, Patrick Huyghe,** and Jerome Clark.

Coleman is an honorary member of cryptozoological organizations like the **British Columbia Scientific Cryptozoology Club,** and he is a life member of the **International Society of Cryptozoology.** He was an early supporter of local cryptozoological efforts, as well as, for example, suggesting to Sanderson that he should create an international organization (which became the Society for the Investigation of the Unexplained).

Coleman, after years of fieldwork and bibliographic research, has written books and more than two hundred articles on the subject, has appeared frequently on radio and television programs, and has lectured from Idaho to London. He has been both on- and off-camera consultant to NBC-TV's *Unsolved Mysteries,* A&E's *Ancient Mysteries,* the History Channel's *In Search of History,* the Discovery Channel's *Into the Unknown,* and other documentary programs. *Strange Magazine* carried his regular column, "The Cryptozoo News," for several years. He contributes a regular cryptozoology column, "On the Trail," to the London-based *Fortean Times,* and "Mysterious World" to St. Paul–based national magazine *Fate.*

Coleman's first articles were published in 1969. He went on to write two books with Jerome Clark (*The Unidentified* [1975] and *Creatures of the Outer Edge* [1978], both published by Warner). In the 1980s, Coleman wrote *Mysterious America* (1983), *Curious Encounters* (1985), and *Tom Slick and the Search for the Yeti* (1989), for Faber and Faber. Coleman's 1999 field guide, with Patrick Huyghe, is *The Field Guide to Bigfoot, Yeti, and Other Mystery Primates Worldwide* (Avon Books).

On October 20, 1997, on the occasion of the thirtieth anniversary of the reported filming of a Californian **Sasquatch,** Coleman was among the first ten inductees into the new Roger Patterson Memorial Hall of Fame at the soon-to-be-open Bigfoot Museum in Portland, Oregon. With appropriate funding, Coleman plans to open an International Cryptozoology Museum in Portland, Maine, to house his vast collection of artifacts, books, and research materials sometime in the next few years. Coleman has perhaps the largest cryptozoological library in North America and an extensive collection of cryptid artifacts.

Coleman has been an author, filmmaker, grants specialist, instructor, professor, and research associate in various academic university settings since 1980. He is the author of several non-cryptozoological books, including *Working with Older Adoptees* (1987) and *Suicide Clusters* (1987).

Loren Coleman can be reached at P.O. Box 360, Portland, Maine 04112, or via E-mail at LCOLEMA1@maine.rr.com. His website is <www.lorencoleman.com>

CONGO PEACOCK

Some animal discoveries are made in museums. In 1913, the New York Zoological Society sent an unsuccessful expedition to the Congo in an attempt to bring back a live **okapi.** Instead, one of the team's members, Dr. James P. Chapin, brought back some native headdresses with curious long reddish-brown feathers striped with black. None of the experts could identify them.

In 1934, on another of his frequent visits to the Congo, Chapin noticed similar feathers on two stuffed birds at the Tervueren Museum. Though labeled "Young Indian Peacocks," he knew they were something else. As it turned out, a mining company in the Congo had donated them to the museum and labeled them "Indian peacocks," but as Chapin soon determined, they were a new species.

The following year he flew down to the Congo and brought back seven birds, known to the natives as *mbulu*. Chapin confirmed them as the first new bird genus discovered in forty years. They were a true African pheasant, a primitive form closely related to the Asiatic peacocks. The Congo peacock (*Afropavo congensis*) is now commonly featured in European and North American zoos.

CON RIT

Con rit is Vietnamese for "millipede," a name applied to the special form of **Sea Serpent** found in the oceans off South East Asia. Initial research on the Con Rit was conducted by Dr. A. Krempf, director of the Oceanographic and Fisheries Service of Indo-China, in the 1920s. He interviewed an eyewitness who reportedly touched a beached Con Rit in

1883. The body was sixty feet long and three feet wide. Dark brown above and yellow below, the animal had regular armored segments every two feet along its body (thus its millipede and centipede names). The Con Rit appears as the dragon of ancient Vietnamese legends, not as a snake but as an animal seen in the Gulf of Tonkin, fabulously long "like a centipede."

Bernard Heuvelmans has formally designated the Con Rit and its relatives, the *Cetioscolopendra aeliani* ("Aelian's cetacean centipede"), and links it to the ancient whales. He views the Con Rit as the prototype for the Oriental dragon. Heuvelmans writes in *Cryptozoology 5* that this type of Sea Serpent is "strangely provided with many lateral fins and with a segmented, jointed armor of bony dermal plaques which were common among archaic whales. It is found only in the belt of tropical and sub-tropical waters around the world."

CORRALES, SCOTT (1963-)

Scott Corrales, a resident of Pennsylvania, is the foremost English/Spanish-language investigator of the **Chupacabras.** A translator and author, he has been interested in natural mysteries since an early age. He attended George Washington and Rutgers Universities. He is the editor of *Inexplicata,* a Hispanic journal on reports of unusual phenomena.

Corrales is the author of *Chupacabras and Other Mysteries* (1997) and *Flashpoint-High Strangeness in Puerto Rico* (1998).

Scott Corrales. (Scott Corrales)

CROOK, CLIFF (1940-)

Cliff Crook is the second half of a trivia question involving the movie *Harry and the Hendersons,* which features a character based on Crook and played by the late Don Ameche. (See **René Dahinden** for the other half.) Crook served as an uncredited technical consultant when the

Cliff Crook at Green Mountain, Washington, making a cast of a Bigfoot track. (FPL)

movie was filmed in 1987. His "Bigfoot Museum," open since 1982, served as the model for the film's museum, and many of Crook's **Bigfoot** track casts were used in the movie.

Crook's interest in the subject grew out of an experience in 1956, when he was sixteen years old. Crook was camping in an isolated section of backwoods near Duvall, Washington, with three other boys and a dog when a Bigfoot approached their campfire. Crook says their German shepherd went after the creature but was picked up and thrown at their feet. They heard a deep, horrendous sound, something like *"Ee-gor lar-gor."* One of the boys started crying. The giant, hair-covered creature came nearer. The boys ran. They left everything behind. The dog awoke. The boys ran all the way home, barefoot.

From then on, the subject of Bigfoot became something of an obsession to Crook. He has produced a variety of commercially available items for tourists and researchers, including the Bigfoot Totem postcard, Wild Creek Bigfoot postcard, Bigfoot bumper stickers, buttons, ribbons, shirts, caps, *Bigfoot Map* (1973, 1975), *Bigfoot Trailblazer* (1980), *Bigfoot Trails Newsletter* (since 1992), and *Bigfoot and the Moon* (1995).

In 1976, Crook developed a seven-point tracking test to detect hoaxed footprints at Bigfoot reporting sites. As the founder of Bigfoot Central, he established North America's first Bigfoot Reports Headquarters and Research Data Base (the so-called Bigfoot Museum), in 1982. Later, in 1991, Bigfoot Central would be the first Bigfoot research organization officially sanctioned by the state of Washington.

The 1990s, however, have seen Crook as the focus of much criticism and controversy. In October 1995, he purchased and promoted what he calls the "clearest known alleged Bigfoot photos," the so-called seven Wild Creek Bigfoot photographs. Critics have charged that these photos—of what looks like a neckless computer-enhanced model—are a transparent hoax. Then in 1998, after promoter Chris Murphy (who had helped sell the **Patterson Film** frames for Dahinden) broke with Dahinden, Murphy and Crook teamed up to debunk the Patterson Film. Crook says he is now working on a book that will expose the Patterson Film as "the Bigfoot Hoax of the Century," although he still believes in the reality of Bigfoot.

CROWE, RAY (1937–)

Ray Crowe was born and raised in Oregon, serving as a weatherman for the U.S. Air Force and the U.S. Weather Bureau, as well as working in a variety of other trades. Today Crowe directs a nonprofit organization, the Western Bigfoot Society (WBS), which he founded in 1991. WBS was located in Portland for almost a decade but has recently moved to Hillsboro, Oregon. Crowe and WBS have played a large role in many of the **Bigfoot** investigations in Oregon and Washington in the 1990s. Holding monthly public meetings, talking to school groups, and publishing a regular newsletter, *Track Record,* Crowe has been a prominent and accessible advocate for laypeople attracted to Bigfoot studies. Crowe is a rarity in the field in openly acknowledging the entertainment potential of Bigfoot research.

In 1997, Crowe created the Bigfoot Information Center, a Bigfoot museum-in-planning, and inducted ten respected hominoid researchers into its Roger Patterson Memorial Hall of Fame. He hopes to open the museum by the year 2000. It will house exhibits on early man, dinosaurs, and local natural history, affording the venture a broad educational mission. Contributions from local herpetologists and the Oregon Archaeological Society are promised.

CRYPTID

"Cryptid" is a relatively new word used among professionals and laypeople to denote an animal of interest to cryptozoology. John E. Wall of Manitoba coined it in a letter published in the summer 1983 issue of the *ISC Newsletter* (vol. 2, no. 2, p. 10), published by the **International Society of Cryptozoology.** Recently "cryptid" was recognized by the lexicographers at Merriam-Webster as a word of legitimate coinage, though it has yet to appear in their dictionary.

Cryptids are either unknown species of animals or animals which, though thought to be extinct, may have survived into modern times and await rediscovery by scientists. "Cryptid" is derived from "crypt," from the Greek *kryptos* (hidden); "id," from the Latin *ides,* a patronymic suffix; and the Greek *"ides,"* which means "in sense." When the suffix *id* is used it typically applies to an implied lineage or similar usages, as in "perseid" (meteors appearing to originate from Perseus, typically around August 11).

Bernard Heuvelmans's definition of cryptozoology itself was exact: "The scientific study of hidden animals, i.e., of still unknown animal forms about which only testimonial and circumstantial evidence is available, or material evidence considered insufficient by some!"

Over the last ten years some have suggested that the science of cryptozoology should be expanded to include many animals as "cryptids," specifically including the study of out-of-place animals, feral animals, and even animal ghosts and apparitions. In *Cryptozoology,* Heuvelmans rejects such notions with typical thoroughness, and not a little wry humor:

> Admittedly, a definition need not conform necessarily to the exact etymology of a word. But it is always preferable when it really does so, which I carefully endeavored to achieve when I coined the term "cryptozoology." All the same being a very tolerant person, even in the strict realm of science, I have never prevented anybody from creating new disciplines of zoology quite distinct from cryptozoology. How could I, in any case?
>
> So, let people who are interested in founding a science of "unexpected animals" feel free to do so, and if they have a smattering of Greek and are not repelled by jawbreakers they may call it "aprosbletozoology" or "apronoeozoology" or even "anelistozoology." Let those who would rather be searching for "bizarre animals" create a "paradoozoology," and those who prefer to go hunting for "monstrous animals," or just plain "monsters," build up a "teratozoology" or more simply a "pelorology."
>
> But for heavens sake, let cryptozoology be what it is, and what I meant it to be when I gave it its name over thirty years ago!

Unfortunately, many of the creatures of most interest to cryptozoologists do not, in themselves, fall under the blanket heading of cryptozoology. Thus many who are interested in such phenomena as the so-called **Beast of Bodmin Moor** (not an unknown species, but a known species in an alien environment) and the Devonshire/Cornwall "devil dogs" (not "animals" or even "animate" in the accepted sense of the word, and thus only of marginal interest to scientific cryptozoologists) think of these creatures as cryptids.

More broadly, then, we do not know whether a cryptid is an unknown species of animal, or a supposedly extinct animal, or a misidentification, or anything more than myth until evidence is gathered and accepted one way or another. Until that proof is found, the supposed animal carries the label "cryptid," regardless of the potential outcome and regardless of various debates concerning its true identity. When it is precisely identified, it is no longer a cryptid, because it is no longer hidden.

While Heuvelmans created cryptozoology as a goal-oriented discipline (endeavoring to prove the existence of hidden animals), the fact that some of these cryptids will turn out not to be new species does not invalidate the process by which that conclusion is reached and does not retroactively discard their prior status as cryptids. For example, the large unknown "monster" in a local lake is a cryptid until it is caught and shown to be a known species such as an alligator. It is no longer hidden and no longer carries the label "cryptid," but that does not mean it never was a cryptid.

It is often impossible to tell which category an unknown animal actually inhabits until you catch it. Until then, it is a cryptid.

D

DAHINDEN, RENÉ (1930–)

Born in Switzerland, René Dahinden moved to Canada in 1953. Two months after he arrived, he heard about the **Sasquatch** and within three years was conducting serious research on the hairy primates.

Since then Dahinden has conducted numerous field investigations throughout the Pacific Northwest, interviewed many witnesses, and examined apparent physical evidence for the legendary creature. He was the first to show the **Patterson Film** of a **Bigfoot** in the former Soviet Union, and he worked hard to see to it that the film got the scientific attention he felt it deserved. In recent years, with Dahinden's acquiring of the photographic images of the Patterson Film, some of his time has been taken up in legal affairs. Declining health due to cancer held in remission until 1999 has greatly reduced Dahinden's recent activities.

His only book, *Sasquatch* (1973), was written with Don Hunter.

In the Hollywood Bigfoot family movie comedy *Harry and the Hendersons* (1987), the Sasquatch hunter, a character played by David Suchet (better known to television viewers through his BBC/PBS *Mystery* series role as Belgian detective Hercule Poirot), was modeled on René Dahinden.

DAO VAN TIEN (1920–1995)

Dao Van Tien was born in Nam Dinh City, Nam Dinh Province, Vietnam, and graduated from Université de l'Indochine in 1942, with a master's degree in zoology in 1944. As a teacher and professor of zoology at Viet Minh and Hanoi Universities from 1946 until his retirement in 1986, Professor Tien was the most important figure in biology in northern Vietnam. He taught three generations of scientists. He sought to persuade others—through his collegial relationships and a series of articles about unknown hairy hominids in Vietnam—to consider the merits of cryptozoology.

From the early 1960s on, Tien journeyed to small villages in Vietnam to interview eyewitnesses who had reportedly seen the local Wildman of the Forests, the **Nguoi Rung.** He headed at least two Vietnamese expeditions in search of this hominoid.

While spending the night at Thuan Chau in the Central Highlands in 1963, Tien learned of a local type of Wildman that foraged at night and sneaked into houses to steal food. His informant said he had himself seen the creature on a moonlit night through a crack in the window. Five feet tall, covered with hair, it walked erect and had a human-like face. When a noise disturbed it, it leaped to the ground, ran off, and disappeared into the bush.

On another research trip in the Sa Thây area (Gia Lai–Kon Tum) in 1979, local people told Tien of another type of Wildman: taller than an ordinary person, ferocious-looking, hairy, and upright. It was said to use its hands and fingers to pierce the trunk of banana trees to get juice, sometimes tearing its flesh in the process and leaving blood on the trunk.

In 1981, coincidentally, Professor Pham Huy Thong read a book titled *L'Homme de Néanderthal est toujours vivant* (Neanderthal Man Is Still Alive, 1974), written by **Bernard Heuvelmans** and **Boris Porshnev.** The book contains a mass of information on worldwide Wildmen traditions. According to Thong, when Heuvelmans sent him the book, he urged him to "try your hardest to provide more information about Wildmen in Vietnam to the science world, because you have the perfect opportunity."

On reading the part of the book dealing with Wildmen in Vietnam, Tien noticed that the exhibitor (and owner?) of the **Minnesota Iceman** was a U.S. Air Force captain, Frank Hansen, who had fought in Vietnam. The book took note of a 1966 American newspaper report alleging that U.S. Marines once shot and killed "a huge ape" in the Highlands not far from Danang, where Captain Hansen had been stationed; since there are no huge apes, such as the gorilla, in Vietnam (only small gibbons), Tien thought this must have been a Wildman. Hansen then supposedly arranged for the body to be flown to the United States in the same manner as the bodies of American soldiers killed in action, refrigerated it, and, having retired from the Air Force, showed it at country fairs. (This claim, it should be noted, is much disputed, and Hansen has never been able to provide convincing evidence that it is true.)

When Tien finished the Heuvelmans and Porshnev book, his reservations about the Wildman's presence in Vietnam diminished. He wondered if the body Hansen had exhibited could have been that of a genuine Wildman. Such speculations influenced a subsequent generation of researchers who would actively search for the Nguoi Rung. From 1980 onward, various zoologists carried out further research in the areas of Gia Lai and Kon Tum.

Tien's series of articles "The Facts About Forest Man" appeared in 1990 in *Tap Chi' Lâm Nghiêp* (Forestry Review), published in Hanoi.

Tien died in May 1995 of a heart attack.

DINSDALE, TIM (1924–1987)

Tim Dinsdale was born into a British family in China. When his parents returned to England, Dinsdale attended and graduated from King's School, Worcester. During World War II he served as a Royal Air Force pilot in Rhodesia (now Zimbabwe) and afterward worked as an aeronautical engineer.

He is remembered, however, because of his research on the **Loch Ness Monsters.** His interest was sparked in 1955, after he read a magazine article on the subject. Unable to get the mystery off his mind, he prepared a "master plan for a campaign of observation," which began in April 1960. In the course of his life, he went on fifty-six treks to the loch.

None of them would ever match what happened to him during his first month as a Ness-watcher. On April 23, 1960, he made a four-minute film of the fast-moving hump of "some huge living creature," apparently twelve to sixteen feet of it underwater, with three feet of it visible. A subsequent analysis of the film by Britain's Joint Air Reconnaissance Intelli-

Tim Dinsdale at Loch Ness. (FPL)

gence Center rejected the skeptical theory that the object was a boat. JARIC declared the object "probably . . . animate"—in other words, a large, unidentified living creature.

Dinsdale's books on Loch Ness's mysterious inhabitants are considered some of the best in the literature of cryptozoology. His first, titled simply *Loch Ness Monster,* went through four editions between 1961 and 1982. In July 1987, a few months before his death, the **International Society of Cryptozoology** made him an honorary member, noting his "dedication to the investigation, and the honesty and integrity with which you have proceeded." After his death, chemist and cryptozoologist Henry H. Bauer wrote, "Tim Dinsdale was a profoundly good influence on many of us."

DOBHAR-CHU

Among the legendary beasts of Ireland is something called the *dobhar-chu* (Gaelic for "water hound"), a mysterious and dangerous creature said to dwell in some lakes. The very sight of one is rumored to cost a witness his or her life. These "water hounds" figure not just in oral tradition but also in claimed experiences from earlier centuries.

Bearing stark testimony to the water hound's bloodthirsty nature is a gravesite in Glenade, County Leitrim. The epitaph notes the death of a woman named Grace (the last name is no longer discernible) on September 27, 1722. On the tombstone is the carving of an unidentified animal with some features of an otter, run through with a spear. The woman is said to have been killed by a water hound as she was washing clothes in nearby Glenade Lake.

When her husband found her bloody clothes with a water hound lying on them, he plunged a knife into the animal's heart. The creature made a whistling sound, and another animal just like it appeared in the lake, swam swiftly toward the husband, and chased him and a friend, who fled on horseback. Eventually, they turned on the creature and stabbed it to death before it could harm either of them.

This is a colorful local legend. As early as 1684 Roderick O'Flaherty, author of a book on his Irish rambles, noted stories of an "Irish crocodile" that witnesses often mistook, at least initially, for an otter. The creature once attacked a man who managed to hit it on the head with a rock and then cut it with a knife, scaring it away. Similar beasts, O'Flaherty wrote, had been observed in other Irish lakes. "They call it *Doyarchu*, i.e., water dog, or *anchu,* which is the same thing." One witness said it had the color "of an ordinary greyhound" and "black slimey skin, without hair."

Dave Walsh, an Irish lough (lake) monster investigator, visited the gravesite and investigated the Dobhar-chu. He felt the identification of the Dobhar-chu with the fairly shy otter (which can be found at lengths of over five feet six inches [1.67 meters], including the tail) seems to be by default—no other known Irish water creature comes as close to a rational zoological explanation. Its general resemblance to an otter notwithstanding, it seems clear it could not have been one of these shy, unaggressive animals. The Dobhar-chu does not seem to have been a **Lake Monster** in the (relatively speaking) conventional sense. Walsh asks whether we can accept the Dobhar-chu as a hungry lake serpent that grows legs occasionally when it feels like eating.

No encounters with water hounds have been reported in a long time. If these creatures had any existence outside the imagination, it is hard to figure out what they could have been.

E

ELLIS, RICHARD (1938-)

Richard Ellis, known to most cryptozoologists through his work on the giant squid and sea monsters, is recognized in the larger world as a much-honored painter of marine natural history subjects. Ellis was born in New York City, and grew up in Belle Harbor, Long Island. He graduated from the University of Pennsylvania in 1959. His paintings of whales have appeared in *Audubon, National Wildlife, Australian Geographic,* the *Encyclopaedia Britannica,* and numerous other national and international publications. His shark paintings have been featured in *Sports Afield, Audubon, Sport Diver, Nautical Quarterly, Reader's Digest,* and of course his own *Book of Sharks,* now in its sixth printing, and called the most popular book on sharks ever written. He has appeared in numerous television specials and has written screenplays on whales for PBS. His research has taken him all over the world.

Although Ellis has had a long-standing interest in mythological animals (he drew unicorns, griffins, winged horses, and dragons as a child), his interest in cryptozoology really began with the 1976 discovery of the first **megamouth.** He had just published *The Book of Sharks* when the new (and totally unexpected) shark was discovered in Hawaiian waters, and eventually he illustrated it for the publication in which it was first described. As soon as he heard about the founding of the **International Society of Cryptozoology** from the shark researcher and cryptozoologist **Eugenie Clark,** Ellis joined.

In the years before writing his first cryptozoological book in 1994, *Monsters of the Sea,* Ellis had devoured the works of Arthur C. Clarke, Ray Bradbury, Herman Melville, Jules Verne, and Victor Hugo. During the writing of that work, Ellis intensively researched mystery whales, sharks (including again the megamouth), **Sea Serpents, Merbeings, Giant Octopuses,** and finally, giant squids, which so piqued his interest that he devoted two years to research on the legend of the **Kraken** and its now modern, scientifically recognized entity, *Architeuthis.*

In 1998, Ellis's book *The Search for the Giant Squid* appeared. The book, favorably reviewed in the *New York Times* and the *Washington Post,* was selected as one of the best books of 1998 by *Publishers Weekly.* He is at work on an encyclopedia of the sea.

EMELA-NTOUKA

Emela-ntouka is Lingala for "Killer of Elephants" or "Water-Elephant." The alleged animal is also referred to as *aseka-moke, ngamba-namae,* and *emia-ntouka.* The Emela-Ntouka is reported to live in the rivers and lakes of the Likouala swamp region of the Republic of the Congo (formerly the People's Republic of the Congo, and before that the French Congo Republic). The senior game inspector in the Likouala area, Lucien Blancou (who first called **Bernard Heuvelmans** the Father of Cryptozoology), was the earliest descriptor of Emela-Ntouka. Writing in a December 1954 article in *Mammalia,* Blancou said the creature was known to disembowel elephants, and a Emela-Ntouka had been killed there (but not scientifically described) around 1934.

These animals are the size of an elephant or larger. Hairless, brown to gray in color, they possess a heavy tail like a crocodile's. The most distinctive feature, a single horn located on the front of the head, resembles the ivory tusk of an elephant.

The Emela-Ntouka's legs are heavy and support the body from beneath. It leaves elephant-sized footprints, with three toes or claw marks. It emits a sound compared to a growl, rumble, howl, or roar. It apparently eats malombo, leafy plants, and leaves. But the animals are known to be violent. Native accounts have them killing elephants, water buffaloes, and other animals with their horn.

The Emela-Ntouka, according to **Roy Mackal, Karl Shuker, Scott Norman,** and others, may be a ceratopsian dinosaur such as the *Monoclonius* or *Centrosaurus.* **Loren Coleman** and more conservative cryptozoologists propose that this cryptid is an unknown form of semiaquatic rhino.

ERNST, WILLIAM "TED" (1945–1998)

W. Ted Ernst and **Robert W. Morgan** incorporated the American Anthropological Research Foundation on July 11, 1974. It is a not-for-profit corporation organized under the laws of the state of Florida. Ernst, an attorney, usually stayed in the background, fielding various cryptozoological expedition operations while the colorful Morgan dealt with media and sought funding for their various treks throughout the world. AARF's 1998 board of directors was comprised of Ernst, Morgan, and Steven Jones.

From 1974 through 1996 Ernst and AARF sponsored four formal expeditions and more than three hundred field studies in North America, Russia, the Crimea, and the Republic of Georgia. All were related to cryptoanthropology. During AARF's heyday in the 1970s, Ernst and Morgan sponsored numerous searches after the **Skunk Ape** of the Florida Everglades. Their efforts in the western United States resulted in a commercially successful documentary film, *The Search for Bigfoot*.

In the late 1970s and 1980s, Ernst and Morgan vanished from the public eye. Morgan had begun a "long and arduous apprentice under the auspices of Native American holy men," according to AARF. Ernst and Morgan resurfaced during the 1990s, after a 1991 trek to the Russian Caucasus Mountains, the Crimea, and Moscow with a refugee Tibetan lama looking for new, metaphysically based answers to the **Bigfoot, Almas,** and **Yeti** mysteries.

Ernst, who was living in Key West, died on May 21, 1998, in a sudden accident, according to an announcement by Morgan. Ernst had hit his head after diving into a Tampa-area motel swimming pool, then drowned. According to Morgan, the accident was "bizarre" since Ernst was an expert swimmer. Press accounts noted that the Tampa police filed the death as "unexplainable."

At the time of his death, Ernst was actively planning for the summer 1999 American Yeti Expedition to Mongolia, hoping to find evidence of the Almas said to inhabit the region.

F

FLATHEAD LAKE MONSTER

Witnesses describe the Flathead Lake Monster, said to inhabit northwestern Montana's Flathead Lake, as more than ten feet long. Some have reported as many as three humps on its back. Since it was first observed in 1889, seventy-eight sightings have been recorded by the state Department of Fish, Wildlife and Parks.

During 1993, a near-record eleven encounters occurred. On August 18, 1998, in the vicinity of Gravel Bay, just north of Skidoo Bay, on the lake's eastern shore, an unusually large animal was spotted. Jim Vashro, regional fisheries manager for the Department of Fish, Wildlife and Parks in Kalispell, got the report from an anonymous angler. As the angler reeled in a small lake trout from 120 feet down, a large form, judged to be several feet long, was visible for a few seconds tracking the hooked fish as it neared the surface. Vashro told the *Billings* (Montana) *Gazette* the "shape . . . and tail fin were characteristic of a sturgeon."

Was it a sturgeon? Was it the Flathead Lake Monster? Vashro said that of the department's record of sightings, no fewer than twenty-five fit the description of a white sturgeon. The other fifty-three reports, again according to Vashro, generally describe "a creature greater than ten feet long"—even up to sixty feet long—characterized by "humps and smooth skin" whose shape is "snakelike or eellike."

"Something certainly seems to be going on," Vashro said. "Very credible people have seen something variously described as a large fish or some kind of monster-like creature, usually quite long in length."

G

GAAL, ARLENE (1937–)

Arlene Gaal was born and raised in a coal-mining town in southeastern British Columbia. In 1968 she and her husband, Joe, along with their three children moved to Kelowna, located on Lake Okanagan in central British Columbia, and home to the famous **Ogopogo.** There, Gaal would make a life for herself as a teacher by profession and author/journalist by choice. She has written a weekly column for the *Kelowna Daily Courier* for the last twenty-three years.

Gaal soon began tracking the many sightings of the creature in Lake

Okanagan. Her intense search led her to the first film footage taken of the animal, the so-called Folden film, which she purchased, and to write her first book, *Beneath the Depths,* in 1976. Soon after, Alan Landsburg Productions from Los Angeles arrived to shoot the first program at Lake Okanagan, *In Search of Ogopogo,* for which Gaal served as a consultant.

Gaal became the reporting station for sightings of Ogopogo, and as the years progressed, the data accumulated would easily fill a moderate-sized room. Not only did she document sightings, but she made certain that any film, video, or still photos were preserved. In 1984 Hancock House Publishers issued her *Ogopogo, the Million Dollar Monster.*

In 1990 and 1991, Tokyo's Nippon Television hired Gaal as consultant to two productions shot on Lake Okanagan. Helicopters and submersibles searched for the creature. Video footage and sonar readings captured images that seemed to be of Ogopogo. Gaal was present for both.

Gaal has been awarded a lifetime honorary membership in the **British Columbia Scientific Cryptozoology Club.**

GIANT ANACONDA

Amazon explorers and local Indians have reported encounters with oversized serpents for over a hundred years. A classic account comes from the colorful Percy H. Fawcett. In 1906, twenty years before he vanished without a trace in the Amazon, Major Fawcett was sent by the Royal Geographic Society to survey the Rio Abuna and Acre rivers. Thirty-nine at the time, Major Fawcett was known for two sometimes contradictory character traits: he was a dreamer whose visionary ideas led him to search for lost jungle cities of fantastic wealth and splendor; he was also a scrupulously matter-of-fact military man who reported exactly what he saw in detailed and down-to-earth observations. His memoirs, striking for their contrast of visionary dreams and earthy frankness, relate many strange adventures—including an encounter with a Giant Anaconda.

It happened in 1907. With his native crew, he was drifting along the Rio Negro when he spotted a great triangular serpentine head appearing at the bow of the boat. Fawcett opened fire, hitting the creature in the spine. In its dying throes the snake thrashed the water all around the boat.

Hunters encounter a Giant Anaconda. (Bernard Heuvelmans)

According to Fawcett, the snake measured forty-five feet out of the water and seventeen in it, a total of sixty-two feet. The diameter was relatively small, only twelve inches. Nevertheless, Fawcett had no way to carry the specimen back from the interior, and his sighting has since been viewed as a wild traveler's tale by conservative zoologists.

An early skeptic, herpetologist Raymond Ditmars, rejected the story on the grounds that anacondas do not get much longer than nineteen feet. Most snake experts now allow for thirty feet. **Bernard Heuvelmans,** in his chapter on Giant Anacondas in *On the Track of Unknown Animals,* remarked that the "American herpetologist Thomas Barbour, the great Brazilian expert Dr. Afranio do Amaral of the Institute at Butantan, and Dr. Jose Candido de Melo of the Rio de Janeiro Zoo all agree on forty-five feet."

In an article in the **International Society of Cryptozoology** newsletter, **J. Richard Greenwell** mentions that "the longest measured and accepted length [for an anaconda]—from a 1940s encounter by a Colombian petroleum geologist—is 'only' thirty-seven feet, six inches, and even this has recently been questioned."

GIANT FOREST HOG

In 1904 zoologists were surprised at the discovery of the giant forest hog (*Hylochoerus meinertzhageni*), only three years after the **okapi** was found. The latter was widely assumed to be the last major mammal yet uncatalogued. Not to be confused with the wild boar of oak woods and warthog of arid lands, the long-rumored giant forest hog of the tropical jungles was discovered and documented in Kenya.

Sightings of the world's largest wild swine had been recorded since 1688, when reports came out of what is now Liberia. Between 1888 and 1890, during his famous expedition to the Congo, Sir Henry Stanley collected accounts. He failed, however, to capture the elusive beast.

Lieutenant Richard Meinertzhagen of the British East African Rifles took up the challenge. On two occasions in early 1904 locals showed him recently killed giant forest hogs on the slopes of Mount Kenya. He obtained two whole skins. Soon afterward, in May, Meinertzhagen finally came upon a dead specimen near Lake Victoria in Nandi country. Its skull was enormous—three feet in length. He sent the evidence (including an older skull) to scientists in London. In response he was shocked to learn that the giant ground hog was an entirely new species; indeed, it constituted a brand-new genus.

The giant forest hog is three feet high and seven feet long. It has a pair of massive, curved tusks from its upper mandibles, and a pair of strange warts that look like fungus under its eyes, covering most of the middle of its face. Highly vocal, the animals emit a barking call that carries over long distances.

Today, three known but rare populations of the giant forest hog exist in the thick jungles of Kenya-Tanzania, bordering Lake Victoria, into northeastern Congo (Zaire) and southern Ethopia; Cameroon and the People's Republic of Congo; and West Africa, from Ghana, through the Ivory Coast into Liberia. The most westerly population is now officially endangered. **Karl Shuker** thinks, based on so-far-unconfirmed reports from Guinea and Guinea-Bissau, that there may be a fourth population.

GIANT MONKEY

Reports from around the globe describe what appear to be enormous monkeys.

Asians give the name for the mountain range that includes Mount

Everest as Mahalanguar Himal, which translates as "The Mountains of the Great Monkeys." South Americans report sightings of Giant Monkeys dating back to the nineteenth century. In North America, these animals are sometimes referred to as "Devil Monkeys" by such researchers as **Mark A. Hall,** while eyewitnesses report having seen "mystery kangaroos." **Loren Coleman** investigated the 1973 case of livestock killings at Albany, Kentucky, caused by three Giant Monkeys, each with a long, black bushy tail. In 1969, **Bigfoot** researchers **John Green** and **René Dahinden** investigated reports of a large, monkey-like animal with a long tail, seen near Mamquam, British Columbia. In both Kentucky and British Columbia, the animals left distinctive three-toed tracks.

Giant Monkeys are said to be four to six feet tall. The smaller juveniles often resemble wallabies or "baby kangaroos." The mode of leaping to move around has also caused them to be confused with kangaroos. They have a barrel chest, thick arms, powerful legs, and a bushy tail. Their faces are baboon- or doglike, with dark, "mean" eyes and pointed ears. They have short to shaggy hair, varying in color from red to black. Their footprints are about twelve inches long, but tracks up to fifteen inches have been found, getting thinner the longer they get. Distinctive footprints show three rounded toes.

The animals can be obstinate toward canines and humans, and eyewitnesses sometimes merely comment on the creatures' aggressive looks. Though generally thought to be vegetarians, they may kill livestock and small game. Giant Monkeys exhibit a wide range of primate hoots, calls, screeches, whistles, and "blood-chilling screams." Their smell has compounded the identification problem, as some are labeled as **Skunk Apes.**

Bernard Heuvelmans, when commenting on Giant Monkey reports he considers valid, points to finds in India of a giant baboon, *Simopithecus,* twice as big as the largest baboon, literally a giant form of *Theropithecus gelada,* the gelada baboon of Ethiopia. He notes that paleontologist Robert Broom found fossils of a similar giant baboon, *Dinopithecus*. Writing in the 1950s, Heuvelmans wondered if these two could have something to do with the native legends of the **Nandi Bear.** From his own later research, Hall concluded that the American version of the Giant Monkey seemed identical to *Simopithecus*. Recent fossil finds of a giant howler-spider monkey in South America may have some bearing on these accounts.

Hall, in decades-long discussions with Loren Coleman, developed the concept of the Giant Monkey. *The Field Guide to Bigfoot, Yeti, and Other Mystery Primates Worldwide,* by Loren Coleman and **Patrick Huyghe** (1999), is the first book to formalize the use of the phrase "Giant Monkey" to describe this group of reports.

GIANT OCTOPUS

A discovery made on Anastasia Island, Florida, on the evening of November 30, 1896, set in motion a controversy that has never been settled. Two young cyclists came upon an immense carcass whose great weight had driven it deep into the sand. Having no idea what it was but sensing it was something important, they alerted others to the presence of the mysterious object. One of them, physician DeWitt Webb of the St. Augustine Historical Society and Institute of Science, arrived the next day with a handful of associates. The group estimated that the object was recently arrived and weighed close to five tons.

A Giant Octopus attacks a ship, a rare sight. (FPL)

When they measured the parts above the sand, the investigators found that the blob was twenty-three feet long, four feet high, and eighteen feet across at its widest point. Its skin was somewhere between light pink and white, with a silvery cast. They were certain that these were not the remains of a whale. As incredible as it seemed, they decided, these were from an octopus of unprecedented dimensions. On a later trip one investigator found fragments of arms. The *American Naturalist* (April 1897) reported that "one arm was lying west of the body, twenty-three feet long; one stump of arm, west of body, about four feet; three arms lying south of body and from appearance attached to same, longest one measured over thirty-two feet, the other arms were three to five feet shorter." It looked as if the animal had been partially dismembered before dying and washing to shore. Subsequently, a storm caused the Globster to wash out to sea again. It resurfaced two miles to the south. (See page 99.)

Yale University zoologist A. E. Verrill and Webb corresponded about the discovery. Though initially skeptical of the octopus identification (octopuses are not believed to exceed twenty-five feet; this creature's arm length was seventy-five feet, Verrill estimated), Verrill soon embraced it, even naming the animal after himself: *Octopus giganteus Verrill*. Meantime, weather conditions had moved the carcass, with even more of its body missing, to a third location. On January 17, 1897, Webb, who was trying to recover it before it was lost forever, wrote W. H. Dall, curator of mollusks at the National Museum, Washington, D.C.:

> Yesterday I took four horses, six men, three sets tackle, a lot of heavy planking, and a rigger to superintend the work and succeeded in rolling the Invertebrate out of the pit and placing it about forty feet higher upon the beach where it now rests on the flooring of heavy plank . . . on being straightened out to measure twenty-one feet instead of eighteen. . . . A good part of the mantle or head remains attached near to the more slender part of the body. . . . The body was then opened for the entire length of twenty-one feet. . . . The slender part of the body was entirely empty of internal organs. And the organs of the remainder were not large and did not look as if the animal had been long dead. . . . The muscular coat which seems to be all there is of the invertebrate is from two and three to six inches in thickness. The fibers of the external coat are longitudinal and the inner transverse . . . no caudal fin or any appearance if there had been any . . . no beak or head or eyes remaining . . . no pen [internal shell of a squid] to be found nor any evidence of any body structure whatever.

Though neither Dall nor Verrill came down to Florida to examine the carcass, Verrill retracted the giant octopus identification and wrote that the carcass was nothing but the "upper part of the head and nose of a sperm whale." The National Museum's Frederic Augustus Lucas called the samples he examined "blubber, nothing more nor less." Webb bitterly disagreed, and Dall and others expressed quiet disbelief in the claim. Nonetheless, it remained the official explanation, and it would not be challenged for decades.

In 1971 marine biologist **Forrest G. Wood** and octopus specialist Joseph F. Gennaro wrote that the samples they had examined provided clear evidence that "the St. Augustine sea monster was in fact an octopus." Though Wood and Gennaro were respected figures in their fields, that did not keep them from being ridiculed and then ignored. A decade and a half later cryptozoologist **Roy P. Mackal** of the University of Chicago analyzed samples. He concluded that they came from a "gigantic cephalopod, probably an octopus, not referable to any known species."

In a disputed study published in 1995 in *Biological Bulletin,* four biologists attacked the Wood/Gennaro and Mackal analyses. Their own study of amino acids from the carcass showed that the animal could not have been a giant octopus or any invertebrate. The remains were probably from a whale, the biologists remarked, and "likely the entire skin"— notwithstanding the fact that whale skin cannot be removed intact, even artificially, from the animal. Even the skeptical marine expert **Richard Ellis** rejected the theory, and French cryptozoologist **Michel Raynal,** in a scathing review of the study, found numerous methodological problems and dubiously substantiated conclusions. As Ellis would write, "the mysteries remain unsolved and the legend endures."

GIANT PANDA

The giant panda (*Ailuropoda melanoleuca*) was not known outside Tibet until March 23, 1869, when native hunters brought a French missionary and naturalist Perè Armand David a dead specimen. In 1914, German zoologist Hugo Weigold became the first Westerner to see a giant panda alive in the wild. Soon museums were sending off expeditions to obtain a specimen for their collections.

Yet nature does not always yield her secrets easily, anthropologist George Agogino observed in 1961, pointing to the example of the giant panda as an object lesson for both cryptozoologists and those who would decry their quest. "From 1869 until 1929, a period of sixty years, a dozen well-staffed and well-equipped professional zoological collecting teams unsuccessfully sought an animal the size of a small bear in a restricted area," Agogino wrote. "The giant panda lives in the same general area and at the same general elevation (six thousand to twelve thousand feet) as the **Yeti,** yet this animal remained hidden for over sixty years."

In 1929, the first Western hunters to kill a giant panda were two sons of a former President, Theodore and Kermit Roosevelt, who shot one out of a hollow pine tree. Finally, eight years later, **Ruth Harkness** and **Gerald Russell** brought out the first live giant panda. It took sixty-seven years from the time of the giant panda's Western "discovery" until its live capture.

GIANT SALAMANDER

The Giant Salamanders of California's Trinity Alps have been reported for more than seven decades. Frank L. Griffith was one of the first modern witnesses. During the 1920s, Griffith was hunting deer near the head of the Trinity Alps' New River. At the bottom of a lake there, Griffith spotted five salamanders ranging five to nine feet long. He caught one on a hook, but he could not pull it out of the river.

After hearing the story of Griffith's Giant Salamanders, biologist Thomas L. Rodgers made four unsuccessful trips in 1948 to try to locate the animals. He had speculated that they might be an isolated group of Pacific giant salamanders, *Dicamptodon,* which never get to be much bigger than a foot long. He also thought they could be a relict population of *Megalobatrachus,* the Asian giant salamander, an animal measuring five to six feet. These inhabit swift-moving mountain streams in Japan and China, similar to those found in the Trinity Alps.

Herpetologist George S. Myers had learned of the Trinity Alps sighting and thought the Asian link made sense. Writing in a 1951 scientific journal, Myers recalled his encounter with a Giant Salamander captured in 1939 in the Sacramento River. Myers was called by a commercial fisherman who had found the animal in one of his catfish nets. Myers was able to examine the specimen carefully for half an hour or so. He noted that it was a different color from those found in the Japanese and Chinese species. It was dark brown, not slaty gray as the Asian types were, and it had dull yellow spots, whereas those on known giant salamanders are a darker gray. He wrote in *Copeia* 2 (1951):

The animal was a fine *Megalobatrachus* (unquestionably identified generically by its closed gill openings), in perfect
condition. . . . It was between twenty-five and thirty inches in
length. . . . The source of the specimen is, of course, unknown.
Its strange coloration even suggested the possibility of a native
Californian *Megalobatrachus,* which would not be zoogeograph-
ically surprising, but no other captures have been reported.

A few years later, animal handler Vern Harden of Pioneer, California, claimed he saw a dozen Giant Salamanders in a remote Trinity
Alps lake called Hubbard Lake. He managed to hook one but had to release it because of a threatening snowstorm. A quick measurement revealed, however, the Giant Salamander's length: an astonishing eight feet
four inches. Though he had no evidence with which to back up his story,
he related it to Stanford University biologist Victory Twitty. Twitty's
comment: "Spectacular, if true." The reaction of Father Hubbard, the
lake's namesake, was: "Yes, I know Harden. He's a nice fellow, and I
think he ought to write fiction."

But Father Hubbard was a formidable character. A Jesuit scholar,
known throughout the world as the "Glacier Priest" because of his pen-
chant for climbing the Alps of Europe, Hubbard was an explorer, naturalist, photographer, and popular lecturer. His best-known expeditions
were made in Alaska during the 1930s.

When Father Hubbard took an interest in the Trinity Alps' Giant
Salamanders, the media listened. Despite Father Hubbard's remark
about Harden's credibility, the priest did send the supposed witness to
his brother, Captain John D. Hubbard. Father Hubbard noted that although the whole thing sounded fantastic, based on his examination of
the growing body of eyewitness reports, he was fairly certain there were
Giant Salamanders. "And next fall we expect to prove it," the seventy-
two-year-old Hubbard said at the time, "if I have to lead an expedition
from the university myself."

During 1958 and 1959, both Hubbards were believed to have been
associated with a couple of expeditions in search of the Giant Salamanders. In 1960 Father Hubbard stated he had established the existence of
huge amphibians in the Trinity region, but unfortunately no record of
the Hubbard expeditions exists. Perhaps they never really occurred.

Tom Slick, though mainly interested in **Bigfoot,** also went looking for Giant Salamanders in 1960. Slick let it be known that he wanted to join the leagues of Giant Salamander seekers, and told the members of Slick's Pacific Northwest Expedition to try to find one. They couldn't. Some of his hired Bigfoot hunters became angry with Slick for what they saw as a silly side trip.

Meanwhile, on September 1, 1960, three zoology professors— Robert C. Stebbins of the University of California–Berkeley, Tom Rodgers of Chico State College, and Nathan Cohen of Modesto Junior College—left Willow Creek, California, on their own Giant Salamander expedition. A few years later Rodgers (who, as noted above, had also looked in 1948) would remember that they were accompanied by "ten laymen," and some of them mistook logs for Giant Salamanders. He said the group collected only about a dozen *Dicamptodons;* the largest was eleven and one-half inches long.

The deeply skeptical Rodgers expressed the hope that "this evidence will kill rumors about any Giant Salamanders (much less *Megalobatrachus*) in the Trinity Mountains of California." Rodgers's official 1962 debunking seems to have ended most zoological interest in the Giant Salamanders of the Trinities.

That is, until recently. In 1997 the Kyle Mizokami Trinity Alps Giant Salamanders Expedition established itself as the latest effort in the area. Mizokami is a Japanese-American writer who has done extensive research on American Indian legends of what may be the Bigfoot. Much like Slick, Mizokami put aside his Bigfoot research to hunt for Giant Salamanders.

Perhaps the Giant Salamanders of the Trinities, if they exist, are American examples of *Megalobatrachus*. The amphibian family to which the Japanese and Chinese *Megalobatrachus* belongs is Cryptobrachidae. It has only one known North American member, *Cryptobranchus,* the Hellbender. It is the largest known American salamander, at some twenty-nine inches, but much smaller than the five and a half feet of the Asian giant salamanders. Like its cousins in China and Japan, the Hellbender is found in the mountains, namely the Appalachians and the Ozarks in the U.S.

Still, nothing like *Megalobatrachus* has been zoologically documented in the American West.

GIANT SLOTH

Giant Sloths of many varieties lived in South America until ten thousand years ago, according to accepted knowledge. But cryptozoologists from **Bernard Heuvelmans** to David Oren find evidence for the Giant Sloth's survival into modern times. There is reason to believe that Indians hunted them; "fresh" skin and dung were discovered in a cave in Argentina in 1895. No less a figure than the governor of Argentina, Ramon Lista, said he saw a creature that might match the description of a medium-sized, hairy Giant Sloth.

GIANT TURTLES

In the third century Aelian wrote: "This sea [the Indian Ocean] produces monstrous turtles, the shells of which can be used as roofs." In 1154, referring to turtles in the same region, in the sea of Herkend, near Sri Lanka, Al Edrisi in his *Geography* mentioned that he had seen turtles thirty feet long. They had, he claimed, laid as many as a thousand eggs apiece.

Icebergs are not the only titanic things, as **Karl Shuker** has amusingly noted, that may be floating around in the Atlantic. Apparently ships of yesteryear had to watch out for Giant Turtles, too. Cryptozoologists have observed that the area off Newfoundland and Nova Scotia, a region with a long history of **Kraken** encounters as well, seems to be a haven for these oceangoing Giant Turtles.

Off Newfoundland's Grand Bank, on March 30, 1883, the schooner *Annie E. Hall* came upon something that its crew first thought was an overturned ship. It turned out to be a giant, and very much alive, turtle. Thirty feet wide and forty feet long, it appeared to have twenty-foot-long flippers.

Near Nova Scotia, in June 1956, the crew of the steamer *Rhapsody* reportedly encountered an enormous white-shelled turtle measuring forty-five feet long, with fifteen-foot-long flippers. The creature raised its head all of eight feet out of the water. Crew members had the Canadian Coast Guard warn away local boats.

In his book *In the Wake of the Sea-Serpents,* **Bernard Heuvelmans** writes of the "Father-of-All-Turtles," borrowing a name from a Sumatran folktale that he thinks refers to Giant Turtles of the sort some witnesses mistake for a **Sea Serpent.** According to Heuvelmans, "This very rare type is described as a gigantic turtle and is sometimes given very specifically turtle-like features, such as a very wide mouth which splits the head in two when it opens, big prominent eyes, and very large scales on the back." Heuvelmans thinks that if these creatures do exist, they live for the most part in temperate waters.

Things also look promising in Vietnam for more new freshwater Giant Turtle discoveries. According to legends associated with Hoan Kiem Lake (located in downtown Hanoi), a giant golden turtle rose from the waters in the mid-fifteenth century to snatch a magical sword from Emperor Ly Thai To, fresh with victory over Chinese invaders. The king and his courtiers were boating on the lake when a Giant Turtle arose, took the magic sword, then plunged to the depths and returned the blade to its divine owners. Since that time the lake's name has been "Ho Hoan Kiem," which means "Lake of the Returned Sword." The story is retold in thousands of schoolbooks and in popular performances at Hanoi's water-puppet theaters.

In recent years the Vietnamese state press has run photographs of crowds gathered at the lakeside pointing excitedly at some fuzzy shapes on the surface. Finally, in December 1996, the legend became real when witnesses reported seeing a large and ancient turtle. A swarm of bubbles would herald its arrival at the murky surface. A flipper would pop out, and part of its shell (estimated to be forty inches across in its entirety) would rise to view. Sometimes its green-and-yellow head, the size of a football, would appear. On one occasion in December 1996, the creature came to within six and one-half feet of the shore, swiveling its head to show a great downcast mouth, its skin peeling.

In early 1998 closer encounters set Hanoi abuzz. The witnesses were numerous pedestrians who noticed unusual activity in the lake. They described one to three turtles. A recent sighting, among the most credible, occurred on March 24, 1998, when passersby caught a glimpse of the turtles as they surfaced to take in the spring air.

An amateur cameraman caught the creatures on video, which subsequently aired on Vietnamese television. The station also claimed the turtles made a second appearance on April 5. Researchers who have been trying to get a glimpse of the turtles believe they could be the only ones of their kind in the world.

Mythology and science mix in the work of Hanoi National Univer-

sity professor Ha Dinh Duc, the world's foremost expert on the turtles of
Hoan Kiem Lake. "The Hoan Kiem turtle is the world's biggest freshwater turtle," he says. "It can measure two meters (six and one-half feet)
long and can weigh as much as two hundred kilograms (440 pounds)
Professor Duc has been studying the turtles for the past decade, sometimes in conjunction with international reptile specialists. A Hoan Kiem
turtle, found and preserved thirty years ago, is now displayed at a small
temple on an island in the lake. The plaque tells visitors it is thought to
be more than five hundred years old—old enough, in fact, to be the turtle of the legend.

Much remains unknown about these ancient monsters living in the
center of downtown Hanoi—their number, reproductive ability, origins,
and especially, the question of whether or not they're unique to the Lake
of the Returned Sword. Duc says, "If we have cooperation from international experts and they determine this is a new species, it will be a significant contribution to world biological diversity. And since the turtles are
right here in the middle of urban Hanoi, many people can easily come to
see them." In this vein, local civic and governmental groups plan to clear
the Lake of the Returned Sword of pollution that may be harmful to the
big turtles. The construction of an artificial beach has been proposed to
facilitate breeding.

GIBBONS, WILLIAM (1958–)

Bill Gibbons first became interested in mystery animals during his child-
hood years in Scotland. After watching an early movie adaptation of Sir
Arthur Conan Doyle's *The Lost World,* the young Gibbons wondered if
perhaps there really are living dinosaurs, or at least animals very much
like them, alive in the remote areas of our planet. His curiosity eventually
resulted in two major expeditions to the Congo, in 1985–86 and 1992, in
search of **Mokele-mbembe.** Two other field investigations were conducted on the island of Mauritius in the southern Indian Ocean in 1990
and 1997, after two European visitors claimed dodo sightings. Operation Congo III and Project Dodo III are currently under development.
Gibbons has set as his goal to go on one cryptozoology expedition per
year, for the next decade. Gibbons is pursuing a doctorate in cultural anthropology from Warnborough College in England and is working on a
series of cryptozoology books.

GLOBSTERS

Ivan T. Sanderson did much to publicize Globsters, a word he coined to describe those unusual beachings of enormous globs of seemingly unidentifiable flesh and bone that are often initially labeled the remains of **Sea Serpents.** Most strandings, of course, are found to be mundane animals. Though such animals have been seen for centuries, the "original" Globster washed ashore in western Tasmania in August 1960, and was later identified as the partial corpse of a whale. Other famous, usually round and large Globsters have beached in Bermuda, Tasmania (again), New Zealand, South Africa, and St. Augustine, Florida. While most Globsters are found to be basking sharks, a few may be cryptozoological surprises, such as the **Giant Octopus.**

Mark Chorvinsky has created an extensive "homepage" for Globster

Dr. DeWitt Webb and the most famous Globster in history, the carcass of a Giant Octopus that washed ashore at Anastasia Beach, St. Augustine, Florida, November 1896. (FPL)

data: http://www.strangemag.com/globhome.html, which wins our prize for the most unique website ever created on one specific cryptozoological topic.

GOBLIN UNIVERSE

The phrase "Goblin Universe" is often applied to the earth's supernatural and otherwise esoteric residents. Long ago classification systems were created for legendary beings and entities of the Goblin Universe. As the anthropologist John Napier points out, this kind of sorting became so detailed that classical Greek mythology, for example, recognized three types of Cyclopes.

"Goblin Universe" was first used popularly in Napier's much-read *Bigfoot* (1972). Nevertheless the Goblin Universe figured in scholarly discussions about **Bigfoot** and, by extension, cryptozoology in general as early as 1964. Among the first places it appeared was in "Unknown Hominids and New World Legends," by Bacil F. Kirtley, *Western Folklore*, vol. XXIII, April 1964, no. 2. Most people, however, incorrectly cite Napier as the source of the phrase.

F. W. Holiday's book *The Goblin Universe* (1986), published seven years after his death, combined the author's early **Lake Monster** research with occult speculations about the nature of the beasts. Soon Goblin Universe came to mean paranormal explanations, though that is not entirely what Napier or Holiday had in mind. Before his death (and too late to put his revised views into print), Holiday would reject such approaches, returning to an earlier conviction that Lake Monsters are animals in the biological sense.

GREEN, JOHN (1927–)

John Green was born in Vancouver, British Columbia. After receiving a master's degree in journalism from Columbia University in 1958, Green was, for more than thirty years, a newspaperman from Harrison Hot Springs, British Columbia.

Green is one of the leading figures in the field, having started investigating **Bigfoot/Sasquatch** reports in 1957, and worked with **Tom Slick, René Dahinden, Bob Titmus,** and others in California and British Columbia in the early days of the inquiries. He is a major influence on Bigfoot researchers because he actively wrote about his and others'

John Green works on his latest data entry project of over three thousand incidents regarding the Sasquatch of the Pacific Northwest. (John Green)

Sasquatch research. He published several monographs that became the standard references for the Canadian cryptid, and wrote the classic book on the North American subject, *Sasquatch: The Apes Among Us* (1978).

Green chronicled some of the more famous cases, such as those of William Roe, who raised his rifle but did not shoot at a female Bigfoot in 1955, and Albert Ostman, who was kidnapped by a family of the unknown hairy giants in 1924. Green reportedly has gathered more than two thousand sightings, and several hundred incidents of giant footprint finds. He speaks frequently at Bigfoot conferences, continues to interview witnesses, and conducts on-site examinations of the Sasquatch phenomenon throughout the Pacific Northwest.

GREENWELL, J. RICHARD (1942–)

J. Richard Greenwell has served as secretary of the **International Society of Cryptozoology** since its founding in 1982. He was instrumental in creating the ISC after given the idea through an introduction to **Roy P. Mackal** by Jerome Clark. Greenwell has been funded in his ISC position to travel to many parts of the world to investigate cryptozoological claims and specimens, including **Mokele-mbembe** in the Congo with Roy P. Mackal, and Ri, a reported **Merbeing** that turned out to be a manatee relative, the dugong, in New Guinea, with anthropologist Roy Wagner. Greenwell has also researched **Onza** (a mystery cat found to be a subspecies of puma) in Mexico, as well as the **Yeren** (Wildmen) in China with anthropologist Frank Poirier.

Originally from Surrey, England, Mr. Greenwell spent six years in South America, after which he was appointed research coordinator of the Office of Arid Lands Studies at the University of Arizona, in Tucson. In 1991, he was awarded an honorary doctorate by Mexico's University of Guadalajara. A member of numerous scientific societies, including the American Society of Mammalogists, Greenwell is a fellow of both the Explorers Club (New York) and the Royal Geographical Society (London). He is the author of more than one hundred scholarly and popular articles, and, since 1993, he has been a columnist for *BBC Wildlife,* Britain's leading animal conservation publication. During the 1990s, Greenwell has frequently been a paid consultant on various television programs dealing with cryptozoology.

GRIMM, JACK (1925–1998)

Jack Grimm, who came to be known through media stories about his "quixotic quests" to find **Bigfoot,** Noah's Ark, the **Loch Ness Monsters,** and the *Titanic* was, with **Tom Slick** and F. Kirk Johnson, among the Texas millionaries who gave financial and other support to cryptozoology.

Founder of Grimm Oil Company, the man known in his native Abilene as "Cadillac Jack" spent a reported $2 million to find and salvage the *Titanic* in the 1980s. He recovered approximately 1,700 artifacts from the wreckage in 1987 but has not been credited with finding the legendary ship first.

In the 1970s Grimm spent millions of dollars in quests for Noah's Ark and Nessie. He hired two photographers to slog through the western Canadian wilderness in a futile hunt for **Sasquatch.**

Grimm died on January 8, 1998.

H

HALL, DENNIS JAY (1956–)

Dennis Jay Hall was born in Middlebury, Vermont. In 1973, he was elected president of the Vergennes Chapter of the Vermont Archeological Society. While he was serving in that capacity, the board of trustees of the Vermont Archeological Society appointed him to a special task force to write laws to protect archaeological sites. A lifelong love of Vermont history has led him to many discoveries, from the sites of the earliest Native Americans to the cellar holes of the first white settlers.

In the summer of 1965, when he was nine years old, Hall had an experience that would change his life. His aunt Shirley and uncle Pete Bigelow had been boating in Plattsburgh Bay. While anchored in the crystal-clear, sandy-bottomed bay, they saw one of the animals known as **Champ** swim under their boat. The tale they told when they came home changed Hall's life.

For the past twenty years Hall has been engaged in the search for the Champ animals that reportedly inhabit Lake Champlain. He has sighted them on no fewer than nineteen occasions. He now directs Champ Quest.

Hall is currently writing a book about Champ titled *The Ultimate Search*. It is a combination field guide and narrative of his two-decade inquiry.

HALL, MARK A. (1946–)

Mark A. Hall, a native Minnesotan, has been intrigued by nature's anomalies all his life. For nearly forty years he has actively pursued historical records, traveled throughout eastern North America, and gathered eye-

Mark A. Hall. (Loren Coleman)

witness testimony concerning cryptozoological phenomena. He coauthored one of the first studies of Native "**Bigfoot**" traditions. Hall, who has formulated unknown hominoid theories for years, proposed that North America is home not only to the Bigfoot of the **Patterson Film** but also to drastically different primates such as the **True Giant** (*Giganto-pithecus*) and the Taller-hominid (a survival of the recorded fossil known as *Homo gardarensis*). He worked closely with **Ivan T. Sanderson** on a variety of projects, including the early investigations of the **Minnesota Iceman,** and served as a director of the Society for the Investigation of the Unexplained during the 1970s. Hall edits and publishes the journal *Wonders,* devoted mostly to cryptozoology. He is the author of *Thunder-birds—The Living Legend!* (2nd edition, 1994), *Natural Mysteries* (2nd edition, 1991), and *The Yeti, Bigfoot and True Giants* (2nd edition, 1997). More books are in progress, including *Living Fossils* (1999).

HARKNESS, RUTH (1900–1947)

Ruth Harkness discovered, captured, and returned to the West with the first **giant panda.**

In the 1930s, the rush was on to be the first to catch a giant panda, known only from dead specimens and still mysterious. The adventurer and live-animal collector William H. Harkness, fresh from the success of his **Komodo dragon** exploits, organized a grueling expedition for the New York Zoological Society and Bronx Zoo in search of the giant panda. The Harkness expedition was to go to Tibet and return with the first legendary and elusive specimen. Instead, Harkness was delayed by permit politics and turned back at one point by the unstable situation in Szechwan. In February 1936, Harkness died in Shanghai.

Ruth Harkness introduces a new giant panda, Diana (in foreground), to her first discovery, Su-Lin, at the Brookfield Zoo, Chicago, in 1938. (Ruth Harkness)

On hearing the news, his widow, Ruth Harkness, socialite, New York clothing designer-turned-adventurer, traveled on a slow boat to China, not arriving until July, and took over the reins of the expedition. Amazingly, her new expedition, after ten fruitless days in the wild, found a live giant panda, a cub kept by a villager. Harkness, with Yang Di Lin and **Gerald Russell,** returned with the panda, named Su-Lin, to Chicago's Brookfield Zoo in 1937.

Pandas became the animal for zoos to acquire. Harkness returned for more giant pandas and on her second expedition quickly brought two back—this after decades of frustration by other searchers. Sadly, she never left any records of her second or third expeditions, according to Richard Perry's *The World of the Giant Panda.*

Three giant pandas were captured and taken to the United States in the 1930s: Mei Mei, Pandora, and Pan. Pao Pei was the last panda to be captured and exported by a Western nation. By 1945 there were only five giant pandas outside China, most of which had been caught by Ruth Harkness, who would die two years later. In 1953, there were no giant pandas alive in captivity anywhere, even in Tibet and China.

Today, the giant panda is still a highly endangered animal, a popular but rare animal in capitivity, and therefore, the logo animal for the World Wildlife Fund. Few know of Ruth Harkness's role in bringing this animal out of folklore into zoological awareness.

Ruth Harkness's giant panda expedition still ranks among the bravest and most important cryptozoological efforts of the last hundred years. Her adventures can be read in her two books, *The Lady and the Panda* and *The Baby Giant Panda* (both published in 1938).

HEUVELMANS, BERNARD (1916–)

Bernard Heuvelmans, the "Father of Cryptozoology," was born in Le Havre, France, and found he had a love of natural history from an early age. His interest in unknown animals was first piqued as a youngster by his reading of science fiction adventures such as Jules Verne's *Twenty Thousand Leagues Under the Sea* and Sir Arthur Conan Doyle's *The Lost World.* After earning his doctoral degree before World War II with a thesis on the classification of the hitherto unclassifiable teeth of the aardvark, Heuvelmans spent the next years writing about the history of science. But when he read a 1948 *Saturday Evening Post* article, in which biologist **Ivan T. Sanderson** sympathetically discussed the evidence for

Bernard Heuvelmans is seen here, in 1961, with the young gorilla Kaisi. (Bernard Heuvelmans)

relict dinosaurs, he decided to pursue a vague, unfocused interest in a systematic way.

From then on, Heuvelmans sought evidence in scientific and literary sources. Within a few years he had amassed so much material that he was ready to write a large book. That book turned out to be *Sur la piste des bêtes ignorées,* published in 1955 and better known in its English translation three years later as *On the Track of Unknown Animals.* More than four decades later, the book remains in print, with an excess of one million copies sold in various translations and editions, including one in 1995 with a large updated introduction.

The book's impact was enormous. As one critic remarked at the time, "Because his research is based on rigorous dedication to scientific method and scholarship and his solid background in zoology, Heuvelmans's findings are respected throughout the scientific community." Soon Heuvelmans was engaged in massive correspondence as his library and other researches continued. In the course of letter-writing, he invented the word "cryptozoology" (it does not appear in *On the Track of Unknown Animals*). That word saw print for the first time in 1959 when

French wildlife official Lucien Blancou dedicated a book to the "master of cryptozoology."

Writing in *Cryptozoology* in 1984, Heuvelmans said, "I tried to write about it according to the rules of scientific documentation." Because of the unorthodox nature of his interests, however, he had no institutional sponsorship and had to support himself with his writing. "That is why," he wrote, "I have always had to make my books fascinating for the largest possible audience."

Heuvelmans and his book influenced the investigative work of cryptozoology supporter **Tom Slick**. Sanderson, who influenced Heuvelmans, in turn was influenced by Heuvelmans. He served as confidential consultant with Sanderson on Slick's secret board of advisers. Heuvelmans was asked to examine a "**Yeti** skullcap" brought back by Sir Edmund Hillary's *World Book* expedition of 1960. He was also one of the first to declare it was a ritual object made from the skin of a serow, a small goatlike animal found in the Himalayas. Over the years, without fanfare, Heuvelmans has journeyed from the shores of Loch Ness to the jungles of Malaysia, interviewing witnesses and examining the evidence for cryptids.

On the Track of Unknown Animals was concerned exclusively with land animals. The second of his works to be translated into English, *In the Wake of the Sea-Serpents* (1968), covered the ocean's unknowns, including the recognized but still in some ways enigmatic giant squid. In 1968, Heuvelmans (at Sanderson's invitation) examined what was represented to be the frozen cadaver of a hairy hominoid, the **Minnesota Iceman,** which was the subject of his *L'homme de Néanderthal est toujours vivant* (with **Boris Porshnev,** 1974). Other books, none yet translated into English, include works on surviving dinosaurs and relict hominids in Africa.

Heuvelmans's Center for Cryptozoology, established in 1975, was first housed near Le Bugue in the south of France, but in recent years moved to LeVesinet, closer to Paris. It consists of his huge private library and his massive files. Heuvelmans was elected president when the **International Society of Cryptozoology** was founded in Washington, D.C., in 1982. He still holds that position. In a 1984 interview he expressed the desire to write a twenty-volume cryptozoology encyclopedia, but no volume has appeared to date, owing to the death of a translator and other problems. Heuvelmans has lapsed into a period of active but mostly unseen writing except for the rare magazine article.

Heuvelmans's health appears to be failing. When in February 1997 he was awarded the Gabriele Peters Prize for Fantastic Science at the Zoological Museum of the University of Hamburg, Germany, he was unable to appear to collect the prize of 10,000 marks (about $6,000) and sent his friend, journalist and cryptozoologist Werner Reichenbach, to accept on his behalf. Heuvelmans has refused television and other journalistic interviews in recent years.

A list of Heuvelmans's books follows:

1955 *Sur la piste des bêtes ignorées*. Paris: Plon.
1958 *Dans le sillage des monstres marins—Le Kraken et le Poulpe Colossal*. Paris: Plon.
1958 *On the Track of Unknown Animals*. London: Hart-Davis.
1959 *On the Track of Unknown Animals*. New York: Hill and Wang.
1965 *Le Grand-Serpent-de-Mer, le problème zoologique et sa solution*. Paris: Plon.
1965 *On the Track of Unknown Animals*. (Abridged, revised.) New York: Hill and Wang.
1968 *In the Wake of the Sea-Serpents*. New York: Hill and Wang.
1974 (with Boris F. Porshnev) *L'homme de Néanderthal est toujours vivant*. Paris: Plon.
1975 *Dans le sillage des monstres marins—Le Kraken et le Poulpe Colossal*. Paris: François Beauval (2nd ed.).
1975 *Le Grand-Serpent-de-Mer, le problème zoologique et sa solution*. Paris: Plon (2nd ed.).
1978 *Les derniers dragons d'Afrique*. Paris: Plon.
1980 *Les bêtes humaines d'Afrique*. Paris: Plon.
1995 *On the Track of Unknown Animals*. London: Kegan Paul International.

HOMINOLOGY

Hominology is an important subcategory of cryptozoology that deserves a moment of explanation. Russian researcher **Dmitri Bayanov** coined the word "hominology" around 1973, to denote those investigations that study humanity's as yet undiscovered near relatives, including **Almas, Yeti, Bigfoot/Sasquatch,** and other unknown hominoids. He further defined hominology as a "branch of primatology, called upon to bridge the gap between zoology and anthropology" in a 1973 letter to the London primatologist John Napier. His English paper on the subject was a major breakthrough contribution after decades of unpublicized Russian research and expeditions. The paper, "A Hominologist View from Moscow, USSR," appeared in *Northwest Anthropological Research Notes* (Moscow, Idaho), vol. 11, no. 1, 1977.

In 1958, the Soviet Academy of Sciences created the Snowman Commission, and later a Relict Hominoid Research Seminar was begun at the Darwin Museum in Moscow. One of the Soviet Union's first hominologists was **Boris Porshnev,** a contemporary of **Odette Tchernine** and **Ivan T. Sanderson,** who also studied unknown hominoids. Porshnev wrote the difficult-to-obtain late 1950s scientific monograph *The Present State of the Question of Relict Hominoids.* The U.S.S.R. allowed only 180 copies to be printed. While some hints of Porshnev's new studies were becoming known in the West by 1960, his work was largely unknown and unavailable to the scientific community in Russia.

The collapse of the Soviet state has changed much, and hominologists have been able to circulate their work freely. For example, Bayanov has recently published two works on hominology: *In the Footsteps of the Russian Snowman* (1996) and *America's Bigfoot: Fact, Not Fiction—U.S. Evidence Verified in Russia* (1997). During a 1997 international hominology conference held in Moscow, attended by North American Sasquatch research notables **John Green** and **Grover Krantz,** Bayanov called for the establishment of a Porshnev World Institute of Hominology to study the creatures' role in the evolutionary process.

HONEY ISLAND SWAMP MONSTER

Near New Orleans, Louisiana, in the wild Honey Island Swamp, there lives—or so tradition has it—a swamp monster, a unique bipedal animal that leaves pointed three-toed footprints. Honey Island is a vast stand of bottomland swamp sitting between the east and west Pearl Rivers. The Honey Island Swamp Monster achieved national notoriety when filmmaker Alan Landsburg and on-camera host Leonard Nimoy featured the creature on the 1970s series *In Search of . . .* In the 1980s, **Loren Coleman** interviewed locals with knowledge about the Honey Island Monster. One man told of past expeditions searching for them, and of finding their huge footprints. Another resident said he thought it looked generally like **Bigfoot**. However, most descriptions and tracks do not link the creature to Bigfoot.

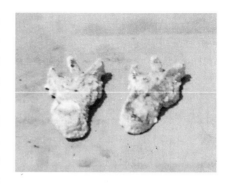

Casts of the distinctive three-toed tracks of the Honey Island Swamp Monster. (Loren Coleman)

HORNED SERPENTS

Centuries-old legends from native sources conjure up encounters with giant "reptiles" with great horns.

In "Water-Monsters of American Aborigines" (*Journal of American Folklore* [1889]), Albert S. Gatschet surveyed stories of these peculiar aquatic beasts, including the Great Horned Reptile of the Ohio River region and the Horned Snake. The Creek Indians, when they lived in Tennessee, spoke of a large, horned snakelike animal that frequented water holes. The deep water hole–dwelling Horned Snake was brought to the shore by the magical singing of Creek elders, and when the creature showed its horn, the Indians would cut it off. The horn was then taken as a fetish and carried into war, to ensure success in battle.

An account from the Oneida branch of the Tuscaroras, collected by David Cusick and published in 1828, tells of the "Mosqueto" which rose from Lake Onondaga (near Syracuse, New York) and slew a number of people. The Indians also said that "2,200 years before the time of Columbus" (approximately 700 B.C.), a great horned serpent appeared on Lake Ontario and killed onlookers with its overpowering stench.

The strikingly similar horned beast of Alkali Lake (now known as Walgren Lake) near Hays Springs, Nebraska, was the subject of tales by the local Indians. These native Nebraskans told the first white settlers to the area to be on the lookout for the monsters. The legends seem to have had some truth, for more modern sightings followed. The *Omaha World-Herald* of July 24, 1923, carried the testimony of J. A. Johnson, who stated: "I saw the monster myself while with two friends last fall. I could name forty other people who have also seen the brute." Johnson claimed that the stubby alligator-like head had a projection like a horn on it, between the eyes and nostrils. The gray-brown creature devoured livestock, gave off dreadful roars, and smelled horribly. News of Alkali Lake's horned wonder spread around the world in 1923.

Michel Meurger and Claude Gagnon underscore the importance of these legends in their book *Lake Monster Traditions* (1988) when they discuss them in their book's section on Native North Americans. "From Alaska to New Mexico the belief in a horned serpent-shaped water beast of enormous dimensions is widespread," Meurger and Gagnon write. They go on to place them into a folkloric framework.

If, on the other hand, we speculate about an underlying zoological signal amid the noise of mythology and folklore, where are those "horned serpents" today? As it turns out, they may be surviving in a few of the lakes in the same regions of contemporary North America. If you look at drawings made of the current eyewitness accounts of, for example, **Ogopogo,** you will immediately notice two bumps on its head. Horns, of course. Several **Lake Monsters** from around the world, from diverse sites, appear to have horns.

While the long-necked Lake Monsters may fit nicely into a classification system with some dinosaurs or seallike mammals, a handful of bold theorists have backed another candidate as an explanation for the many reports of more upright, stockier, horned lake **cryptids.** Could these creatures, they ask, possibly be the crested, duck-billed dinosaurs—the hadrosaurs, a group of prehistoric animals that survived relatively late as dinosaurs go?

Duck-billed dinosaurs also serve as the model for a few Lake Monsters in other locations around the globe. Take, for example, the 1980 descriptions of the Lake Tian Chai monster, a big creature with a long neck topped by a squarish head and, to quote **Karl Shuker**'s *In Search of Prehistoric Survivors*: "most memorable of all, a flat ducklike beak (an unusual characteristic recalling to mind the familiar duck-billed dinosaurs or hadrosaurs)." Reports of horned dinosaur-like beasts also have been heard from Africa for years.

HUYGHE, PATRICK (1952–)

Patrick Huyghe is a science writer whose articles on cryptozoology have reached a large public through their appearance in a number of mainstream magazines. His contributions have included analyses of the American Northeast cougar in *Audubon*, **Grover Krantz**'s **Bigfoot** research in *Science Digest,* and Scottish and Idaho **Lake Monsters** in *Omni.*

Patrick Huyghe. (Patrick Huyghe)

Following a casual conversation with the **International Society of Cryptozoology**'s **J. Richard Greenwell** in 1993, he managed to track down the present whereabouts of the only known evidence of a **pygmy elephant**. The remains of this pygmy elephant, which was exhibited live at the Bronx Zoo in the early part of the twentieth century, now lie in the collection of the American Museum of Natural History in New York City. His primary work in cryptozoology is *The Field Guide to Bigfoot, Yeti, and Other Mystery Primates Worldwide*, coauthored with **Loren Coleman** and published by Avon in 1999. This is the second volume in the Field Guides to the Unknown series, which Huyghe began producing for Avon in 1996.

Born in Newport News, Virginia, Huyghe holds an undergraduate degree in social psychology from the University of Virginia and a graduate degree in journalism from Syracuse University. After working on the staffs of *Us* and *Newsweek* magazines, he turned freelance in 1980. Since then he has written for dozens of magazines, from the *New York Times Sunday Magazine* and *Discover* to *Psychology Today* and *Reader's Digest, Health, Omni, Audubon,* and many others. His books include *Glowing Birds: Stories from the Edge of Science* (1985), *The Big Splash* (with Louis A. Frank, 1990), and *Columbus Was Last* (1992).

Huyghe has contributed to Time-Life, Reader's Digest, and Scribner's book series, taught science writing at the college level, produced public-TV programs for WGBH-Boston and WNET-New York, and written exhibit text for the Liberty Science Center in New Jersey and the Petrosains Discovery Center in Malaysia. Huyghe has also been a contributing editor of *Omni* magazine on-line. Today he edits and publishes a twice-yearly journal, *The Anomalist,* on the mysteries of nature, science, and history.

I

IGOPOGO

Lake Simcoe, Ontario, is where a monster the locals call Igopogo (it is a play on the popular British Columbia **Lake Monster, Ogopogo**) supposedly dwells. Seen for more than a century, the creature is described as a large, "dog-faced" animal. Most often it is seen in Kempenfelt Bay, near Barrie. A believable videotape of Igopogo swimming at the southern end of the lake was taken in 1991 by unidentified visitors. It appeared to be a "relict seal," according to one chronicler.

A similar Lake Monster in nearby Muskrat Lake, Ontario, was captured on film at about the same time by Dana Rogers. The unknown animal appeared to be at least ten feet long and swimming up and down like a seal, even though it was apparently not one. Muskrat Lake has hosted many sightings, including some of the creature (called Mussie or the Hapyxelor) on the shore. Michael Bradley wrote of the history of the encounters in *More Than a Myth: The Search for the Monster of the Muskrat Lake* (1989).

Both Lake Monsters are described as up to twenty feet long and gray. They resemble giant seals with strange heads.

ILIAMNA LAKE MONSTER

Iliamna Lake, near Alaska's southern coast, is eighty miles long and twenty-five miles wide in spots; it covers 1,033 square miles. The depth average is 660 feet; in Pile Bay at the eastern end, on one sounding, the lead dropped to 1,350 feet, and then the line ran out. Once part of the ocean, the lake is now less than a hundred feet above sea level.

The January 1959 issue of *Sports Afield* carried an article titled "Alaska's Monster Mystery Fish." The story, by Gil Paust, chronicled more than thirty years of reports of huge fish in Lake Iliamna. In breathless fashion the author details his adventures in trying to catch this mysterious monster fish. Paust, along with Iliamna **Lake Monster** hunters Slim Beck, John Walatka, and Bill Hammersley, used a Bushmaster seaplane as a dock and some homemade monster-fishing gear. The four attempted to catch "the big one" with a hook made from a foot-long, quarter-inch-thick iron rod baited with a chuck of moose flank. Their line was several hundred feet of sixteenth-inch stainless-steel aircraft cable. A fifty-five-gallon oil drum was the bobber. The thing snapped the line.

For some three decades before this report appeared, sightings of the monster fish had circulated around the shores of Lake Iliamna. At first the stories were assumed to be Inuit (Eskimo) folklore, and local whites did not take them seriously. But then well-regarded local people and visiting sportsmen claimed to have seen the fish, and the word spread.

Perhaps local guide Babe Aylesworth and fisherman Bill Hammersley made the best sighting in September 1942. Crossing at Big Mountain, they were on a direct flight over the lake to get to the village of Iliamna. Bush pilot Aylesworth was taking his Stinson ferry plane across at a steady pace over the deep, blue-black water when he noticed some unusual specks in the water near the unnamed island in the middle of the lake. Suddenly Aylesworth shouted "Oh, my God, what big fish!" and swirled the plane around for a closer look. Both Hammersley and Aylesworth got a good look. They described the things as dull aluminum in color with heads that were broad and blunt. The width of the long tapered bodies was the same as that of their heads, and vertical tails slowly waved side to side. (Whale tails go up and down. Fish and reptile tails go side to side.) They saw several dozen of them.

Spiraling the plane from one thousand feet down to three hundred feet, they soon saw that Aylesworth's estimate of their length at ten feet was low. The fish were easily longer than the plane's pontoon; they looked like minisubmarines. They circled for several minutes, then suddenly surged in the water and disappeared in a distinct wave disturbance. As they continued on their journey, the two men discussed and debated. No, it couldn't have been a whale, walrus, or seal, because they never blew or surfaced. Sharks would have been much smaller.

Local people, most notably the outspokenly skeptical Arthur Lee, thought they might be cod, a theory the witnesses emphatically rejected. Once word got around Iliamna, authorities told Hammersley that he had seen only belugas. Hammersley countered that he had seen thousands of belugas (native white whales) during his years of fishing Bristol Bay and their white backs, tapering heads, and horizontal tails were in no way like what he and Aylesworth had seen.

The lake's close proximity to the ocean has fueled speculation that the monster fish are landlocked sturgeon or some unknown prehistoric fish, but no dead sturgeon or even landlocked belugas have ever washed up on the shores of Iliamna.

In 1947, after leaving his defense job, Hammersley published a short piece on the mystery fish to try to get others to investigate the matter or to come forward with reports. One who did was Larry Rost, a U.S. Coast and Geodetic Survey pilot. Flying across Lake Iliamna in the fall of 1945, he had been so startled by what he saw in the water that he had turned around and passed over it at one hundred feet. What he saw was a giant fish, more than twenty feet long, the color of dull aluminum.

Aylesworth reaffirmed the details of his 1942 sighting in a 1988 interview with **Loren Coleman**. He added that he thought that most of the animals were well over ten feet long, swimming in water that was only forty feet deep. Aylesworth recalled that cryptozoological sponsor and adventurer **Tom Slick** hired him several times to fly Slick and his boys to moose hunting sites, and in the fall of 1959 to attempt specifically to find the monsters of Lake Iliamna. Slick had offered a reward of $1,000 to anyone who could catch one of the mystery creatures, and Slick himself was in charge of getting lines set with barrels for buoys. He even hired a helicopter to hover over the exact spot where Aylesworth had had his encounter. Aylesworth and Slick never saw the big unknown animals on these flights and, indeed, the pilot said he went over that place in the lake more than one hundred times without seeing them again.

In 1967, in his book *"Things,"* **Ivan T. Sanderson** wrote of Slick's teaming up with one Stanley Lee to look for the monsters in Lake Iliamna. Elwood Baumann noted in *Monsters of North America* that "Texan Tom R. [*sic*] Slick spent thousands of dollars in search of strange creatures in Lake Iliamna, Alaska." As Michael Newton observed in his book *Monsters, Mysteries and Man*, Slick and Lee "organized an expedition to search for the elusive creatures. Slick was unsuccessful, and after his tragic death, Commander Lee teamed up with others to continue the hunt. Still the monsters remain unidentified."

Newton appears to have picked up Sanderson's lead here: "Captain Lee of Kodiak, Alaska, together with the well-known nature photographer, Leonard Rue of New Jersey, made still another stab at the monsters of Lake Iliamna in 1966."

The cause of the monster fish sightings remains a mystery.

INDONESIAN COELACANTHS

To the considerable surprise of Western scientists at least, a second population of **coelacanths** has been discovered off the coast of Indonesia, some seven thousand miles from their only previously known location near Madagascar. Of course, local people knew about them all along. And where was the first specimen of this new population found? In a case where history repeated itself, the first Indonesian specimen turned up in a fish market, as had the 1938 specimen.

Forty-six years after the "discovery" of coelacanths in the Comoros Islands, the new population has now been identified by at least two spec-

The second coelacanth discovered in Indonesian waters in 1998 is shown with the fishermen who caught it. (Mark and Arnaz Mehta Erdmann)

imens caught off North Sulawesi, Indonesia. Postdoctoral research fellow Mark Erdmann, on a honeymoon trip to the area in September 1997, investigated a coral-reef research site, when his wife, Arnaz Mehta, spotted a strange fish being wheeled in the fish market. Recognizing it as a coelacanth, they snapped a picture of it before it was sold. Assuming the fish to be already known from Indonesia, the two later posted the picture on their honeymoon website. As soon as he saw it, E. K. Balon of the University of Guelph, a longtime coelacanth specialist, advised Erdmann, a marine biologist attached to the University of California–Berkeley, to withdraw the picture and pursue further funding to confirm a second specimen.

The National Geographic Society and the Smithsonian Institution were eager to help, but as a condition for funding they insisted on a news blackout. Consequently, the coelacanth research community was kept in the dark for another year.

When they saw the coelacanth, Mehta and Erdmann had been living for the past seven years in Indonesia, where Erdmann studies the health of Indonesia's coral reefs. Mehta is a nature guide. They were at a traditional market when they made the discovery. Mehta gave this account to **Loren Coleman:**

> I was the first to see a fish being wheeled by on a handcart. I could only see the head portion of the fish as it was being pushed away but it caught my attention as being something I didn't recognize. I went out to take a closer look at it and, admittedly, I was at a loss to its identity. I called Mark over to see the fish and Mark immediately recognized it as a coelacanth. Mark said that he read all about the coelacanth as a boy and that it was only known from the Western Indian Ocean, but had not kept up with coelacanth news for over fifteen years and assumed that the fish must have since been discovered in other areas of the world. After all, how could we literally step out of a taxi and think that we have immediately stumbled on such a significant discovery! . . .
>
> We turned the possibilities of keeping the fish over and over in our minds, but Mark had disappointing memories of going out of his way to preserve specimens that he thought were new or special only to find that all his trouble (and the life of an animal) were all for nothing.

So we opted to take a couple of quick photos instead and find out more about the distribution of the fish when we returned to the States. Furthermore, we rationalized that we would be living in Manado for two years and surely, we would find another coelacanth. That was a decision that Mark agonized over for the next ten months after he found out that no other coelacanths had been found within ten thousand kilometers [6,200 miles] off Manado.

Soon, Erdmann was able to use his grant money to return to Indonesia in search of further coelacanths. His team quickly set to work among the fishermen of the North Sulawesi region. He and his associates asked them if any had seen the fish before, duplicating the efforts J. L. B. Smith, a professor-turned-coelacanth-hunter, had used in uncovering the second specimen in 1952.

Erdmann's investigation turned up reports of a big but rare fish, up to six feet long and very heavy. It was known locally as *rajalaut*, "king of the sea." Finally, at sunrise on July 30, 1998, Om Lameh Sonathan and his crew of ten fishermen netting for deepwater shark off the young volcanic island of Manado Tua, caught and delivered a *rajalaut* to Erdmann. An attempt was made to keep the fish alive by dragging it through the water. Although nearly dead, the coelacanth remained alive long enough for Erdmann to film it swimming for three hours before freezing it for later analysis. This second specimen led to the press release of late 1998, and subsequent new worldwide attention.

Erdmann and his coauthors, Roy Caldwell and M. Kasim Moosa, reported on the remarkable discovery in the September 24, 1998, issue of the influential British journal *Nature*. They wrote that the coelacanths recently found in Indonesia apparently live in the same type of environment as those found in the Comoros, caves about six hundred feet deep along the steep sides of underwater volcanoes. They hope that many more colonies will be found now that scientists know where to look. The fish were probably "habitat specialists," choosing young volcanic islands with steep sides full of crevices and caves, conditions that exist in both Manado Tua and the Comoros.

The new population of Indonesian coelacanths seems centered on the island of Manado Tua in North Sulawesi. Because of its beautiful coral reefs the island is a popular diving spot. North Sulawesi is some seven

thousand miles from the Comoros with no apparent water current interactions. This population appears completely isolated from the Comoran
coelacanths, whereas recent catches off Madagascar and East Africa have
not been eliminated as possible strays or satellite colonies. The observed
specimens appear identical to the Comoran coelacanth, *Latimeria chalumnae,* except that they are brown rather than blue and have gold flecks on
their sides. During April 1999, news reports stated that early DNA tests
had found the Indonesian coelacanths to be a separate species. But while
Mark Erdmann notes that the fish is substantially genetically divergent
from Comoran specimens, enough so to raise the question of separate
species status, its naming as *Latimeria menadoensis* may be premature.

INTERNATIONAL SOCIETY OF CRYPTOZOOLOGY

Founded in January 1982 at a gathering held at the National Museum of
Natural History of the Smithsonian Institution and hosted by zoologist
George Zug, the International Society of Cryptozoology (ISC) brought
scientists, wildlife professionals, and lay investigators together to formalize the study of hidden animals. The moving forces behind the ISC were
University of Chicago biologist **Roy P. Mackal** and University of Arizona
ecologist **J. Richard Greenwell,** who over a year-and-a-half period had
contacted scientists who in one way or another had expressed interest in
cryptozoological concerns and asked if they would be willing to participate in a professional organization dedicated to the subject. The suggestion for the ISC had come out of a Chicago-based conversation between
writer Jerome Clark and Greenwell, when Clark had introduced Greenwell to his friend Mackal.

The new organization drafted a statement defining cryptozoology as
the study of "unexpected animals." It would promote "scientific inquiry,
education, and communication among people interested in animals of unexpected form or size, or unexpected occurrence in time and space." It
elected **Bernard Heuvelmans** its first president. Heuvelmans still serves in
that post. Mackal is still vice president and Greenwell secretary and editor.

In its early years the ISC published a yearly refereed journal, *Cryptozoology,* and a quarterly newsletter, though with the passage of time these
appeared irregularly. The ISC holds an annual meeting at a chosen university or scientific institute. It has had as many as 850 members.

The address of the ISC is P.O. Box 43070, Tucson, AZ 85733.

J

JERSEY DEVIL

The Jersey Devil is one of those localized names that residents and written histories have applied to any **cryptids** seen in the state of New Jersey. The legendary creature, in fact, is an unofficial state mascot, and the state's National Hockey League team is named in its honor. The Jersey Devil, a feral human first thought to be a **Bigfoot,** was also featured in the third episode of *The X-Files* as its first "monster of the week," and a Sony PlayStation game has turned the savage beast into a video game character.

The Jersey Devil legend dates back to at least 1735, when a Leeds Point woman in the Pine Barrens of southern New Jersey allegedly gave birth to a cursed child. It was born, so the story goes, a hideous monster, combining a horse's head, the wings of a bat, cloven hooves, and a serpent's tail. This being, which flew off to haunt the Barrens ever after, was first called the Leeds Devil, and in the nineteenth century it came to be known as the Jersey Devil.

In 1909, nearly two centuries after the creature's reputed birth, a rash of bizarre reports erupted. The episode has been dubbed the Jersey Devil's "finest hour." In the course of five January days, more than one hundred persons across eastern Pennsylvania and southern New Jersey swore they had seen the beast. All over the region, accounts of such a creature or creatures were heard, as well as the discoveries of bizarre, unidentifiable hoofprints in the snow. Schools and businesses closed, and Jacob Hope and Norman Jeffries hoaxed a capture of the monster. They charged a small fee for a look at a kangaroo they had disguised with green paint, feathers, and antlers.

A climax to the events took place on January 21 in West Collingswood, when the town's fire department supposedly confronted the monster and sprayed it with firehoses as it swooped menacingly overhead. The next morning, a Camden woman said the Jersey Devil attacked her pet dog. Another sighting occurred in February, marking the end of the 1909 incident.

Years later, **Loren Coleman** and **Ivan T. Sanderson** offered a likely explanation for the scare: apparently an elaborate real estate hoax. Scared residents would be more likely to sell the property at lower prices to developers. Sanderson even found the fake feet used to make the footprints in the snow. Hoofprints and other evidence were faked or misidentified. The stories of sightings seem to have been a combination of planted stories, hoaxes, and imaginations fueled by fear.

The Jersey Devil would surely be no more than an obscure piece of colonial folklore today, if not for the sensational "sightings" of 1909. More modern sightings, if taken seriously, tell us that a diverse number of creatures have been lumped under the Jersey Devil rubric. In one recent report of a sighting December 1993, a witness named John Irwin, a summer park ranger in the Wharton State Forest of New Jersey and a respected figure in the community, was patrolling at night when he noticed a large, dark figure emerging from the woods. It stood like a human, over six feet tall, and had black fur that looked wet and matted. The Forest Service report of the incident went on to state, "John sat in his car only a few feet away from the monster. His initial shock soon turned to fear when the creature turned its deerlike head and stared through the windshield. But instead of gazing into the bright yellow glow of a deer's eyes, John found himself the subject of a deep glare from two piercing red eyes." Some New Jersey researchers compared what Irwin saw to the Australian **Bunyip** in overall looks.

Mystery cryptids of many kinds, from little otter-shaped animals to hairy bipeds, from strange birds to unknown panthers, seen in New Jersey are always called Jersey Devils, though surely none really is.

KEATING, DONALD (1962–)

Donald Keating was born in Columbus, Ohio. In 1984, after reading one of **John Green**'s **Sasquatch** books, Keating became fascinated with Midwestern **Bigfoot** activity. He went on to found and direct the Eastern Ohio Bigfoot Investigation Center, headquartered in Newcomerstown

and consisting of a network of active researchers. Since 1992 he has published *Monthly Bigfoot Report,* which discusses regional as well as international events dealing with unknown hairy hominids. He produced a
video documentary, *Sasquatch: The Mounting Evidence* (1998), and has
written *The Sasquatch Triangle* (1987), *The Eastern Ohio Sasquatch*
(1989), and *The Buckeye Bigfoot* (1993).

Keating has been frequently interviewed by radio programs, has a
website, holds monthly meetings, and hosts the largest annual Bigfoot
conference in the United States.

In December 1998, **Daniel Perez**'s *Bigfoot Times* named Keating
"Bigfooter of the Year."

KING CHEETAH

For years, intrigued by legends, the appearance of strange skins, and reports of an unusual-looking giant cheetah in Africa, cryptozoologists
Paul and Lena Bottriell searched for the King Cheetah. Then in 1975, in
Kruger Park, South Africa, they observed and photographed one of
these rare animals. Larger than a regular cheetah, it had a distinctive set
of unique stripes and spots on its coat. In the course of that same expedition, sponsored by Coca-Cola and other corporate entities, the couple
obtained mounted specimens and skin and hair samples. They were on
their way to solving the mystery of the King Cheetah.

As long ago as the 1950s, in *On the Track of Unknown Animals,*
Bernard Heuvelmans had predicted the outcome of the King Cheetah
riddle. He considered it likely that the sightings were only of a series of
abnormally marked local individuals. Heuvelmans wrote, "These abnor-
malities could be connected with the genetic ancestry of a group of animals in a confined area."

This proved to be exactly the case. The King Cheetah was neither a
new species nor a new subspecies, but a variation of the standard cheetah. King Cheetahs could seem to appear and disappear within a population and thus be reported as "elusive," because their appearances were
tied to a recessive gene that would only occasionally stand out in any
given group of normally patterned cheetahs.

King Cheetahs do seem to turn up in clumps. For example, in the
1980s, thirty-eight specimens were recorded far south of the Zambezi, in
southern Africa, in an area where the common cheetah had been nearly

exterminated. The King Cheetah is found widespread throughout the common cheetah's range.

Lena Godsall Bottriell eventually wrote a book, *King Cheetah: The Story of the Quest* (1987), which documents her and her husband's findings of mounted specimens, skins, and live animal specimens. It also contains a five-page foreword by Heuvelmans.

KIRK, JOHN (1955–)

John Kirk is the president of the **British Columbia Scientific Cryptozoology Club** (BCSCC), an international organization whose status has grown as the **International Society of Cryptozoology** (ISC) has lapsed into relative inactivity in recent years.

Kirk became interested in cryptozoology in 1987 after two sightings of **Ogopogo.** The BCSCC was founded by **Paul LeBlond, Jim Clark,** and

John Kirk. (John Kirk)

Kirk in May 1989, with the inaugural meeting held at Simon Fraser University. The BCSCC newsletter, which Kirk edits, has published thirty-four issues through 1998.

Kirk has had a varied career in mass communication. Previously a television producer and on-camera presenter with Asia Television and a broadcaster and producer with the British Forces Broadcasting Service, Kirk has also produced and presented numerous documentaries, corporate videos, commercials, and educational programs. Kirk has appeared on many programs on TV and radio to discuss cryptozoology, including *Myths and Mysteries* and *Strange Science,* both on the Learning Channel.

His fieldwork reports have also been published in *Cryptozoology,* the journal of the International Society of Cryptozoology. He is the author of *In the Domain of the Lake Monsters* (1998). Currently he is writing books on topics as wide-ranging as dragons and **Sasquatch.**

As president of the BCSCC, Kirk oversees the activities of one of the most fieldwork-oriented cryptozoological clubs in the world today. The BCSCC has staged numerous expeditions to Okanagan Lake in search of **Ogopogo,** the resident monster, and has conducted surveys of witnesses and investigated the **Sea Serpent** dubbed **Caddy,** or Cadborosaurus. It has also launched forays into the montane forests of the Pacific Northwest in search of **Bigfoot**/Sasquatch.

KOFFMANN, MARIE-JEANNE (1919–)

Born in France, Marie-Jeanne Koffmann spent most of her life in the U.S.S.R., as a surgeon at Moscow hospitals and as a mountaineer. She became interested in the "Snowman" in the 1950s, particularly in Kabarda (Caucasus), where she recorded hundreds of sightings of the *almasty,* the local variety of the **Almas.** From 1948 to 1954, Koffmann was held in a gulag (Soviet labor camp) after being accused of spying for the French. Four years after her release, she was picked to be on the Soviet Union's first official expedition to the Pamirs. She published a synthesis of her remarkable fieldwork research in the magazine *Archéologia.* Koffmann was also the president of the Russian Society of Cryptozoology for a time.

KOMODO DRAGON

In 1910, it is said, a Dutch pilot crash-landed on Komodo, a rugged, volcanic Indonesian island. After his rescue he claimed to have seen an incredibly large lizard, about thirteen feet long. Another story, equally murky in origin, has it that in 1912, a pilot who had safely landed on Komodo returned with stories of monstrous dragons that ate goats and pigs and even attacked horses. Nobody believed him.

What we do know for certain is that in 1912, Lieutenant Van Steyn van Hensbroek killed a Komodo dragon measuring seven feet long. He sent a photograph and skin to Major P. A. Ouwens, director of the Zoological Museum and Botanical Gardens in Buitenzorg, Java. Ouwens was the first to write a scientific description of the Komodo dragon, as it was called.

The heyday of Komodo dragon hunting was to come in the late 1920s. While those early pilot stories are difficult to confirm, it is known that in 1926 an English aviator named Cobham, who had flown to the nearby island of Sumbawa, sighted a captive Komodo dragon there. He wrote a letter to the *London Times* about it, and it caused quite a stir.

During the early 1920s the Dutch had tried and failed to capture live Komodo dragons. The dragon that Cobham saw on Sumbawa chained to a tree may have been the one that arrived at the Amsterdam Zoological Garden at the end of 1926. But before its arrival, the press was to have a field day with the dragons.

Openly, with the whole world watching, Douglas Burden, along with a professional herpetologist, a Pathé cameraman, and a skilled hunter, led an expedition in 1926 with the avowed purpose of capturing live dragons. Pathé newsreels of the Komodo dragon captured the public fancy, and the Komodo dragon became an international zoological superstar. When Burden brought back two live Komodo dragons to the Bronx Zoo in New York City—the first in the New World—the lines to see them stretched for blocks.

Expeditions sponsored by museums and zoos went off in search of more Komodo dragons. Newspapers around the world told of the dramatic capture of two Komodo dragons in 1933, by two young men collecting for the St. Louis Zoo. In the following years, dragons were added to the London Zoo as well as other locations.

The story, cryptozoologically speaking, does not end there. One of the young men who captured live Komodo dragons was William H. Harkness. "Wild Bill" Harkness then went on to try to catch the first live **giant panda.** He died in the attempt. But his widow, **Ruth Harkness,** continued the hunt, and did capture the first giant panda, Su-Lin, in 1936.

KONGAMATO

A large flying animal, possibly a giant unknown bat or more improbably a Jurassic pterosaur (which includes the subgroup of animals called pterodactyls) seen throughout sub-Saharan Africa, is called Kongamato or, less frequently, Olitiau or Sasabonsam. *Kongamato,* which means "overwhelmer of boats," appears in a magic spell of the Kaonde tribe, natives of Zambia (formerly Northern Rhodesia). The charm, *muchi wa kongamato,* is used to protect travelers from floods, which are blamed on the creature. Olitiau's origins, apparently localized from the Cameroons, appear to be a misunderstanding for *ole ntya,* "the forked one." The use of Sasabonsam seems restricted to Ghana.

Today, Kongamato is the word of choice, because it received the ear-

The Kongamato appears to be a form of giant bat, despite some interpretations of it as a prehistoric reptilian creature. (William M. Rebsamen)

liest and most widespread publicity. The giant flying monster got its first Western attention when Frank H. Melland wrote about it in his book *In Witchbound Africa* in 1923. When Melland asked local informants about the Kongamato, he was told it was a huge flying animal with membranes on its wings instead of feathers, teeth in its mouth, generally red, and from four to seven feet across. Melland showed them a picture of an extinct, prehistoric pterodactyl, and the locals identified it as a Kongamato. Melland, who apparently felt he was dealing with reports of a flying reptile, showed the witnesses only the pterodactyl drawing.

Other accounts of pterosaur-like flying monsters came from the distinguished British newspaperman G. Ward Price. Price was with the future Duke of Windsor in Southern Rhodesia in 1925 when they learned of the recent attacks of one of these creatures on a local man in a swamp. Here again, shown a book of animals, the man picked out the pterodactyl.

In 1928, game warden A. Blayney Percival found tracks of a strange creature that the Kitui Wakama tribespeople told him flew down from nearby Mount Kenya at night. In 1942, Captain Charles Pitman wrote in his book *A Game Warden Takes Stock* that a large pterodactyl-like beast existed in the swamps near the Angola-Zaire border. In the 1950s, the man connected to the **coelacanth,** Dr. J. L. B. Smith, investigated, then wrote in his book *Old Fourlegs* about the superstition—circulating near Mount Kilimanjaro—of flying dragons.

The Kongamato received the most widespread notice, however, when a well-publicized sighting was featured in newspapers in 1956. Engineer J. P. F. Brown saw two prehistoric-looking creatures flying overhead along a rural road near Lake Bangweulu, Northern Rhodesia. They had a wingspan of about three and a half feet, a long narrow tail, and a dog-like muzzle. When they circled around and flew over again, he saw that they had a mouth full of sharp teeth. Quickly, other credible witnesses in Northern and Southern Rhodesia came forth with their own sightings.

More modern accounts of the Kongamato have been recorded in Namibia. These southwestern African sightings so interested University of Chicago biologist **Roy Mackal** that he traveled to Namibia in the summer of 1988 to investigate. Mackal managed to collect many accounts of the giant flying beast, but left before he spied one. However, one of his party stayed behind, and James Kosi reported he saw a giant black glider with white markings. Reportedly these Kongamatos liked to fly between the local hilltops.

The ostensibly related Olitiau is featured in only one well-known sighting, but since it was seen in Africa by the author **Ivan T. Sanderson,** it generally is discussed in conjunction with the Kongamato. In 1932, zoologist Sanderson was leading an expedition with naturalist **Gerald Russell** in the Assumbo Mountains of Cameroon. When crossing a river, Sanderson and Russell witnessed the passage of a creature nearly the size of an eagle. It dived at them, then flew away. That evening, Sanderson, Russell, and their party saw the black, sharp-toothed animal again. Locals called the animal *olitiau.*

Sanderson theorized that this unknown flying monster was an exceptionally large specimen of the hammerhead bat (*Hypsignathus monstrosus*), a particularly ugly-looking fruit bat. **Bernard Heuvelmans** agrees that the Kongamato may actually be an unknown huge variety of bat or the hammerhead bat. Other cryptozoologists, such as **Karl Shuker** and Mackal, have toyed with the idea, perhaps not too seriously, that the Kongamato may be a surviving pterosaur.

KOUPREY

Before the wealth of cryptozoological discoveries in Vietnam, the most recent large animal to be discovered in Asia was the kouprey. In its day this animal, found along the Mekong River in Cambodia and Laos, generated considerable controversy.

In 1937, the director of the Paris Vincennes Zoo, Professor Achille Urbain, journeyed to North Cambodia and learned of a large wild ox, unlike the gaur and the banteng. Native people called it the *kouprey*. Other naturalists, however, were certain that he was wrong, and they suggested that the kouprey might be no more than a hybrid of the gaur and the banteng.

Finally, in 1961, a detailed anatomical study of the kouprey (*Bos sauveli*) proved it to be so different from the area's other wild oxen that it was declared a new animal, upholding Urbain's 1937 conclusion. Harvard mammalogist Harold J. Coolidge proposed that the kouprey be placed in a new genus, *Novibos*.

Southeast Asia's wars killed off many koupreys, and some regional zoologists fear that not more than three hundred now exist in the wild. Between 1953 and 1980 koupreys were thought extinct in Thailand until a small group was rediscovered in the Dongrak mountains. A 1975 New York Zoological Society expedition failed to capture any, though members did observe a herd of fifty.

In November 1988, Hanoi University zoologist Vo Quy led a well-funded capture team to begin a captive breeding population, but specimens eluded him and his party. Koupreys remain one of Asia's most elusive larger mammals.

KRAKEN

The Bishop of Bergen, Erik Pontoppidan, writing in *The Natural History of Norway* (1723), told of the largest "Sea-Monster in the world," the many-armed Kraken. The giant squid—once known as the Kraken—was considered an absurd fiction until indisputable physical evidence of its existence became available in the 1870s. Before then, however, respectable opinion thought Kraken as fabulous a creature as the **Mer-beings,** and those who claimed to have seen it could count on being ridiculed if they took their sightings to scientists.

Scientific investigation of the animal did not begin until the 1840s,

On November 30, 1861, near the Canary Islands, sailors aboard the French gunboat Alecton *tried to capture a giant squid, but when the body broke, all they recovered was a small portion of the tail.* (FPL)

when Danish zoologist Johan Japetus Steenstrup took up the subject, looking for reports in printed sources. In an indifferently received 1847 lecture to the Society of Scandinavian Naturalists, he took note of beach strandings of giant squids going back to 1639, when one was found on an Icelandic beach. In 1853, after Jutland fishermen caught and cut up a giant squid (they used the pieces for bait), Steenstrup secured the pharynx and the beak. In a scientific paper published in 1857, he described the remains and gave the giant squid its scientific name, still in use: *Architeuthis.* Even so, his colleagues remained skeptical, and as late as 1861, when the crew of the French gunboat *Alecton* encountered and tried to capture a specimen in the Canary Islands, the report was laughed or shrugged off. A member of the French Academy of Sciences thundered that giant squids, along with **Sea Serpents,** amounted to a "contradiction of the great laws of harmony and equilibrium which have sovereign rule over living nature."

But in the next decade, after a series of strandings in Labrador and Newfoundland, the sneering stopped. In a particularly crucial incident, a fisherman and his son spotted a giant squid off Great Bell Island, near St. John's, Newfoundland, in October 1873. They cut off a tentacle ten feet from the body and showed it to Alexander Murray of the Geological Commission of Canada. Murray deduced that the whole tentacle must have been thirty-five feet long and the creature to which it was attached some sixty feet long and five to ten feet across.

More than a century later much remains unknown or obscure about giant squids. Little has been determined about their eating and reproductive habits, for example. A raging controversy, the one of most interest to cryptozoologists, concerns their size. How giant can a giant squid be? A specimen from a New Zealand beach in 1880 measured sixty-five feet, most of that length (up to about forty feet) taken up with tentacles. (All squids, of whatever size, have eight arms and two tentacles.) That is the largest documented specimen, but intriguing eyewitness reports describe squids as long as ninety feet.

A related controversy has to do with the meaning of giant-squid scars on sperm whales. The two sea creatures are enemies and engage in what must be titanic (though seldom witnessed) battles, with squids usually the losers. Some scars are eighteen inches around. **Bernard Heuvelmans** argues that the "diameter of the largest suckers is one hundredth of the length of the body and the head"; if true, that means staggeringly immense squids lurk in the ocean depths. On the other hand, conservative zoologists argue that scars grow as a whale grows and consequently their size is not a reliable guide. Heuvelmans counters that because they are guarding the young while the adult males do the fighting, "scars are rare on female whales. . . . A baby whale would be kept well away from such huge brutes and, if attacked, would hardly survive."

Richard Ellis has written the most recent full-scale examination on the Kraken, *The Search for the Giant Squid* (1998).

KRANTZ, GROVER S. (1931–)

A retired anthropologist at Washington State University in Pullman, Grover S. Krantz is the author of many academic works on physical anthropology. One of a very small number of academics actively involved in **Bigfoot/Sasquatch** research, he is one of the most quoted experts on the

Here Grover Krantz (left) is shown examining a Bigfoot sighting location with Robert Morgan. (Robert Morgan)

status of the controversy. He has written several papers of exemplary rigor (published in *Northwest Anthropological Research Notes*) and two books, *The Sasquatch and Other Unknown Hominoids* (1984, with Vladimir Markotic) and *Big Footprints* (1992), revised as *Bigfoot Sasquatch Evidence* (1999). Krantz is the foremost proponent of the theory that the survival of the giant ape *Gigantopithecus,* recently thought to be extinct, is the source of Bigfoot reports.

KRUMBIEGEL, INGO (n.d.–1992)

A German mammalogist, Ingo Krumbiegel published a number of cryptozoological articles: on the **Waitoreke** from New Zealand (an unknown aquatic mammal), on the *coje ya menia* from Angola (a saber-toothed cat for which he proposed the name *Machairodontids*), and on Wood's argus (*Argusianus bipunctatus,* a bird of the Phasianidae family, known from a single feather). He also wrote a basic book, *Von neueun und unentdeckten Tierarten* (*Concerning New and Undiscovered Animals,* 1950), which anticipated some of the **cryptids** of the discipline that would later be called cryptozoology.

L

LAKE MONSTERS

According to one estimate, more than three hundred lakes around the world harbor large, unknown animals unrecognized by conventional zoology. Such claims have a long history and a rich representation in the world's mythology and folklore. "Lake Monsters" is a relatively recent appellation; traditionally, such creatures have gone by a variety of names, including great serpents, dragons, water horses, worms, and others.

Probably the issue of Lake Monsters would be of concern only to antiquarians were it not for a large body of modern reports from seemingly credible eyewitnesses, most prominently at Loch Ness in Scotland. Besides these, there are unexplained instrumented observations of large, moving bodies under the water's surface as well as a small number of intriguing photographs that seem neither to be fraudulent nor to depict mundane objects. In other words, the evidence is not conclusive and probably will not be until incontrovertible physical evidence is available. Nonetheless, it is suggestive enough to keep the issue very much alive. As recently as the summer of 1998, two well-equipped expeditions sought— without success, unfortunately—to establish the presence of a monster in Storion in Norway and in the Swedish lake Seljordsvatnet. In 1999 another expedition, the Nessa Project of **Dan Taylor,** with a small submarine engineered for the purpose, will attempt to get close enough to a **Loch Ness Monster** to obtain a sample of its flesh.

The scientific investigation of Lake Monsters began in the early nineteenth century, and it had much to do with the controversy surrounding **Sea Serpents.** It was assumed that Lake Monsters were Sea Serpents that had entered freshwater bodies from the ocean, either temporarily or permanently. It was further reasoned that a Sea Serpent could be more easily captured in a much more accessible place—a lake or river—than a vast one such as the ocean. This, of course, has proved not to be true, but it was hardly an unreasonable conclusion.

Typical of nineteenth-century references to Lake Monsters is an article from the *Inverness Courier* (Inverness is a small city north of Loch Ness), reprinted in the *London Times* in March 1856:

> The appearance in one of the inland freshwater lakes of an animal which from its great size and dimensions has not a little puzzled our island naturalists. Some suppose him to be a description of the hitherto mythical water-kelpie [a dangerous shape-shifting monster which would appear as a horse to lure unsuspecting travelers onto its back, after which it would plunge into the water to drown them]; while others refer it to the minute descriptions of the "sea serpent," which are revived from time to time in newspaper columns. It has been repeatedly seen within the last fortnight by crowds of people, many of whom have come from the remotest places of the parish to witness the uncommon spectacle.

Though the *Courier* correspondent suggested that the witnesses had seen an oversized conger eel, later theorists took their cue from the Dutch zoologist **Antoon Cornelis Oudemans** (1858–1943), author of the influential *The Great Sea Serpent* (1892). Oudemans believed that huge long-necked seals were responsible for "serpent" sightings. That, for example, was the conclusion the investigator Peter Olsson came to in 1898 after studying reports from Storsjo, a deep mountain lake in central Sweden.

Though the long-necked seal theory has long been out of fashion, it did anticipate subsequent speculations that held mammals, rather than reptiles, to be the animals people were sighting. By the 1970s many cryptozoologists sided with the University of Chicago biologist **Roy P. Mackal**'s notion that the creatures were most likely **zeuglodons,** primitive, snakelike whales that disappeared from the fossil record some 20 million years ago. Mackal thought zeuglodons might live on in certain lakes in the world's northern regions. To some considerable extent, zeuglodons have eclipsed plesiosaurs as the cryptozoologists' favorite candidate for the allegedly extinct animals behind Lake Monster sightings.

There is much to be said for the zeuglodon hypothesis. Many of the reports describe animals that at least look like zeuglodons. Moreover, the undulating motion noted in sightings widely distributed in time and space is characteristic of mammals but not of reptiles. Like whales, Lake Monsters are said to have lateral rather than vertical tails. Also in common with whales, Lake Monster tails are forked. After a careful analysis of Canadian reports, including those of the celebrated **Ogopogo** of British Columbia's Lake Okanagan, Mackal declared that the characteristics recounted "fit one and only one known creature": the zeuglodon, or at least a freshwater evolutionary variant.

On the other hand, hoaxes, mirages, observations of objects as commonplace as logs and waves, and the occurrence of known animals in unexpected places complicate the picture. Nineteenth-century American newspapers delighted in concocting bogus tales of water serpents, and consequently some reported Lake Monsters—for example, Lake Champlain's **Champ**—giving researchers a false sense of history if they are not properly cautious and skeptical. There is no evidence of any American Lake Monster stronger than striking eyewitness testimony and the rare photograph.

This does not mean that more compelling evidence is not out there to be uncovered. All it may mean is that the proper resources, funding, and expertise have not been brought to bear on the question. Real science is expensive, and because of the ridicule associated with the subject of Lake Monsters, few scientists have investigated, and those few have acted largely on their own, without institutional support. In the end, science has little to say about Lake Monsters because science has paid no— or, at best, rare, scattered, and brief—attention to them. These animals, if they exist, need not remain forever enigmatic and elusive. The answers—and the proof—may be as close as the first concerted, sustained scientific effort to get to the bottom of the mystery.

LAWNDALE INCIDENT

The Lawndale, Illinois, incident is among the most important avian cryptozoological events ever to have been investigated. It is a modern, real-life enactment of a kind of episode portrayed in folklore all over the world: the attempted abduction of a child by a **Thunderbird.** Its status was recently reinforced when it was highlighted on the 1998 Yorkshire Television/Discovery Channel series on **cryptids,** *Into the Unknown.*

On July 25, 1977, as ten-year-old Marlon Lowe played outside his family home along open fields near Kickapoo Creek, two giant birds passed over. One suddenly swooped down to grab the boy, carrying him a few feet before dropping him, apparently because of his frightened mother's screams. The incident occurred in front of seven witnesses, all of whom described exactly the same thing: two huge, coal-black birds with long, white-ringed necks, long curled beaks, and wingspans of ten or more feet.

Jerry Coleman of Decatur, Illinois, was able to interview Marlon and his parents, Jake and Ruth Lowe, within hours of the incident. Two years later, he conducted a follow-up interview, this time accompanied by his brother Loren. In 1996 Jerry Coleman, accompanied by a crew from Yorkshire Television, spoke again with Marlon and his mother.

"I'll always remember how that huge thing was bending its white ringed neck," Ruth Lowe remarked. It "seemed to be trying to peck at Marlon as it was flying away." Though she compared the bird's size to that of an ostrich, she said it looked more like a condor. After the incident she spent many hours in the library trying to identify the bird, without success. She rejected a local sheriff's speculation that it had been no more than a turkey vulture. "I was standing at the door, and all I saw was Marlon's feet dangling in the air," she recalled, adding the obvious: "There just aren't any birds around here that could lift him up like that."

Several other incidents followed quickly in the wake of the one at Lawndale. Sightings occurred in late July and early August in locations throughout central and southern Illinois. On Thursday, August 11, in southwestern Illinois, near Odin, the 1977 series of Thunderbird sightings publicly ceased.

Officials had begun telling the newspapers that people were seeing turkey vultures and letting their imaginations run away with them. The Lowe report, impossible to square with turkey vultures, was dismissed out of hand. As public ridicule was setting in, witnesses grew quiet about what they were seeing.

Mark A. Hall, author of *Thunderbirds—The Living Legend!* (1994), concludes an extended discussion of the Lawndale incident thus: "The final word on the Illinois wonder deservedly goes to Ruth Lowe. After all the experts had their say, Mrs. Lowe, who spoke from personal experience, has made the most perceptive comment on the appearance of two extraordinary birds in Illinois. She was quoted as saying: 'The game warden said there wasn't anything like this ever reported in the county. Maybe there wasn't, but there is now. Two came through here last night.'"

LEBLOND, PAUL H. (1938–)

Paul H. LeBlond, coleader of the **British Columbia Scientific Cryptozoology Club,** is an oceanographer at the University of British Columbia in Vancouver. LeBlond has conducted field investigations of large marine animals sighted off the coasts of western Canada, including the local **Sea Serpent,** nicknamed Cadborosaurus or **Caddy.** He has written articles on this and other aspects of cryptozoology, and has estimated the size of **Champ,** the Lake Champlain Monster photographed by Sandra Mansi in 1977. With Dr. Edward Bousfield he has written a book, *Cadborosaurus: Survivor from the Deep* (1995).

LEY, WILLY (1906–1969)

In 1941, the young scientist and scholar Willy Ley, German-born and educated, wrote his first book in the field of popular science, initiating a lifelong exploration of cryptozoological matters. (His other passion, about which he wrote and was internationally famous, especially after escaping from Nazi Germany, was rocketry and space travel.) The book was an adventure story about his own first love, paleontology, but also included his thoughts on **"living fossils."** Called *The Lungfish and the Unicorn: An Excursion into Romantic Zoology,* it reached a relatively small but immensely delighted coterie of readers. Ley's talent for conveying wonder, curiosity, and humor was evident from the beginning.

Ley wrote other books on what he called "romantic zoology," his early way to convey one aspect of what would become known as cryptozoology. In 1948 his first book was revised and expanded into *The Lungfish, the Dodo and the Unicorn: An Excursion into Romantic Zoology.* Later, *Dragons in Amber: Further Adventures of a Romantic Naturalist* (1951), about survivors from antiquity, animals and plants with wanderlust, and vanished flora and fauna, appeared. *Salamanders and Other Wonders* (1955), about other unique animals and plants, expressed his thoughts on other cryptids. Finally, his compilation volume, *Exotic Zoology* (1959), gathered all that he had written before on **Yeti, Mokelembembe,** and **Sea Serpents.**

As Ley was writing before **Bernard Heuvelmans** had published on similar topics, Ley's books are viewed today as popular classics and he is seen as one of the great "popularizers" of the late 1940s and early 1950s of the soon-to-be new science of cryptozoology.

LINDORM

Lindorm is a Swedish word for dragon, a creature which even in nineteenth-century Scandinavia was no mythological beast. It was something people could encounter in the countryside, especially in or near marshes, caves, and bodies of water. (Some thought it to be a landlocked **Sea Serpent.**) In 1885, in a book on the subject, scientist and folklorist Gunnar Olaf Hylten-Cavallius collected forty-eight first-person accounts, one from a member of the Swedish parliament. Half of the accounts claimed multiple witnesses.

Hylten-Cavallius's informants described Lindorms as ten to twenty feet in length. The body of a Lindorm "is as thick as a man's thigh; his color is black with a yellow-flamed belly. . . . He has a flat, round or square head, a divided tongue, and a mouth full of white, shining teeth."

The "heavy and unwieldy" creature had a stubby tail and wild, hypnotic eyes as large as saucers. Aggressive and powerful, it would hiss and contract until its body "lies in billows; then he raises himself on his tail four or five feet up and pounces upon his prey," according to Hylten-Cavallius. It was possible, though difficult, to kill a Lindorm. In its death throes it would emit an overwhelmingly foul odor. Encounters were terrifying to witnesses who, often for years afterward, suffered what today would be called post-traumatic stress disorder.

Hylten-Cavallius's offer of a reward for a dead Lindorm found no takers. He would be the last scientist to take the reports seriously. Lindorms, whatever they may or may not have been, are seen no more.

LIVING FOSSILS

A favorite theory, often expressed in the cryptozoological literature of the 1950s, is that **cryptids** may be "living fossils." As the zoologist Maurice Burton wrote in his 1956 book of the same name, "a living fossil is an organism that has survived beyond its era."

The 1938 discovery and 1952 second finding of the **coelacanth,** a prehistoric fish supposed to have vanished 65 million years ago, gave living fossils a specific and precise point of reference.

Maurice Burton, in *Living Fossils,* had this to say about the problem of the changing fossil record:

> As in all other living fossils, there have been constant, but small, changes throughout its history, but these changes have been so slight that we have no difficulty, at any stage, in recognising a coelacanth for what it is. This is [all] the more striking since the coelacanths have so often changed their habitat. Their ancestors in the Carboniferous [period] were living for the most part in the freshwaters. The coelacanths of the Triassic, on the other hand, had returned to salt water and were living in the shallow waters.

The fossil record is incomplete. It does not follow that just because there is a gap in the fossil record of, for example, the horseshoe crab, the **okapi,** or the coelacanth, the term "living fossil" is necessarily inaccurate. The phrase remains a useful, if overused, one.

LOCH NESS MONSTERS

The world learned of something unusual in Scotland's Loch Ness in the spring of 1933, after the *Inverness Courier* reported the experience a couple had undergone while traveling along the lake's northwest edge two weeks earlier. On April 14, the sight of an "enormous animal rolling and plunging" in the water caught their attention. Stopping their car, they watched the strange sight over the next few minutes. The newspaper account called the object a "monster," and the episode was covered in other Scottish papers.

Not long before, and not coincidentally, an older road running along the north end of Ness had been expanded through the use of dynamite. Construction workers removed trees and other obstructions to a view of the water. The explosive disturbances and ability to see clearly the surface of the loch while driving on the new road appeared to be related directly to a sudden proliferation of reports like the one above. Six months and twenty sightings later, the legend of the "Loch Ness Monster" was born, and the story became an international sensation.

The first photograph of the Loch Ness Monster was taken near Foyers by Hugh Gray, November 12, 1933. (FPL)

This is the famous "Surgeon's Photograph" of the Loch Ness Monster taken by London surgeon Lt. Col. Robert Kenneth Wilson on April 19, 1934. Despite recent claims of a hoax, most researchers have always considered that this and the second photograph Wilson took show nothing more than a diving bird or otter. (Robert Kenneth Wilson)

Monster or no monster, Ness is a remarkable lake. The largest freshwater body in Scotland, it is more than twenty miles long; at its deepest it is one thousand feet down. It is also narrow, no more than a mile and a half at its widest. It was formed ten thousand years ago during the last Ice Age, at the end of which glaciers melted and sea water flowed in to fill up the fjords they had created. With the disappearance of the ice, the land rose, and the salty sea waters trapped in the fjords became lakes. Over time the water turned fresh, and the descendants of the animals that had washed in from the North Atlantic adapted to the new environment.

Whether these animals included large beasts either uncatalogued by science or generally thought long extinct, no one knows. What we do know is that an earlier printed reference to an unknown in the loch appeared in another Inverness paper, the *Northern Chronicle,* on August 27, 1930. (An early medieval legend, set in A.D. 565, has St. Columba confronting a man-killing dragon in River Ness and causing it to flee "backwards more rapidly than he came.") Three years later, in 1933, as

"Nessie" was entering the world's popular culture, a number of persons came forward to recount alleged sightings going back to the middle of the nineteenth century. Most—albeit (as we shall see) not all—of the sightings concerned a large animal whose black or gray back resembled an overturned boat in the water. Sometimes the back was visible only as two or three humps. It had a long, thin neck and a small head of horse-like appearance. On occasion its long, tapered body could be seen, with finlike attachments and an extended, thick tail.

Though often called "the monster"—and even thought by one early chronicler, Rupert T. Gould, to be a single stranded **Sea Serpent**—a handful of sightings confirmed what common sense would have dictated: that to survive there would have to be a breeding population of Nessies. In other words, more than one "Loch Ness Monster." Sometimes, as in a 1937 sighting, multiple creatures of varying size have been observed: "three Monsters about three hundred yards out in the loch . . . two black shiny humps, five feet long and protruding two feet out of the water and on either side . . . a smaller Monster," according to the *Scottish Daily Press* (July 14, 1937). Sixty years later a journalist for London's *Financial Times* would write—apparently seriously—of seeing five "plesiosaur-type monsters," including a small, juvenile specimen, at a distance of no more than fifteen feet.

Estimates of the animals' size range from three to sixty-five feet, more evidence suggesting a breeding population. Most, however, are in the range of fifteen to thirty feet.

Aside from the reports of witnesses, evidence for the existence of Nessies comes from photographs and sonar trackings. The former has proved problematic in some important regards. The most celebrated of pictures, taken in April 1934 by physician R. K. Wilson, shows what is supposed to be the long-necked profile of a plesiosaur-like Nessie. It is more likely (as a second, much less-publicized photo suggests) to be an otter or a seal, though there was an unsubstantiated allegation in 1994 that it was a hoaxed image of a doctored plastic toy submarine. There have been several notorious hoaxed photographs of Nessie through the years.

The best photographs were taken underwater in 1972 and 1975. In the first case, a sonar-bearing boat patroling the waters near Urquhart Bay, along with a companion vessel with strobe and camera, tracked an unidentified target 120 feet away. An underwater strobe camera missed the object, however, evidently because it passed above or below its beam. Less than an hour later two more objects, apparently twenty to thirty feet long and within twelve feet of each other, appeared on the sonar screen, just behind an apparently fleeing school of salmon.

When developed, the underwater-camera film was found to have preserved some highly interesting images. On two frames what looked like a flipper attached to a roughly textured body could be seen; a third carried an out-of-focus picture of two objects, the nearer and clearer of which bore an unmistakable resemblance to what witnesses had been reporting for decades. The sonar records, in the judgment of Jet Propulsion Laboratory analysts, confirmed the presence of unknowns in the loch and indicated that these were the objects in the photographs.

The researchers, sponsored by the Massachusetts-based Academy of Applied Sciences, returned to Ness in 1975 and captured an even more dramatic image, showing what an article in *Technology Review* characterized as the "upper torso, neck and head of a living creature" in Ness's murky, peat-sogged waters. A second photograph showed what appeared to be the animal's horselike face at a distance of five feet from the camera. It also caught two small horns that many witnesses had noted. According to analysts, "Measurements indicated the 'neck' to be about one-and-a-half feet thick, the 'mouth' nine inches long and five inches wide, and the horn on the central ridge six inches long."

Though zoologists from a range of prestigious scientific and academic bodies (including the Smithsonian Institution and Harvard University) seemed ready to endorse the reality of Nessies on the strength of this evidence, the skeptics eventually triumphed. Because the images were not crystal-clear, it was possible for them to argue that they were something else—something conventional—such as a rotting tree stump or a floating engine block. Though the images did not look much like either of these, it turned out to be impossible to prove the extraordinary alternative. Eventually, perhaps sensing the impossibility of their supposed identifications, debunkers were reduced to leveling baseless charges of hoaxing against the investigators.

The rarest type of evidence, films of the Loch Ness Monster, have existed from the beginning of this phenomenon. Researcher Mike Dash, for example, is on the track of the reputed films of the elusive Dr.

MacRae. The MacRae films are close-up cinema films shot in the 1930s, of a Sea Serpent and the Loch Ness Monster. Dash has always been surprised that so little has been pursued on the reputed existence of these films, and he has been in communication with the MacRae family to recover any surviving evidence that the trust may have. Dash notes that if the films turn up they could help solve two of the greatest cryptozoological mysteries at a stroke.

The single best piece of photographic evidence is a film taken on April 23, 1960, from the loch's eastern shore. **Tim Dinsdale,** perhaps the most respected of all Ness investigators, was on a Nessie watch when through binoculars he noticed a "long oval shape, a distinct mahogany color . . . well above the water." Suddenly, as it began to move, Dinsdale realized that he was looking at the back of "some huge living creature." He managed to get four minutes of it on film before the object submerged.

In a subsequent analysis Britain's Joint Air Reconnaissance Intelligence Center (JARIC) used a second film, also taken by Dinsdale for purposes of comparison, of a boat sailing in the same direction the presumed Nessie had taken. JARIC was able to disprove the skeptics' theory that the first film had been of a boat. It concluded that the thing was "probably . . . an animate object," twelve to sixteen feet in length, three feet above the water, moving at ten miles per hour. JARIC's analysis has yet to be challenged successfully. If it is possible to prove that Nessies exist without producing the actual physical remains of one, the Dinsdale film is that proof.

Occasional, rare land sightings—the last was reported in February 1960—are associated with the plesiosaur-like Nessie described in the water sightings. Some sightings, however, are not. These witnesses describe creatures that could have stepped out of *The Twilight Zone.*

For example, there is the testimony of Colonel L. McP. Fordyce, who wrote in 1990 that one night in April 1932, as he and his wife were driving through woods at the loch's south edge, they saw a weird creature "like a cross between a very large horse and a camel. . . . Its long, thin neck gave it the appearance of an elephant with its trunk raised." Its tail was narrow and hairy, and it walked on long, thin legs. It is worth noting that this was not the only alleged sighting of this sort of bizarre apparition. In 1771 someone spotted a monstrous creature "which was a cross between a horse and a camel" in or near the loch. Children playing at Inchnacardoch Bay in 1912 told of seeing, from no more than a few yards away, an animal that looked like a long-necked camel. It entered the water, then disappeared into it.

Two other land reports, from 1923 and 1933, speak of what witnesses compared to a giant hippopotamus. (Land sightings may not be as rare as one might assume. Dash says that fifty-five land sightings, in total, have been recorded for **Lake Monsters** worldwide.)

These sorts of stories make scientifically oriented Ness proponents and cryptozoologists understandably uneasy. One of them, chemist and Ness sympathizer Henry H. Bauer, observes, "One is brought squarely up against the phenomenon of apparently responsible and plausible individuals who insist on the reality of experiences of the most extremely improbable sort."

Even waterbound sightings sometimes betray anomalies. Reports of a creature likened to a "great salamander," a "large alligator," or a "crocodile" have been logged. These are rare, true, but they are not nonexistent, and their occurrence is both puzzling and resistant to any imaginable solution that involves conventional biology.

Still, the considerable majority of reports are of things—presumed animals—that conventional zoology could accommodate: in other words, reptiles or mammals, either new species or (more likely) species thought extinct, such as plesiosaurs or **zeuglodons** (snakelike whales believed to have vanished 20 million years ago). As we have seen, a body of seemingly solid evidence, from witness testimony, photograph and film, and instrumented observation, underscores what seems a real and distinct possibility.

LOOFS-WISSOWA, HELMUT (1927-)

Helmut Loofs-Wissowa was born in Halle, Germany, of Belgian-German-Polish ancestry. Growing up in Leipzig, he was drafted into the German army at the end of the war, shipped to the Eastern front, spent two years under Russian occupation, and escaped to the French zone where he worked as a documentary film cameraman.

On joining the French Foreign Legion, he served in Vietnam as a regular French army war correspondent, remaining there until 1954. Back in Europe Loofs-Wissowa obtained his education at the University of Tübingen, Germany, at Musée de l'Homme in Paris, and received a Ph.D. in anthropology at the University of Fribourg, Switzerland, in 1960, for his thesis on the mountain tribes of southern Indochina. He worked as a lecturer, reader, and finally professor at the Australian National University in Canberra from 1964 until his retirement in 1992. He still holds the post of Visiting Fellow in the Faculty of Asian Studies at the university there.

Loofs-Wissowa's interest in cryptozoology was kindled by his encounter with **Bernard Heuvelmans** in 1957 when, as a student in Paris about to leave on an expedition to Patagonia and Tierra del Fuego, he met with Heuvelmans. Loofs-Wissowa vowed to look into cryptozoological mysteries in his travels. Nevertheless, it was his Southeast Asian expertise that propelled Loofs-Wissowa into a longer, active role in cryptozoology. Loofs-Wissowa and his mentor Heuvelmans became frequent correspondents during the ensuing years.

Helmut Loofs-Wissowa appears with a drawing of the Minnesota Iceman in the background. (Helmut Loofs-Wissowa)

In 1978, Loofs-Wissowa was the first "nonsocialist" to be invited to Vietnam, where he briefed his Vietnamese colleagues on Heuvelmans's 1974 book on *Homo pondoides,* Heuvelmans's scientific name for the **Minnesota Iceman.** The Minnesota Iceman launched Loofs-Wissowa into some of his most productive work on the Vietnamese Wildman and the related reports of the semi-erect penis of the Minnesota Iceman as a marker of the **Neandertal,** shown in the cave art of Europe, in the traditions of the Sumerian *Gilgamesh*'s wild man Enkidu, and through the descriptions of the classical Greek Satyrs.

His contacts in Southeast Asia and Australia served him well, and he created a network of scholars and researchers interested in cryptozoology. During the 1990s, Loofs-Wissowa took a leadership role in research into **Nguoi Rung,** the Wildman of the Forest of Southeast Asia, and has discussed his findings in Australian, German, and Japanese documentaries. In 1995, in Laos, he interviewed locals about their sightings of their version of the Nguoi Rung, a gorilla-like creature called the *briau.* Loofs-Wissowa is writing a history of Nguoi Rung research in Australasia.

"LOST WORLD" OF VIETNAM

In July 1992, global news organizations introduced everyone to the startling discovery of a so-called lost world of animals living in Vietnam's Vu Quang Nature Reserve, a sixty-five-square-mile area near the Laotian border. The knowledge of the faunal diversity of Vietnam was impeded by years of war and limited international contacts. Scientists have described the reserve as a "lost world seemingly untouched by the war," and possibly teeming with new species. The Vu Quang Reserve has one of the country's richest and most pristine forests.

The first and most exciting animal discovery announced was a creature known locally as the **saola** ("forest goat"). While investigating scientists did not observe a living specimen, they did find three sets of upper skulls and horns. One of the skulls was from a recently deceased animal, enough to establish its existence and scientifically describe it. The saola or Vu Quang ox (*Pseudoryx nghetinhensis*) had been officially discovered.

The Lost World has produced several other recent discoveries, including evidence of a new species of fish, two previously unknown bird species, and an unknown tortoise with a striking yellow shell. Meanwhile, the search is on for a new reptile known as the burrowing Vietnamese sharp-nosed snake. During the Vietnam War, U.S. Navy officers gathered and photographed specimens of this snake, but the specimens were lost. A recent issue of *Cryptozoology* (dated 1992 but published in 1994) offers a scientific description of this reported, but so far unproved, animal.

In addition to these, Dr. Ha Dinh Duc of the National University of Hanoi reports that a colleague at Hue University has seen another goat-like animal near A Luoi in Thua Thien Province. Dr. Pham Nhat

(Forestry University, Xuan Mai) reports two unusual civet (a catlike animal) specimens from Lao Cai Province in the far northwest.

In Vietnam, zoologists and biologists are discovering new animals at an amazing rate in what has become known as their very special Indochinese "lost world." Needless to say, much credit must go to the Vietnamese researchers, specifically Do Tuoc, and their associate, **John MacKinnon.**

One thing is certain: The discoveries issuing from the Lost World of Vietnam seem far from over.

LUSCA

Largest and least explored of the many isles of the Bahamas is the mysterious, mangrove-choked Andros, 104 by 40 miles in size. Off the coast of Andros are deepwater "blue holes," said to be inhabited by **cryptids** called Lusca. Described as many-armed animals resembling oversized octopuses, divers have reported attacks and near-encounters that have made the "blue holes" a risky challenge.

The zoologist **Bruce S. Wright**'s on-site investigations also determined that in the "banana holes," the deep brackish, semi-freshwater pools and small lakes on the Andros, similar monsters reportedly live. He theorized that the Lusca could be a **Giant Octopus** or a rare variety of giant squid, harking back to the tales of the **Kraken.**

MACFARLANE'S BEAR

In 1864, Inuit (Eskimo) hunters in Canada's Northwest Territories killed an "enormous" yellow-furred bear. Naturalist Robert MacFarlane obtained the bear's skin and skull and shipped the remains to the Smithsonian Institution, where they were placed in storage and forgotten.

Decades later, Dr. C. Hart Merriam found the specimen while conducting research at the Smithsonian. Upon closer study, he deduced that MacFarlane's animal belonged to a new species. While the specimen resembled the grizzly more than the polar bear, the skull and teeth were different from those of all other living bears. The skull most closely resembled prehistoric species. Merriam named the animal *Ursus inopinatus,* the "unexpected bear." In 1918 he went further, placing it in the newly created genus *Vetularctos.*

While Inuit stories about such bears continue, no other specimen has been collected. Theories concerning MacFarlane's bear suggest that it is a freak grizzly, a grizzly-polar bear cross, or a surviving representative—maybe the very last—of a type that should have become extinct during the Pleistocene.

Dr. James Halfpenny, a polar bear specialist, disputes the notion of a "throwback" grizzly but remarks that grizzly-polar crosses are documented. No one, however, has properly compared this specimen's remains to those of a known hybrid. The matter remains unsettled.

MacFarlane's Bear is different from any known "giant" bear. That much, at least, is certain. The brown bear (*Ursus arctos*), varieties or subspecies of which include the grizzly, the Kodiak, the Peninsula, and the Kamchatka bear, is only one species of "giant" bear. Nineteenth-century hunter John "Grizzly" Adams once captured a live grizzly weighing 1,510 pounds. The other giant is the polar bear (*U. maritimus*). One outsized specimen measured more than eleven feet tall and weighed 2,200 pounds.

MACKAL, ROY P. (1925–)

Roy P. Mackal is a distinguished biochemist, engineer, and biologist who has spent most of his academic life at the University of Chicago, where he obtained his B.A. in 1949 and a Ph.D. in 1953.

His biochemical research, much of it DNA-related, has brought him international recognition. As an engineer he has developed numerous technical innovations, including the design and construction of automatic parachute and recovery systems for sounding rockets and a hydrogen-generation device for weather balloons.

As a biologist he has become well known for his sometimes controversial involvement with cryptozoology. He participated in several important cryptozoological expeditions. One took him to Scotland in the 1960s, to study the **Loch Ness Monster,** and to the Congo in the 1980s, in search of the supposedly brontosaurus-like **Mokele-mbembe.** Another African trek in 1988 had Mackal pursuing the **Kongamato.** He is

Roy Mackal at Loch Ness. (FPL)

the vice president of the **International Society of Cryptozoology,** having been involved in its founding at the suggestion of his friend Jerome Clark and new associate **J. Richard Greenwell.** Between 1965 and 1975 he was scientific director of the Loch Ness Phenomena Investigation Bureau. The titles of his books, *The Monsters of Loch Ness* (1976), *Searching for Hidden Animals* (1980), and *A Living Dinosaur? In Search of Mokele-Mbembe* (1987), suggest his dedication to cryptozoology, to which he brings a healthy and enthusiastic optimism as well as an analytical and practical intellect.

MACKINNON, JOHN (1947–)

John MacKinnon, discoverer of the **saola** and other new species from the **"Lost World" of Vietnam,** grew up deeply interested in wildlife. The grandson of a British prime minister, James Ramsay MacDonald, he was born into a large family in Leeds. Early in his career, he spent a year in Tanzania studying insect behavior, as well as chimpanzees with Jane Goodall. MacKinnon went on to Oxford for a zoology degree, receiving his Ph. D. while working under Nikolaas Tinbergen and Desmond Morris.

From 1968 through 1970, MacKinnon was in Borneo on a one-man expedition studying orangutans, and later was in Sumatra observing the native orangs there. In 1970, while in the Malaysian state of Sabah, he recorded his own finds of footprints of the mysterious apelike **Batutut.** MacKinnon eventually would study all the other apes of Asia and Africa.

MacKinnon is a flashback to the great animal discoverers of the past, like **Gerald Russell** and Carl Hagenbeck, but he is a modern conservationist, too. His unique combination of instincts and field training makes him one of the best field cryptozoologists alive at the end of the twentieth century. Through his current work in Vietnam under the sponsorship of the World Wildlife Fund, MacKinnon continues to make amazing discoveries of new animals.

MANGIACOPRA, GARY (1960-)

Gary Mangiacopra, a New Englander with a master's degree in biology, has been interested in doing archival cryptozoological investigations since he was a teen. Today he is seen as one of the foremost specialists in the study of eighteenth- and nineteenth-century reports of the **Sea Serpent** in New England. He has also studied American **Lake Monsters.** He has published many articles on these two subjects in journals like *Of Sea and Shore,* and he is preparing separate books on Sea Serpents and Lake Monsters.

In 1995, Mangiacopra wrote a major article, "Connecticut's Mystery Felines: The Glastonbury Glawackus" (*The Anomalist*) on his decades-long investigation of his home state's **Black Panther** accounts.

MANIPOGO

Manipogo—a name inspired by British Columbia's **Ogopogo**—is the moniker given to the **Lake Monster** that allegedly roars and lives in Lake Manitoba. Seen many times during the 1950s, it was described as black-brown and some thirty feet long. In 1957, a group of journalists organized a quasi-official expedition that found a cave full of the remains of small animals and traces left by a heavy serpentine animal.

The chairman of the Department of Zoology at the University of Manitoba, James McLeod (not to be confused with the other Professor **James McLeod,** who investigates **Paddler** in Idaho), took the reports of twenty picnickers who all saw Manipogo on July 24, 1960, and he led two expeditions that year. McLeod has collected sightings as well as an intriguing 1962 photograph. The Manipogo photograph, one of the few ever taken of a not-so-famous **cryptid,** shows a still-unexplained animal, if it is not a hoax. **John Kirk** points out in his book *In the Domain of the Lake Monsters* (1998) that routine sightings of Manipogo ceased after 1962.

MAPINGUARY

The issue of South America's unknown primate population is confused by credible reports of giant **Bigfoot**-like beasts from the Andes, the **Ucu,** as well as by accounts of **Giant Monkeys.** Even so, a number of sightings as well as other evidence keep the question of human-sized and smaller apelike creatures very much alive in the various regions of the continent. Some are called Mapinguary, a term that merges with another local moniker, Didi.

The Didi is a site-specific name for a red-haired bulky anthropoid restricted to a narrow strip of northwestern South America. It appears to be shorter than the Mapinguary of Brazil, but both are unknown hominoids, and both sometimes are described as having red fur. For hundreds of years, native peoples in the Guyanese montane forests from the highlands of Brazil over through Suriname and Guyana have reported encounters with little hooting creatures they call *didi, dru-di-di, or didi-aguiri.* Once they had penetrated these areas, Westerners heard and recorded comparable accounts. In the course of the European discovery of British Guiana (now Guyana) in 1596–97, Sir Walter Raleigh and Laurence Keymis recorded rumors of the creatures. In 1769, Dr. Edward Bancroft, Benjamin Franklin's friend and later a British spy in Paris, took note of stories of what he assumed were five-foot-tall apes with short black hair.

In 1910, the resident magistrate of British Guiana, a man named Haines, saw two Didis along the Konowaruk, near the junction of the Potato River. Eight years later the guide Miegam and three others were up the Berbice River, a little beyond Mambaca (in what was then British Guiana), when they spotted two figures they first took to be men on a beach. Soon, however, they "were staggered to find that the footprints were apes', not men's." The Didi and Mapinguary, it seems, have similar feet, more anthropoid than human. Both also reportedly emit a similar range of whistles and sounds.

Typically, the Mapinguary is described in native traditions throughout southern Brazil as a mostly red-haired, sloping, bipedal, long-armed giant ape associated with unique "bottle" footprints. Most cryptozoologists, including **Bernard Heuvelmans, Ivan T. Sanderson,** and **Loren Coleman,** have written of the Mapinguary as a form of primate. But biologist David Oren told *The New York Times* in 1994 that Amazonians were in fact seeing supposedly extinct medium-sized giant **Ground Sloths.** Though some ostensible Mapinguary sightings may be of such an animal, others clearly are not. **Mark A. Hall** has written, "The popular discussions of David Oren's research have done nothing to clear up the picture [regarding Mapinguary]. They may have only confused the issue all the more for the time being."

Likewise, Sanderson found the Didi a confusing creature to classify. He wondered if it was a regional version of the Mapinguary. But the Didi are smaller and usually darker than the Brazilian rainforest-dwelling Mapinguary. So we are left with questions. Are the Didi a small, dark, localized montane population of apes—or are they **Proto-Pygmies?**

MARKED HOMINID

From Siberia to infrequent appearances in places like Monroe, Michigan, one remarkable feature seems to set apart a group of seven-foot hairy hominids usually seen in and near the subpolar regions of the world. In this population, the individuals tend to be piebald—exhibiting either a two-toned, multicolored hair pattern, a lighter-haired mane, a near-albino appearance, or a white patch in the midst of a field of darker hair. The Siberians called one such individual Mecheny, meaning the Marked One. **Loren Coleman,** in his field guide to unknown hominoids written with **Patrick Huyghe,** used that name as a basis for calling these beings the Marked Hominids. Additionally, he saw this naming as a fitting tribute to his fellow researcher **Mark A. Hall,** who had first identified these beings as markedly different from **Bigfoot.**

Though often mistaken for Bigfoot, Marked Hominids are actually more human-looking and somewhat shorter than those classic neo-giants. They average about seven feet tall and have firm, powerful bodies with well-developed legs and shoulder muscles. Their arms do not reach below the knees, and they have flat buttocks, visible genitalia, and sometimes a protruding stomach, which is probably indicative of the individual's age and well-fed condition. Also characteristic is a foot that measures ten to fourteen and one-half inches long and has a narrow curving impression and a three-to-five inch width. Its five toes are splayed; often, even the outside, or little, toe appears splayed.

Essentially neckless, the Marked Hominid has large eyes set in a rounded face with a calm, almost pleasant, appearance. It does not look apelike at all. In males, the face has hair, or a beard, from the eyes down, giving the impression of a mask. The hair is short brown, or dark, and slightly longer on the head, under the arms, and in the pubic area. As noted, they have a tendency to piebald, showing lighter patches among the darker colors. Some are albino or lightly maned.

The Marked Hominid, while perhaps existing globally, appears to live mainly on the wooded mountainsides and tundra in the subpolar regions of North America, Europe, and Asia. This howling nocturnal creature sometimes wears skins and often smells like a wet dog. Though they may live in groups, the Marked Hominids do not appear to be as intelligent as the native peoples with whom they have shared similar harsh living conditions. The Marked Hominids have been known to approach human housing and livestock, trade with humans, and communicate with them nonverbally. A by-product of their close association with humans is their natural annoyance with dogs which, according to reports, they have sometimes killed.

The diet of the Marked Hominid shows a preference for larger mammals, small game, and plants. In April 1992, Vyacheslav Oparin,

The Siberian Marked Hominid named Mecheny was six and a half feet tall and had a distinctive patch of white hair on its forearm. Mecheny's appearance is based on Russian scientist Maya Bykova's 1987 sightings. (N. Potapov/D. Bayanov)

a Karelian journalist, was promoting the idea that Finland's Abominable Snowman should be renamed the Forest Monster or Tree Eater because, he claimed, the tall and hairy animal living along the Finnish border climbed trees and lived off bark.

One of the most remarkable series of close-up sightings of these Marked Hominids occurred in the 1980s in Siberia, as reported by Maya Bykova, who described the creature portrayed on page 152.

MAROZI

The *marozi* ("spotted lion"), which has been given the scientific name *Panthera leo maculatus,* has been reported from the montane forests of East Africa.

The animals, heretofore unknown by Western observers, came to the fore beginning in 1903, with sightings of darker and beautifully spotted lions in the Kenyan mountains. The natives called them the *marozi.* Then farmer Michael Trent killed two three-year-old individuals in 1931. The published photograph of the skin is a well-known cryptozoological archival illustration. As **Bernard Heuvelmans** has noted, a lion of that

The marozi, or spotted lion, of East Africa has been seen alive, though is also described from the skins of two killed in 1934 by Michael Trent, which are still preserved in London. (William M. Rebsamen)

age should have lost its spots. Suspecting that a subspecies is in the making, he has given these cats the formal subspecies name *maculatus.*

No live specimens have been captured to date, and thus the *marozi* remains an active candidate for cryptozoological pursuits.

MCLEOD, JAMES (1946–)

James McLeod founded one of the earliest university-based cryptozoology organizations, the now-defunct North Idaho College Cryptozoology Club (NICCC), located at Coeur d'Alene. He created the NICCC in 1983, when he began investigating his local **Lake Monster** after he found it noted in an appendix to **Loren Coleman**'s *Mysterious America* (1983). The NICCC's "Cryptoquest" received national attention in 1984 when it searched Lake Pend Oreille for the monster **Paddler.**

Soon afterward McLeod wrote a limited-edition report, *Mysterious Lake Pend Oreille and Its "Monster,"* regarded as a model for cryptozoological investigations. From his examination of the material, McLeod said, "We concluded that about 98 percent of the sightings could be [of] sturgeon." Articles by **Patrick Huyghe** about his collection of Pend Oreille Paddler lore have been published in *Omni* and *The Anomalist.*

A Spokane native, McLeod earned his undergraduate degree from the University of Washington in 1964, and a graduate degree from Eastern Washington University in 1969. He has been a professor at North Idaho College since 1970, teaching English, literature, folklore, and religion. He directed NIC's highly respected Scottish Studies Program in Idaho and Scotland for many years, traveling to Loch Ness several times to look into Nessie, the **Loch Ness Monster,** as well as conduct more mainstream scholarly inquiries. McLeod has also taught at the University of Idaho and has won teaching and leadership awards.

MEGALODON

Recent popular curiosity in the survival of a giant prehistoric shark, known generally under the name Megalodon, has been sparked by a series of popular novels including Robin Brown's *Megalodon,* Steve Alten's *Meg,* Charles Wilson's *Extinct,* and Tom Dade's *Quest for Megalodon.*

A few cryptozoologists have toyed with the idea that the giant great white shark, *Carcharodon megalodon,* thought to be extinct, still exists. But these sharks supposedly died out 1.5 million years ago.

There are two radically conflicting views about the Megalodon. *Exotic Zoology* editor **Matt Bille** states that the evidence supporting the "Megalodon is alive" school consists of two items. The first is a pair of fossilized teeth, estimated by mineral deposits on them to be only eleven thousand and twenty-four thousand years old, respectively. The second

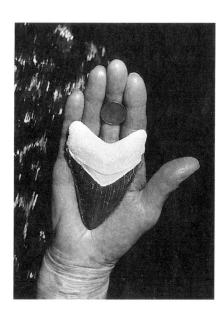

is an assortment of sightings, one of which stands out: the claim by New Zealand lobstermen to have met an all-white shark in 1918; they thought it was one hundred feet long.

On the other hand, **Ben S. Roesch,** editor of *The Cryptozoology Review* and a shark specialist, rejects such claims. He says there is no reason to believe that Megalodon is still alive, despite what he calls "overzealous cryptozoologists" think. The only "evidence" for alleged Megalodon survival is some supposedly fresh teeth, which Roesch says are actually fossils and erroneously dated. Only a few alleged sightings are on record, and they are easily explained as arising either from misidentification of known animals or from yarn-spinning.

Fossil tooth of the giant prehistoric shark, Megalodon. (FPL)

Roesch contends that proponents of Megalodon survival fail to acknowledge that Megalodon was an inhabitant of coastal near-surface waters, much like the extant great white shark. Megalodon did not dwell in the depths of the sea, as proponents of the survival theory contend. If Megalodon was still alive today, we would see unambiguous evidence of its existence.

Concluding their chapter on Megalodon in *Great White Shark,* **Richard Ellis** and John E. McCosker offer this wry observation: "To date, no concrete evidence has surfaced to substantiate the continued existence of these giants. But there will always be those who keep hoping that one will appear. Let us hope we are not in the water when it does."

MEGAMOUTH

This species of shark was unknown until 1976 when one was caught by pure chance. In 1976, a team from the Hawaii Laboratory of the Naval Undersea Center were working around the Hawaiian islands, spending a few days aboard a research vessel, carrying out work in deep waters. Two large parachutes employed as sea anchors were dropped overboard to a depth of five hundred feet. On the day of the team's departure they hauled the parachutes in, only to discover that they had caught a gigantic shark. It measured 14.5 feet in length and weighed 1,650 pounds. Dr. Leighton R. Taylor, director of the University of Hawaii's Waikiki Aquarium, recognized it as a heretofore-unsuspected new species. The newspapers soon dubbed the creature "megamouth," due to its extremely large mouth. Taylor and his colleagues incorporated the name "megamouth" by making it the basis of the species' scientific name, christening it *Megachasma pelagios* ("great yawning mouth of the open water").

For years, only male megamouths were found, but in 1994, a female, the seventh specimen ever seen, was washed ashore in Japan.

Cryptozoology played a role in identifying the most recent verified megamouth from the Philippines. Researcher Elson T. Elizaga E-mailed photographs of the shark caught by three fishermen in Macajalar Bay, Cagayan de Oro, Philippines. Cryptozoologist and shark researcher **Ben S. Roesch** from Toronto, Ontario, was the first to identify the shark as megamouth. Elizaga then heard from Dr. John F. Morrissey, associate professor in the Department of Biology at Hofstra University, Hempstead, New York. Morrissey wrote, "No question! That is megamouth #11! Congratulations!!"

On March 21, 1998, Dr. Leonard Compagno, curator of fishes and head of the Shark Research Center, Division of Life Sciences, South African Museum, Cape Town, South Africa, wrote: "I received the three photographs [from Elizaga] via E-mail. The photos appear to show a large megamouth shark (*Megachasma pelagios*). Apparently, this is the first recorded discovery of the species in the Philippines."

The Florida Museum of Natural History and Dr. Morrissey confirmed and updated his following table of megamouths to include the new Philippines find:

DISTRIBUTION TABLE OF MEGAMOUTH SHARKS

NUMBER	LOCATION	DATE	SEX	LENGTH*
1	Oahu (HI)	15 Nov. 76	M	446 cm
2	Catalina Island (CA)	29 Nov. 84	M	449 cm
3	Mandurah (Australia)	18 Aug. 88	M	515 cm
4	Hamamatsu City (Japan)	23 Jan. 89	M	400+ cm
5	Suruga Bay (Japan)	June 89	?	490 cm
6	Dana Point (CA)	21 Oct. 90	M	494 cm
7	Hakata Bay (Japan)	29 Nov. 94	F	471 cm
8	Dakar (Senegal)	4 May 95	?	180 (?) cm
9	Southern Brazil	18 Sept. 95	M	190 cm
10	Toba (Japan)	1 May 97	F	500+ cm
11	Cagayan de Oro (Philippines)	21 Feb. 98	?	ca 549 cm

*1 cm = 2.54 in.

MELDRUM, D. JEFFREY (1958–)

Jeffrey Meldrum, associate professor of anatomy and anthropology at Idaho State University and affiliate curator of vertebrate paleontology at

Jeffrey Meldrum shown here with a frame from the disputed Redwoods Bigfoot video. (Jeffrey Meldrum)

the Idaho Museum of Natural History, is one of the new breed of young primatologists who have an open-minded approach to cryptozoology, especially relating to **Bigfoot.** After graduating with a Ph.D. in physical anthropology in 1989 from the State University of New York at Stony Brook, Meldrum specialized, through his initial fieldwork with African monkeys, in foot mechanics. He studied the implications for bipedal adaption and locomotion in early hominids. Meldrum also participated in paleontological field projects to South America, collecting new fossil primate specimens from the Miocene of Columbia and Argentina.

Because he grew up in the Pacific Northwest, Meldrum heard about Bigfoot at an early age and has long been interested in the controversy surrounding this fabled creature. His research involvement in **hominology,** however, was rekindled in 1996, when he found and cast a series of Bigfoot prints in Washington. The next year, in northern California, he came across fresh tracks. Meldrum has since gathered and purchased collections of Bigfoot track casts as part of a project to study the anatomy of the creature's foot.

Meldrum has appeared frequently, often with **J. Richard Greenwell,** in documentaries discussing his insights into amateur videotapes allegedly taken of Bigfoot and **Yeti.** Meldrum is at work on an ambitious and potentially groundbreaking book that will address the anatomy, physiology, phylogenetics, and morphology of the **Sasquatch** foot.

MERBEING

The Merbeing, or water creature, is a staple of world mythology and folklore. Few people are aware that reports of generally similar creatures are still being made, though apparently less frequently than in the past. Our concern here is not just with the fabled half-human/half-fish (and zoologically impossible) figure of tradition but also with the Sea-Ape of the Bering Sea, the scaly-looking but actually hairy misnamed Lizard Men, and the fiery-eyed Latino phenomenon known as the **Chupacabras**. While a growing Hispanic population in the Americas is only now actively examining and discussing its Merbeing beliefs and sightings, Asians have been aware of what they call Kappas and other Merbeings for centuries.

Merbeings, according to the classification system developed by **Loren Coleman** and **Patrick Huyghe,** based on some initial thoughts and ideas exchanged with **Mark A. Hall,** appear to come in two varieties. The marine subclass is distinguished by a finlike appendage, while the other, mostly freshwater, subclass is characterized by an angular foot with a high instep and three pointed toes. The freshwater subtypes often venture onto land. They are far more aggressive and dangerous, being carnivorous, than their calmer marine cousins.

Varying in height from dwarf to man-sized, their bodies are strong, but not stocky or bulky. The marine variety has smooth skin, sometimes with a very short "fur," while the freshwater variety may have patchy hair growths like "leaves" or "scaly." In both subclasses, the hair is often maned, though some exhibit almost complete hair cover, especially in the Chupacabras kin. Merbeings in general have eyes that are usually oval or almond-shaped, perhaps due to their watery origins. These mostly nocturnal creatures have a singsong vocalization, reported from Eurasia to Africa.

Freshwater Merbeings often display a row of spikes down along the back, an uncommon but not unknown feature among primates. In the potto (*Periodicticus*), a known cat-sized and monkey-like loris from south-central Africa, the spines of the last neck vertebrae and first vertebrae of the thorax penetrate the skin and are capped with horny spines. When threatened, the spikes stand up so a predator cannot bite the potto on the neck. So it appears to be with some Merbeings. In fact, the resemblance between freshwater Merbeings and the potto nearly extends down to the toes of their feet. While Merbeings appear to be three-toed, the potto has an enormous big toe pointing in the opposite direction to its third, fourth, and fifth toes, and its second toe is nothing more than a lump bearing a cleaning claw.

Merbeing lore may have some basis in reality. Perhaps it is not all myth. Genuinely puzzling sightings have occurred. A series of sightings of a creature that appeared to be half woman and half fish occurred off Scotland's west coast in 1814. On the other hand, the increased activity or visibility of the Chupacabras and the diminishing accounts of ocean-dwelling Mermaids and Mermen may signal a shift toward the successful survival of the more aggressive freshwater, land-oriented subclass. Sightings of the scary, triple-toed **Honey Island Swamp Monster** in Louisiana, the three-fingered and three-toed Thetis Lake Monster in Canada, and similarly digited Scape Ore Swamp Lizard Man in South Carolina, plus the Chupacabras, suggest that the most dangerous Merbeing variety to-day is the more land-based, freshwater variety.

MINHOCAO

Accounts of an unknown type of giant earthworm, or perhaps giant snake, circulated during the eighteenth century from the highlands of Brazil. The creature was called a Minhocao. One writer in *Nature* (February 21, 1878) theorized the animal could be a Pleistocene giant armadillo, the glyptodont.

MINNESOTA ICEMAN

During the autumn of 1967, University of Minnesota zoology major Terry Cullen, visiting the Milwaukee area, saw an extraordinary exhibit. It appeared to be an authentic corpse of a recently killed **Bigfoot**-like animal.

Cullen followed the exhibit around Wisconsin, Illinois, and Minnesota, to the many shopping malls and state fairs at which it was exhibited. Toward the end of the 1968 exhibiting season, after attempting without success to get various local anthropology professors interested

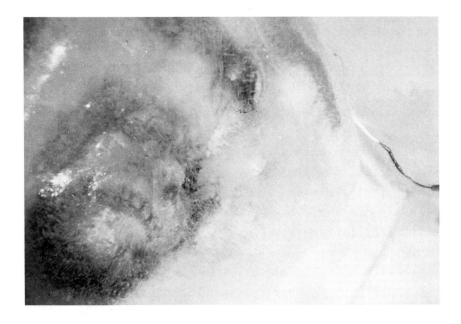

Close-up of the Minnesota Iceman's head. (Mark A. Hall)

in investigating the exhibit, Cullen finally alerted **Ivan T. Sanderson,** author of a book on **Abominable Snowmen.** Sanderson asked contacts of his to examine it at the Chicago Stock Fair.

At the time, by chance, Sanderson's house guest in New Jersey was **Bernard Heuvelmans,** the "Father of Cryptozoology." Intrigued by what they had heard from Cullen, they traveled to see firsthand what exhibitor Frank Hansen was showing across the Midwest. Hansen, who claimed that it was a "man left over from the Ice Age," charged twenty-five cents for a look at the thing frozen in a block of ice, in a refrigerated, glass coffin.

Sanderson and Heuvelmans drove to Hansen's farm, near Rollingstone, Minnesota, where the thing had been stored for the winter. In a cramped trailer they examined the creature. They were soon convinced that they had found the discovery of the century. After three days of study and detailed photography, Heuvelmans and Sanderson believed the beast was authentic. Both smelled the putrefaction where some of the flesh had been exposed from the melted ice. They noted that the thing had apparently been shot through the eye, and that eye dangled on the face. Through the ice, they could hardly believe what they saw.

Heuvelmans described it this way:

> The specimen at first looks like a man, or, if you prefer, an adult human being of the male sex, of rather normal height (six feet) and proportions but excessively hairy. It is entirely covered with very dark brown hair three to four inches long. Its skin appears waxlike, similar in color to the cadavers of white men not tanned by the sun. . . . The specimen is lying on its back . . . the left arm is twisted behind the head with the palm of the hand upward. The arm makes a strange curve, as if it were that of a sawdust doll, but this curvature is due to an open fracture midway between the wrist and the elbow where one can distinguish the broken ulna in a gaping wound. The right arm is twisted and held tightly against the flank, with the hand spread palm down over the right side of the abdomen. Between the right finger and the medius the penis is visible, lying obliquely on the groin. The testicles are vaguely distinguishable at the juncture of the thighs.

Hansen's desire that they keep the discovery quiet notwithstanding, Sanderson and Heuvelmans could hardly contain themselves. It was so real to Sanderson that he started talking about it affectionately to his friends as "Bozo." Sanderson (at the time a popular television nature personality who brought exotic animals to various programs) mentioned the Iceman on the *Tonight Show* with Johnny Carson during Christmas week 1968.

Over the next year the two cryptozoologists wrote scientific papers (Heuvelmans formally named the creature *Homo pongoides*), and Sanderson published an article in the men's magazine *Argosy*. Soon, under still-cloudy circumstances, the original body disappeared, and a model, apparently made in California, replaced the "real" creature. Rumors circulated that various Hollywood makeup artists were privately claiming to have been the actual producer of the Iceman. But Sanderson and Heuvelmans insisted that at least fifteen technical differences existed between the original and the replacement model, citing photographs taken by **Mark A. Hall** in Minnesota and by **Loren Coleman** in Illinois of the traveling exhibit.

Hall offers this speculation:

"It is likely that the rotting corpse of the famous Iceman was in early 1969 deposited into an unmarked and now forgotten grave by agents of the owner. . . . Many have hoped that one day a fortunate accident or an incident of the demise of a 'Wildman' would one day provide a corpse and confirm the existence of such relatives of humankind. The history of the Iceman, if accurate, is harmful to this expectation."

The Smithsonian Institution got involved when Sanderson approached its chief primatologist, John Napier, and urged a scientific examination of the creature. Hansen, the original exhibitor, had neither confirmed nor denied that the original creature was a model; all he would say was that the creature was "really" owned by a mysterious millionaire. He declined to have it examined further. The Smithsonian, suspecting a hoax, lost interest in the matter. Hansen removed the replacement model from exhibition for a while and even reported destroying it. It or a similar figure still shows up at mall exhibits on occasion.

The origins and nature of the creature are the source of continuing debate. Sanderson often said the creature could be North American, but was unsure. Heuvelmans would theorize later that it was a **Neandertal** that had been murdered in Vietnam during the war and smuggled into the United States in a "body bag." Heuvelmans and **Boris Porshnev,** in their 1974 book, *L'Homme de Néanderthal est toujours vivant,* wrote that it may indeed have been possible for Captain Hansen to have obtained the body and arranged to have it flown back in the same manner as the bodies of American soldiers killed in action. As history now reveals, this is the way that many kilos of heroin were slipped into the U.S. from Asia's Golden Triangle during the Vietnam War. The "transport" system was very much a reality. In the scholarly book *Other Origins* (1990; about *Gigantopithecus*), the anthropologist authors, Russell Ciochon, John Olsen, and Jamie James, discuss how they were surprised to hear their Vietnamese colleagues talk with familiarity about this alleged Vietnamese origin for the Minnesota Iceman. **Helmut Loofs-Wissowa** also supports the Indochinese link.

Others have debated Heuvelmans's theory. Hall questions the Iceman's supposed Vietnamese origin and alleged Neandertal affinity and today feels the original Minnesota Iceman was of south-central Asian *Homo erectus* origin.

But the evidence that would resolve the issue is no longer with us. Hall's final words on the matter, from *Wonders 3* (1994), are worth quoting: "We have seen in the Iceman what happens when a specimen of this kind is finally preserved. . . . Among them the only three who saw the importance of the specimen were powerless to influence his fate. His destiny was to be valueless and to disappear entirely from within our midst. He ended his career as a public entertainment most probably in an unmarked grave."

In 1997, what looked like a new version of the affair of the Minnesota Iceman occurred in France, in the heart of the country at Bourganeuf. According to French cryptozoologist **Michel Raynal,** it was indeed a hoax, and amusingly, the Belgium publisher of the journal *Cryptozoologia* was unwittingly responsible. Soon, the media had created a flap with stories of a "frozen man" of Bourganeuf, whose creator had obviously read Heuvelmans and Porshnev's 1974 book.

MNGWA

The Mngwa ("the strange one") is the "great gray ghost" of East Africa. Natives of the former Tanganyika (now Tanzania) inisist that the *mngwa* is not *simba* (the lion). They have known of the Mngwa for hundreds of years, describing the animal as an extremely aggressive, gigantic, unknown felid the size of a donkey.

English contact with the animal began, in earnest, in the 1900s. During the 1930s and 1940s, the Mngwa was commonly known by the name Nunda, but because of the books of Gardner Soule (*The Mystery Monsters* and *The Maybe Monsters*) and **Bernard Heuvelmans,** Mngwa is the appellation now more frequently employed. An influential, open-minded discussion of this **cryptid** appeared in the then-world-famous British scientific journal *Discovery* in 1938.

In his *Nature Parade* (1954) romantic naturalist Frank W. Lane writes of his interview with Patrick Bowen, a hunter, who tracked a Mngwa. Bowen remarked that the spoor were like a leopard's but much larger. The fur was brindled but visibly different from a leopard's. Lane, a cryptozoologist before the label even existed, speculated that nineteenth-century reports of attacks by the South African *chimiset,* usually associated with the **Nandi Bear,** might more plausibly be linked to the Mngwa.

Bernard Heuvelmans theorizes that the Mngwa may be an abnormally colored specimen of some known species or that it may be a larger subspecies of the golden cat (*Profelis aurata*).

MOAS

In 1958 **Bernard Heuvelmans** titled a chapter of his *On the Track of Unknown Animals* "The Moa, a Fossil That May Still Thrive." Moas, both medium-sized and giant forms, have been reported periodically in New Zealand since their supposed extinction five hundred years ago. Moas, flightless birds, are related to New Zealand's kiwis, to Australian emus, to Australian and New Guinea cassowaries, to African ostriches, and to South American rheas.

Writing in the 1960s, **Ivan T. Sanderson** took note of continuing—albeit rare—sightings of Moas on New Zealand's South Island. The most recent alleged sighting of a large Moa took place on January 20, 1993, in the Craigieburn Range. Three individuals sighted and photographed what they insisted was a six-foot-tall bird. They swore it was a Moa, not an emu, ostrich, red deer, or any of the other expert-proposed animal candidates.

Paddy Freaney, hotel owner and former instructor with the British

Army's elite Special Air Service, and his companions Sam Waby and Rochelle Rafferly were tramping—a New Zealand term for hiking in rugged terrain—in the Canterbury high country when they came upon a large bird. "The minute I saw it, I knew what it was," Freaney said soon afterward. "I believe it was a moa."

Moa with kiwis. (FPL)

It was about a meter (39 inches) off the ground, with a long, thin neck of another meter's length, ending in a small head and beak. It was covered in reddish-brown and gray feathers. The large, thick legs were covered with feathers almost to the knee joint, with bare legs below, and huge feet. (Interestingly, in his revised reconstruction of the Moa based on descriptions of aboriginal sightings, Heuvelmans broke with the traditional bare-legged, ostrich-like drawings of what Moas supposedly looked like and instead showed them with feathers down to their knees. Heuvelmans writes on this point: "There is no evidence that the Moa did not have feathered legs like a Cochin hen and like the kiwi itself. Only the fast-running bird of the plains has any advantage in bare legs, and the Moa was not one.")

The large bird ran off across a stream when the witnesses disturbed it. An outdoor survival expert with the SAS, Freaney dashed after the animal and took a photograph of it at a distance of thirty-five to forty meters (115 to 130 feet). He also snapped a picture a minute later of what he thought was the bird's wet footprint on a rock, and he took photographs of similar prints in shingle by the riverbed.

The out-of-focus view of the bird has a rock formation obscuring its legs. From what can be seen, the Moa appears to be medium brown, with a horizontal body, a tall, erect neck, and a head that may have been looking toward the camera. An image-processing group at the University of Canterbury's electrical and electronic engineering department spent three days analyzing the blurred photograph. On behalf of the group, spokesperson Kevin Taylor said the analysis had gone as far as it could go, but in his judgment it confirmed that the object was a large bird. On the other hand, Richard Holdaway, a former University of Canterbury postgraduate zoology student and currently a paleoecologist, stated flatly that the photograph showed a red deer. The neck was too thick for a bird's, he said, adding, "When you look at it at a distance like that, to me it looks like a poor image of the back end of a red deer going west."

After the Department of Conservation (DOC) backed away from its announced plan to search the area immediately, Freaney offered to mount an expedition himself, in some respects to clear his name after hoax charges circulated. Meantime, the experts' claim that the sighted bird was an emu was rapidly laid to rest when all captive emus in New Zealand were officially accounted for.

But the damage had been done, discouraging the DOC from its launching a serious search. And time was running out for the collection of the verifying evidence. A week after the sighting, Freaney remarked that bad weather in the back country may have already eliminated some of the proofs of the Moa, especially the prints in the shingle.

Loren Coleman interviewed Freaney on February 22, 1993, to clarify some points of the report. Freaney said he had turned over the original negative for analysis, but apparently the New Zealand resources for computer enhancement were more limited than initially claimed. The results proved inconclusive. According to Freaney, the bird was definitely larger than any emu he has ever seen in Australia; the feathers looked darker in the shade but basically were light brown most of the time they were in the sun; and the feathers appeared to stop at the knees. He also said no investigator before Coleman had expressed interest in the footprint photos.

Months later, it was revealed that two German trekkers in New Zealand, writing in a hiking outpost logbook, recorded a Moa sighting in the same general region as the earlier reports. German cryptozoologist Ulrich Magin confirmed that the two Germans had been in New Zealand at the time of their reported encounter. He suspected, however, that a hoaxer had simply appropriated their names. The German witnesses did not respond to a letter from Magin. Freaney soon grew dismayed by various "expert" attempts at debunking the account. These included a newspaperman's slander about a nonexistent liars club and the related brief false claim by a publicity seeker that the affair was a hoax. Freaney stood by his story, and he remained determined to find a living Moa. In the mid-1990s he organized several mini-expeditions in an unsuccessful attempt to capture a live specimen.

Despite suggestions by **Karl Shuker** and *Strange Magazine* editor Mark Chorvinsky about the Freaney case's being a hoax, which it may be, Moa sightings in New Zealand do take place and appear to point to undiscovered survivors on the islands.

MOKELE-MBEMBE

For hundreds of years, stories of surviving dinosaurs have come out of the jungles of central Africa. The first printed reference, in a 1776 book, relates Abbe Proyhart's discovery of giant, clawed animal footprints in west central Africa, tracks that he claimed were three feet across. In 1913, a German expedition in the Congo met a band of pygmies who described an animal they called *mokele-mbembe,* which means "one who stops the flow of rivers." They said this beast was about the size of an elephant or hippopotamus, with a long, flexible neck and a long tail like an alligator's. This description would be repeated by numerous witnesses since. It is consistent with a sauropod or other small dinosaur.

Mokele-mbembe reportedly does not like hippopotamuses and will kill them on sight, but it does not eat them. Perhaps lending credence to this allegation, cryptozoologist **Roy Mackal** has found that hippos are curiously absent from areas where Mokele-mbembe is said to live. Pygmies claim that Mokele-mbembe attacks and kills any humans who get too close to it, but it would not eat them, because of its strictly herbivorous diet. The pygmies of the Likouala swamp region report that the essential diet of Mokele-mbembe consists of the Malombo plant. (The term "Malombo plant" actually denotes two plants: *Landolphia mannii* and *Landolphia owariensis.*)

Numerous expeditions have been mounted in search of Mokele-mbembe. In 1980 and 1981, monster-hunter Mackal headed explorations into the Likouala and Lake Tele regions of the Congo, reputed hot spots of dinosaur sightings. Mackal documented a number of past

Mokele-mbembe. (FPL)

eyewitness accounts, including one dramatic story of how one Mokele-mbembe was attacked and killed. Pascal Moteka, who lived near Lake Tele, said that his people had once constructed a barrier of wooden spikes across a river to keep the giant beasts from interfering with their fishing. When Mokele-mbembe tried to break through the barrier, the assembled villagers managed to kill it with spears. Celebrating their triumph, the people butchered and cooked the carcass, but everyone who ate the dinosaur meat reportedly died soon afterward.

Mackal never saw the creature himself, though he says he did have one close call. One day while paddling down the Likouala River in dugout canoes, his group heard a loud "plop" sound, and a large wake splashed up on the far bank. The pygmy guides cried out frightfully, "Mokele-mbembe! Mokele-mbembe!" Mackal and his colleagues believed that only a large animal diving under the water could have caused such a wake, and since hippos are not present in the Likouala area, they suspected that they narrowly missed seeing the elusive cryptid.

Marcellin Agnagna, a Congolese biologist who had accompanied Mackal on his searches, led his own expedition in 1983. Agnagna claimed to have a firsthand sighting of a Mokele-mbembe as it waded in Lake Tele. He described it as having the long-necked form typically attributed to the creature, though he could not see its legs or tail, which remained underwater. Agnagna had a movie camera, but he later reported that there was little film left when the creature appeared, and he began filming it without realizing that the lens cap was still on. Thus, even though he says he observed the animal for about twenty minutes before it submerged and vanished, Agnagna was sadly left with no photographic evidence.

In 1992, members of a Japanese film crew captured some of the best photographic evidence of a Mokele-mbembe. As they were filming aerial footage from a small plane over the area of Lake Tele, intending to obtain some panoramic landscape shots for a documentary, they noticed a large shape moving across the surface of the lake and leaving a V-shaped wake behind itself. The cameraman zoomed in and got about fifteen seconds of the object in motion before it dived under the surface.

The resulting footage, though jumpy and indistinct, shows a vertical protuberance at the front of the object—possibly a long neck. A second, shorter projection could be a humped back or a tail. If the object is not a dinosaur, it's difficult to say what animal it could be, since a crocodile would not have two such protrusions above the water, and an elephant would not submerge in the way the object does. The explanation that makes the best visual match is actually two men paddling a canoe, though the object's speed is too fast to be a nonpowered boat.

The existence of dinosaurs in central Africa is unlikely, but not a total scientific impossibility. According to cryptozoologist **Karl Shuker,** "If dinosaurs could exist unknown to science anywhere in the world, the Likouala is where they would be."

MOMO

Momo ("Missouri Monster") is another of the localized names given to hairy bipedal creatures sighted in specific geographic locations much like the **Jersey Devil.**

Reports of hairy half-human creatures in the area of Louisiana, Missouri (pop. 4,600), had circulated since the 1940s, and in July 1971, Joan Mills and Mary Ryan allegedly encountered a hairy half-ape, half-man on River Road near Louisiana. On August 13, 1965, a similar-looking huge, dark, hairy creature attacked Christine Van Acker as she sat with her mother in their car near Monroe, Michigan. A picture of Christine's face with its highly visible black eye appeared in many newspapers around the country the next day.

The real Momo scare began on July 11, 1972, at about 3:30 P.M. on a relatively sunny day near the outskirts of Louisiana. After Terry Harrison and his brother Wally had gone off to look at some rabbit pens at the foot of Marzolf Hill, their older sister, Doris, who was inside, heard a scream. Looking out the bathroom window, she saw a creature standing by a tree, flecked with blood, with a dead dog under its arm. Doris and Terry described it as six or seven feet tall, black, and hairy. Its head and face were covered with hair, and no neck was visible.

It "stood like a man but it didn't look like one," Doris said. It soon waddled off, still with the dog under its arm. The Harrisons's own dog grew violently ill and vomited for three hours.

Neighbors told of dogs that had disappeared. On July 14, terrible odors emanated from the sighting area, and the children's father, Edgar Harrison, heard eerie howls as he and investigators prowled the site. On July 21, Ellis Minor, who lived on nearby River Road, heard his dogs bark; thinking it was another dog, he flashed a light out in his yard, then stepped outside to observe a six-foot-tall creature with black hair. It was standing erect in his yard. Shortly thereafter, it dashed into the woods.

After two weeks, the scare—which had attracted national attention—ended.

Similar creatures, reported throughout the Midwest and eastern United States and Canada, are often referred to as "Eastern Bigfoot." But in temperament, overall descriptions, body build, and the clear lack of similar facial features, these nonmontane, unknown hairy hominoids seem unlike the Pacific Northwest's classic **Bigfoot/Sasquatch,** and may be a hybrid of these classic Neo-Giants and the **Marked Hominids.**

MORAG

Another body of water near Loch Ness, Loch Morar, located just seventy miles away, has become mildly famous for encounters with creatures similar to the **Loch Ness Monsters.** Sightings of Morag, as the creature has been named, occurred throughout the 1800s and 1900s. Some link the sightings to folk traditions of the Water Horse or Kelpie of Morar.

Morag. (FPL)

In 1970 and 1971 the Loch Ness Investigation Bureau conducted research on Morag, during what it called the Loch Morar Survey. One
member, Neil Bass, spotted a "hump-shaped black object" in the course
of the project's observations. The survey produced a great deal of eyewitness testimony and a well-regarded book, *The Search for Morag*
(1974), by two members of the expedition, Elizabeth Montgomery
Campbell and David Solomon.

MORGAN, ROBERT W. (1935–)

Robert Morgan was born in Canton, Ohio, and has spent most of his
professional career in the film industry and tracking **Bigfoot/Sasquatch.**

Morgan has been involved as the founder and director of several Bigfoot organizations since the early 1970s. His roles have included being
the director of the American **Yeti** Expeditions during the 1970s; founder
and president of Vanguard Research (1972–74); and cofounder (with
Ted Ernst) and executive director of the American Anthropological Research Foundation (1974–present).

Robert Morgan is an activist in Bigfoot and related research, has directed six formal expeditions, and was responsible for instigating county commissioners to create the first ordinance in the U.S. protecting the legendary Bigfoot in Skamania County, Washington State, in 1969, with a

$10,000 fine for shooting a Bigfoot. He has searched for the creatures in Florida, the Pacific Northwest, and Asia. In 1999, he plans to go to Mongolia in search of **Almas.**

Morgan was the subject of the 1975 film *The Search for Bigfoot* (still shown frequently on cable channels) and featured in the Smithsonian series, *Monsters: Myth or Mystery* (1975). He is the author/producer of such Bigfoot material as *The Ultimate Legend Quest* (1992), *Bigfoot: The Ultimate Adventure* (1996), and *The Bigfoot Pocket Field Manual* (1997).

Morgan has appeared as a featured guest on *Montel Williams*

Robert Morgan examines some Bigfoot tracks at the site of an incident in Washington State. (Robert Morgan)

Show, Larry King, Tom Snyder, Howard Cosell, and numerous radio and local TV shows. Articles about his Bigfoot exploits have appeared in the *Wall Street Journal, Miami Herald, Washington Post, Seattle Intelligencer, Parade Magazine,* and many more.

MOUNTAIN GORILLA

The mountain gorilla is another large animal that has become known to Western science only during the last century. Today, we know there are two types of gorillas (separate species or subspecies depending upon which primatologist is making the distinction). The massive mountain gorilla with its rich black crown of head hair is easy to distinguish from the lowland gorilla whose cap of hair is clearly red. (The silverback gorillas seen in television documentaries are older male mountain gorillas, though white-tipped or silver-tinted hair is infrequently found on the backs of some male lowland gorillas.)

Though the lowland gorilla (*Gorilla gorilla*) was officially recognized only as late as 1847, the mountain gorilla (*Gorilla beringa*) was not discovered until the twentieth century—despite many expeditions mounted by universities, zoos, and museums specifically sent to Africa to kill or capture gorillas. It was only in 1861 that the first native accounts of a monster ape (*ngagi* and *ngila*) came to the attention of Western scientists. The animal was said to live on the misty heights of the Virunga Volcanoes of eastern Africa. Westerners, however, refused to credit what seemed like absurd legends.

Then, in 1898, a trekker named Ewart Grogan found a mountain gorilla skeleton—but as in so many other tales of the finds of pieces of unknown hairy primates, Grogan failed to bring the skeleton out of the mountains. Finally, in October 1902, a Belgian army captain named von Beringe and his companion killed two gorillas on the Virungas' Mount Sabinio.

Beringe almost missed his chance of proving the mountain gorilla's existence. When he shot his two mountain gorillas, both the animals fell into a valley. Only after great difficulty were Beringe and his companion able to recover one of the great apes and prove the species' reality to a skeptical world.

The first expeditions to study mountain gorillas in Africa in their natural habitat failed. Late in the 1960s, however, Dr. Dian Fossey founded the Karisoke Research Centre in Rwanda and launched a long-running study of the creature. Today, no more than 350 mountain gorillas survive in the wild.

MOUNTAIN NYALA

Discovered by Major Ivor Buxton in the high mountains of southern Ethiopia in the summer of 1910, the mountain nyalas (*Tragelaphus buxtoni*) are a relatively unknown species. They are a specific type of bovid related to the bongos and kudus. The male, which has gently twisting horns almost four feet long, can weigh up to 450 pounds. The mountain nyala's shaggy coat is a majestic grayish brown. Nyalas have a white chevron between the eyes, two white spots on the cheek, poorly defined white vertical stripes on the back and upper flanks, and a short brown mane on the neck.

After the mountain nayala was first described by Richard Lydekker, the eminent British naturalist, it was ruthlessly hunted by field biologists and trophy seekers through some of the most inhospitable terrain on earth.

The mountain nyala lives at heights above nine thousand feet, where the sun burns harshly in the day and the night temperatures fall to freezing. Illegal hunting and habitat destruction now threatens its existence. From eight thousand in the 1960s, their number declined to three thousand in the 1980s. None are in capitivity. According to zoologist **Karl Shuker,** the animal remains one of Africa's least studied antelopes.

ℕ

NAHUELITO

A **Lake Monster** reported in the Nahuel Huapí Lake of Argentina and Patagonia is called Nahuelito (after the lake where it lives). The huge lake covers over two hundred square miles at the base of the Patagonian mountains, a perfect site for a watery **cryptid,** variously described as a giant serpent or a huge hump.

The "Patagonian plesiosaur"—as it is sometimes called—apparently first attracted press coverage only in the 1920s, though sightings go back well into the previous century. The international search for the Nahuelito began in 1922, when Clementi Onelli, the Buenos Aires Zoo director, was sent accounts of large unknown tracks and matted weeds on shore at the same time locals claimed to be seeing a monster in the middle of the lake. They said the creature had a swanlike neck. A subsequent expedition, led by zoo superintendent José Cihagi, produced nothing of consequence. Writing in the July 22, 1922, issue of *Scientific American,* Leonard Matters remarked that the plesiosaur, "if it ever existed, appears to have fled to parts unknown."

Though little known elsewhere, the Naheulito is something of a cryptozoological celebrity in South America. This mysterious inhabitant of one of the world's most beautiful lakes is still being seen frequently. **Jacques Barloy** has written of sightings from the 1970s, and **John Kirk**'s *In the Domain of the Lake Monsters* (1998) cites several reports from the 1990s.

NANDI BEAR

"What the **Abominable Snowman** is to Asia, or the great **Sea Serpent** is to the oceans," writes natural historian Frank W. Lane, the Nandi Bear "is to Africa. It is one of the most notorious of those legendary beasts which have, so far, eluded capture and the collector's rifle."

Africa is the only continent officially without a member of the bear family Ursidae. Unofficially, it has the Nandi Bear, which is indeed a misnomer. Since the time of Herodotus, natives and colonists through-out East Africa have reported confrontations with a huge, dangerous part-bear/part-hyena. Reputed to kill both people and livestock, it is called—depending upon the particular region—*chimisit, kerit, shivu-verre, sabrookoo, koddoelo, ikimizi,* or *kikambangwe.* More commonly, it is known simply as the Nandi Bear, after the local Kenyan tribe.

In the *Journal of the East Africa and Uganda Natural History Society,* Geoffrey Williams of the Nandi Expedition wrote of his sighting in the early 1900s:

> I was travelling with a cousin on the Uasingishu just after the Nandi expedition, and, of course, long before there was any set-tlement up there. We had been camped . . . near the Mataye and were marching towards the Sirgoit Rock when we saw the beast. . . . I saw a large animal sitting up on its haunches no more than 30 yards away. . . . I should say it must have been nearly 5 feet high. . . . it dropped forward and shambled away towards the Sirgoit with what my cousin always describes as a sort of sideways canter. . . . I snatched my rifle and took a snapshot at it as it was disappearing among the rocks, and, though I missed it, it stopped and turned its head round to look at us. . . . In size it was, I should say, larger than the bear that lives in the pit at the "Zoo" and it was quite as heavily built. The fore quarters were very thickly furred, as were all four legs, but the hind quarters were comparatively speaking smooth or bare. . . . the head was long and pointed and exactly like that of a bear. . . . I have not a very clear recollection of the ears beyond the fact that they were small, and the tail, if any, was very small and practically unno-ticeable. The colour was dark. . . .

Other reports come from the workers on the Magadi Railway then under construction. Railway employee Schindler came upon a series of clear canine-like, 8.5-inch-long tracks with five toes instead of four and a long heel. Sketches of these tracks show their unique character. On March 8, 1913, G. W. Hickes, the engineer in charge of building this railway through East Africa, saw a Nandi Bear. While traveling on a motor trolley at twenty-five miles per hour, he spotted what first appeared to be a hyena about fifty yards straight ahead. Though the "hyena" had seen Hickes and was heading off the line at a right angle, the trolley was approaching faster than the animal could make its escape through the eighteen-inch-high grass of the open country.

Hickes wondered what a "hyena" was doing out at nine in the morning, then realized that it was not a hyena. The animal was about as tall as a lion and tawny in color. Its thick-set body had high withers and a broad rump. Its neck was short, its nose stumpy, its ears short. As it ran off with its forelegs and both hind legs rising at the same time, Hickes noted that its shaggy hair reached right down to its large, mud-covered feet.

Once past, Hickes realized that what he had seen was the strange beast that many had either heard of or reported seeing during the railway's construction. He recalled that engineers had first spotted a strange footprint in the mud. Not long afterward, a native servant had seen such an animal much like the one Hickes had just observed standing on its hind legs. Subsequently a subcontractor had seen it or an identical specimen. Then as now, witnesses mentioned a thick mane, long claws, large teeth, and an upright stance of six feet.

Hickes's account, which was collected by the anthropologist C. W. Hobley who traveled about Africa gathering native traditions in 1912–13, is but one element of this strange beast's confusing history. What the local people, the Nandi, had long called the *chimisit* or the *chemosit,* the British named the Nandi Bear because of its footprint and tendency to rise up on its hind legs, and of course its association with the Nandi tribe.

Mixed into reports of this large baboon-like beast are also sightings of what may be large black honey badgers (*Mellivora capensis*) and the savage deeds of spotted hyenas (*Crocuta crocuta*) of unusual size or color. Some reports argue for identification of the animal as a hyena, possibly an undiscovered species. **Bernard Heuvelmans** senses some may be related to the aardvark (*Orycteropus*), possibly a third species (two, *O. capensis* and *O. aethiopicus,* are already known), or a form of fossil baboon. The Nandi tribal members tend to think of the Nandi Bear as a primate, specifically a huge baboon. **Mark A. Hall** and **Loren Coleman** concur that the Nandi Bear may be a variety of unknown giant baboon.

NAPES

North American Apes, or Napes (a name coined by **Loren Coleman** in the 1960s), have been reported from the southeastern and midwestern United States from at least the 1800s to the present. Other reports speak of similar apelike animals in specific bottomland swamps. For example, Howard Dreeson gave bananas to a "chimpanzee" that visited him regularly near his Oklahoma home from 1967 through 1970. During 1979, North Carolina witnesses claimed encounters with "Knobby."

Napes appear to be a population of chimpanzee-like apes that inhabit the bottomlands and vast network of closed-canopy deciduous and mixed forests of the Mississippi Valley and its tributaries. Some are dimly

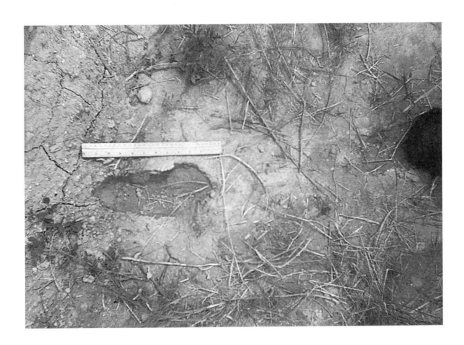

Evidence for the Napes, or North American Apes, takes many forms, but perhaps the best is their footprints. Loren Coleman found one such series of apelike tracks in a creek bed near Decatur, Illinois, in 1962. (Loren Coleman)

remembered in regional folklore and twentieth-century reports of "gorillas" and "chimps."

In 1962, Jerry, Bill, and Loren Coleman found a footprint complete with an opposed left toe (characteristic of the footprint of a **mountain gorilla** or a chimpanzee) in a dry creek bed near Decatur, Illinois. Similar prints have been reported from such diverse locations as Florida, Alabama, and Oklahoma. During a series of August 1971 sightings of two chimpanzee-like apes (termed **Skunk Apes** in some press accounts), a Broward County, Florida, rabies control officer "found nothing but a bunch of strange tracks, like someone was walking around on his knuckles." Of course, this is far from "nothing"—knuckle-walking is exactly what would be expected of an unknown anthropoid ape.

Loren Coleman has proposed a theory that this and similar footprints found in the South belong to Napes, possible specimens of the genus *Dryopithecus.* From their own independent researches into comparable evidence around the world, **Bernard Heuvelmans** and **Mark A. Hall** have come to much the same conclusion for other forms of similar apes.

NEANDERTALS

According to researchers such as **Ivan T. Sanderson,** John Pfeiffer, Myra Shackley, **Dmitri Bayanov,** Igor Bourtsev, **Boris Porshnev,** and **Bernard Heuvelmans,** relict populations of Neandertals may still be roaming Asia and parts of the rest of the world, leaving classic Neandertal (*Homo neanderthalensis*) tracks and being seen as hairy "Bushmen" or "Wildmen."

Neandertals are seldom seen, if we are to believe the reports. Perhaps they manage to stay well hidden from *Homo sapiens,* or perhaps their numbers are few. Their large footprints are rarely found, but when they are, they are so remarkably different they get noticed. Modern sightings of Neandertals and Neandertaloids suggest that their distribution is limited to a small band of forests in Central Asia and wilderness areas in North America's Pacific Northwest, as well as occasional appearances elsewhere in wild North America.

Neandertals are human-sized but have superhuman strength. Covered in red hair, the males have characteristic fringe beards. They have heavy brow ridges and a large nose. Their footprints exactly match those of prehistoric Neandertals found on the floors of caves in Europe. The surviving Neandertals use weapons and materials from the modern wilderness environments where they live to protect and clothe themselves.

Archaeologists tell us that the Neandertals, whose fossils were discovered in Germany about 150 years ago, were a successful species or subspecies. In the 1990s, new fossil finds confirmed that Neandertals were contemporaries with modern humans and in some locations survived alongside moderns until about thirty thousand years ago. But ancient legends and folklore suggest that Neandertal interactions with modern man may have occurred much more recently. For example, *The Epic of Gilgamesh,* a classic story from southern Babylonia, produced some four thousand years ago, is the earliest hairy-hominid story to appear in human literature. Gilgamesh's captured "friend," whom he named "Enkidu," may have been a Neandertal, some cryptozoologists have speculated. The hairy, wild-with-the-gazelles Enkidu was first seduced by a modern Babylonian woman, then "trained" to associate with King Gilgamesh and to do the king's bidding in battle.

Though the first artistic reconstructions of Neandertal were based on a modern human with a form of bone disease, there is no mistaking the striking pose these heavily built men and women took. With thicker bones, larger brow ridges, and larger brains by volume than *Homo sapiens,* Neandertals are in some ways "subhuman" in looks but perhaps not so in intelligence. In any case, with a body so much hairier than those of modern humans, the Neandertal answers generally to the description some witnesses give to the unknown primates that figure in some Wildman reports.

NELLIE

An aggressive and elusive creature terrified the Decatur, Illinois, area in July 1917. Called "Nellie" by reporters, it was said to look like a large female African lion. It attacked Thomas Gullett, a butler at the Robert Allerton estate, southwest of Monticello, as he was picking flowers in the garden. Over the next month, three-hundred-man posses searched for the beast. Sightings continued, and hunters found two sets of catlike prints.

At 10:30 on the evening of July 29, 1917, Chester Osborn, Earl Hill, and their wives were driving near Decatur. The two men, sitting in the front, spotted Nellie standing in the weeds next to the road. It leaped, crashed into the car's side, and fell onto the highway. The party rushed back to Decatur to summon the police. Nellie was still there when they returned, but it soon was lost to sight over an embankment and thereafter managed to elude searchers. Soon after that, Nellie vanished forever.

Today a debate rages among those who feel incidents such as the Nellie sightings are misidentifications. Many think they may be records of the recovery of the Eastern puma, evidence of an undiscovered Pleistocene survival (**Panthera atrox**), or merely escaped zoologically recognized animals.

NGUOI RUNG

In 1982, Professor Tran Hong Viet, now at the Pedagogic University of Hanoi, made a cast of a footprint that looked human but was much wider; the toes were longer than a modern human's. The footprint was found on the slopes of Chu Mo Ray (Mom Ray mountain), near the Cambodian border. Viet has only recently returned to his research on this subject, through the instigation of Nippon Television, which aired a show on the Nguoi Rung (Wildman of the Forest) question in March 1996.

According to Viet and some other Vietnamese scientists, this area, the so-called three borders region where Vietnam, Cambodia, and Laos converge, is where most reports of the Vietnamese Nguoi Rung occur. So frequent were reports that in 1974, during the height of the war, General Hoang Minh Thao, commander of northern forces in the Central Highlands, asked for a scientific survey of the region north of Kontum for what the natives called *nguoi rung*. Scientists who were part of this dangerous expedition included Professors Vo Quy and Le Vu Khoi from Hanoi University and Professor Hoang Xuan Chinh from the Institute of Archaeology in Hanoi. No Nguoi Rung were found—though the expedition returned north with two new circus elephants.

Reports of Nguoi Rung vary from large to small, with body hair from gray to brown or black, sighted in a group or alone. They are always reported to walk bipedally. They go by many names among highlands minority people; most are terms of respect. The Vietnamese name Nguoi Rung means "Forest People"—the direct equivalent of the name for an ape known from Indonesia, the orangutan. The people of Kontum are certain that the forest people existed in their forests in the recent past. They differentiate their forest people from forest spirits or genies, some of which they also describe as hairy bipeds. Visiting near the Laotian border, Vu Ngoc Thanh heard another local term for the Nguoi Rung, the *khi trau,* literally "buffalo monkey" or "big monkey."

Anthropologist Dang Nghiem Van, director of Hanoi's Institute for Religious Studies, has collected many stories of Nguoi Rung from northern Vietnam to the central highlands. These include myths of small but powerful beings knowing the use of fire and eating forest mollusks. There are also stories of a different, much larger being.

Van says that at night Nguoi Rung come to places where people have fires. They sit beside men but do not speak, or speak unintelligibly. There are stories of couples of Nguoi Rung moving rapidly, easily climbing trees, shaking trees for insects, and sleeping in grottos on mountain slopes. Professor Van's detailed notes, some of them from locations near Sa Thay, have yet to be published. Also, several reports have been made in the last fifteen years in the region of Kontum–Sa Thay. These have recently been investigated by Vietnamese scientist Nguyen Dinh Khoa and others.

But if Nguoi Rung exist, what are they? Some, such as cryptozoologist **Bernard Heuvelmans** and **Helmut Loofs-Wissowa** think that at least some forms may be remnants of an early human population. Heuvelmans's candidate is the specimen *Homo pongoides,* the name he gave to the **Minnesota Iceman.**

Many questions remain, and so far no specimens of Nguoi Rung have been recovered.

NITTAEWO

The country of Ceylon, now known as Sri Lanka, is said to have once housed a small, hairy tribe of people called the Nittaewo, first mentioned by Pliny the Elder near the beginning of the Christian era.

In 1887, British explorer Hugh Nevill brought out recent tales of the warfare occurring between the short, primitive but well-known tribal people, the Veddahs, and the even smaller, hairy unknown Nittaewo which inhabited the almost inaccessible Leanama mountains of Ceylon. Nevill wrote that the name "Nittaewo" was derived from *nishada,* the name given by the Aryan invaders of India to the more primitive tribes, citing *nigadiwa* or *nishadiwa* as the Sinhalese form which the Veddah would change into *nittaewo*.

The Nittaewo males were said to be three to four feet tall, with females being smaller. They walked upright, had no tail, and had hair-covered legs. Some reports had them covered with thick reddish fur over their entire bodies. They had short but powerful arms.

The Nittaewo appeared to be already extinct by the time Nevill heard the tales. The Veddahs, who hated the Nittaewo, claimed to have forced the last Nittaewo into a cave, piled brushwood in the entrance, and set fire to the pile. The three-day bonfire killed all of the Nittaewo. This event apparently happened late in the eighteenth century.

When they wrote about the Nittaewo in the 1940s and 1950s, the British primatologist W. C. Osman Hill and **Bernard Heuvelmans** were certain the Nittaewo were real. On a fact-finding trip to Ceylon in 1945, Hill found widespread belief in the Nittaewo's habitation of the island in recent times. He concluded that Dubois's *Pithecanthropus erectus* of Java (the Java ape-man, since renamed *Homo erectus*) matched the tradition of the Nittaewo.

The rumors of hairy pygmies in other parts of Southeast Asia, nevertheless, persist. Around 1900 reports of small Wildmen with thick reddish hair came out of Laos. Today, cryptozoologists link the extinct Nittaewo to the Asian **Teh-lma** and Sumatra's **Orang Pendek.** Hill speculated that *Homo erectus* might also be responsible for the stories of the Orang Pendek, the Nittaewo's apparent Sumatran counterpart.

NORMAN, SCOTT T. (1964–)

Scott T. Norman, born in Salinas, California, has always had a strong fascination with dinosaurs. In the early 1990s, a coworker introduced Norman to Herman Regusters, who had been to the Congo in search of **Mokele-mbembe,** a possible living dinosaur. Regusters had put together a video from his trip, which Norman found intriguing, and he listened with interest as Regusters discussed a possible future expedition.

Then, in early 1996, Norman read **Roy P. Mackal**'s *A Living Dinosaur? In Search of Mokele-Mbembe.* Excited, Norman looked for other printed accounts of the supposed Congo dinosaur. Soon he developed an interest in all of cryptozoology.

In July of the same year, Scott decided to create a website on

Mokele-mbembe. At the same time he was trying to find general information about cryptozoology on the Internet, with little result. He started
a website on general cryptozoology. In this way the website Cryptozoological Realms (http://hometown.aol.com/mokele/cryptozoological_
realms/html_3.2/english/index.html) was born. Through *Cryptozoological Realms,* Norman has met many people, including **William Rebsamen,**
a wildlife artist, who now does original artwork for the site. In exchange,
Norman designed a website for Rebsamen to showcase his cryptozoology and wildlife artwork. He also met **Karl Shuker,** assisting him with information on black tigers in India, and designed Shuker's website.

Norman is currently working with **William Gibbons** on potential
cryptozoology expeditions.

O

OGOPOGO

The monsters of Lake Okanagan, British Columbia, are known both as
Ogopogo and by their native name, *naitakas.* They were first encoun-

*The author surveys the surface of Lake
Okanagan, British Columbia, Canada, for
evidence of Ogopogo.* (Loren Coleman)

tered by Indians and then by the
earliest white settlers in the 1860s.
Ogopogo is described as loglike,
about forty feet long, with dark
green, black or brown skin, and
sometimes with serrations on its
back and/or a mane on its head.
Kelowna, British Columbia's Annual Regatta, celebrates Ogopogo.

The first chronicler of Ogopogo, British Columbian **Arlene
Gaal,** did much to gather sightings, films, photographs, and
aboriginal evidence that other researchers have used for decades to

analyze the Ogopogo mystery. Cryptozoologist **Gary Mangiacopra** and retired University of Chicago biologist **Roy Mackal** relate Ogopogo to the ancient extinct elongated whales, the **zeuglodons.** Another cryptozoological theory holds that Cadborosaurus ("**Caddy**") and Ogopogo may be related and reptilian. Retired Royal British Columbia. Museum cryptozoologist Dr. Ed Bousfield, a relentless researcher in the field, makes the reasonable assumption that both animals may have eaten salmon ten thousand years ago. Thus Ogopogo, he reasons, could have become landlocked in Lake Okanagan, where Columbia River dams have blocked direct access to the ocean for both salmon and serpents. Eyewitness descriptions of both animals describe a horselike head, snakelike body, flippers, and a split tail.

"Glacial and post-glacial evidence suggests that Okanagan's Ogopogo is probably a freshwater form or variant of the reptilian species *Cadborosaurus willsi*," says Bousfield. He adds that it bears no resemblance to whales, seals, or otters. From his reading of the sighting, Native Canadian folklore, and film evidence, Caddy and Ogopogo are a separate unknown reptilian species.

OKAPI

The okapi (*Okapia johnstoni*) is the animal used to symbolize the **International Society of Cryptozoology** and is the centerpiece of the organization's logo. Indeed, a 1978 children's book by Miriam Schlein, *The Search for a Mystery Animal,* details the discovery of the okapi and serves as a good introduction to cryptozoology, although the word is never used in the book.

For years Europeans brushed aside tales from the native peoples of the Congo, the pygmies, about a creature said to look like a cross between a zebra and a giraffe. That would change at the turn of the twentieth century. Sir Harry Johnston gained the trust of a band of Congolese pygmies when he rescued them from a German showman who had abducted them and planned to take them to the 1900 Paris Exhibition. The pygmies then began to tell Johnston stories about the okapi, a mule-sized animal with zebra stripes. In 1901, Johnston secured and sent a whole skin, two skulls, and a detailed description of the okapi to London.

Scientists, who believe the okapi are the closest living relative of the giraffe, call them "**living fossils**" in the many references made to them af-

A 1920s tobacco card speaks to the popularity of this "new" animal soon after the okapi's discovery in 1901 and first live capture in 1918. (Loren Coleman)

ter their 1901 "discovery." The popularity of the okapi can be seen in such works as Ernest Glanville's 1904 boys' adventure book, *In Search of the Okapi,* a 381-page book that was very popular in its day. In 1918, the first live okapi was brought out of the Congo River basin and reached Europe. In 1941, the Stanleyville Zoo witnessed the first birth of an okapi in captivity. It is one of the world's rarest animals both in captivity and in the wild. In 1993, the St. Louis Zoo established a breeding program for okapis. As of 1998, there were fifty-eight okapis in North American zoos and about as many in European zoos.

Okapis are today found only in the tropical Ituri rainforests of the northeastern part of the Democratic Republic of the Congo, formerly Zaire. They prefer altitudes between fifteen hundred and three thousand feet, though they may venture above three thousand feet on Mount Hoyo, in the upper Ituri. The range of the okapi is limited by high montane forests to the east, swamp forests below fifteen hundred feet to the west, savannas of the Sahel/Soudan to the north, and open woodlands to the south. Okapis are most common in the Wamba and Epulu areas. The okapi was driven into extinction in Uganda during the 1970s. However, since 1933, it has been protected by law in the former Zaire, and it lives on shyly and secretly in the dense rainforests of that country. The okapi is one of the last large mammals "discovered" by the scientific community, and little is known of its habits and behavior in the wild.

The most valuable lesson from the okapi is that descriptions of creatures from native folklore and/or experience should be taken seriously.

OLD YELLOW TOP

Hairy bipedal animals allegedly encountered in eastern regions of North America often are given nicknames. One such creature is "Old Yellow Top," so called because of its lightly colored mane. Reports come from the area around Cobalt, Ontario. Accounts of a shaggy **Bigfoot**-type creature with a yellow head of hair have circulated thereabouts since the 1920s. Old Yellow Top, as well as other location-specific creatures such as Fluorescent Freddie of French Lick, Indiana, and Orange Eyes near Black River, Ohio, seem to be special regional populations of eastern North American unknown hairy hominids, perhaps **Marked Hominids,** exhibiting wide diversity in appearance. Then again, some or all may be localized pranks.

OLGOI-KHORKHOI

A mysterious, deadly creature called Olgoi-Khorkhoi, also known as the Mongolian death worm, reportedly lives in the Gobi Desert. Sounding like a mini-version of the giant worms from *Dune,* the Olgoi-Khorkhoi appears to be wormlike, about two feet long, headless, thick, and dark red. The name Olgoi-Khorkhoi means "intestine worm." The death worm is feared among the people of Mongolia, as it supposedly has the terrifying ability to kill people and animals instantly at a range of several feet. It is believed that the worm sprays an immensely lethal poison, or that it somehow transmits high-voltage electrical charges into its victims.

The foremost investigator of the Mongolian death worm, Czech author Ivan Mackerle, learned about the creature from a student from Mongolia. After Mackerle told her about a diving expedition he had made in search of the **Loch Ness Monster,** she told him in a conspiratorial whisper, "We, too, have a horrible creature living in Mongolia. We call it the Olgoi-Khorkhoi monster, and it lives buried in the Gobi Desert sand dunes. It can kill a man, a horse, even a camel."

Intrigued, Mackerle set out to learn more about this Mongolian monster, but information on the topic was hard to come by. As he would soon learn, most Mongolians were afraid to discuss the death worm. In addition, the government of Mongolia outlawed the search for Olgoi-Khorkhoi, which the authorities deemed a "fairy tale." After Communism collapsed in Mongolia in 1990, the new political climate provided Mackerle the freedom to mount an expedition to the country's desert wastes to hunt for the worm. He gathered many stories which convinced him that the creature might be real.

Extending a hypothesis proposed by Czech cryptozoologist Jaroslav Mares in 1993, French cryptozoologist **Michel Raynal** has suggested in recent years that the Olgoi-Khorkhoi might be a highly specialized reptile, belonging to the suborder of the amphisbaenians: specialized burrowing reptiles that generally have no limbs and are reddish-brown in color. It is difficult to distinguish the head from the tail in many amphisbaenians, some of which can reach two and one-half feet in length.

Another possibility is that the death worm is a member of the cobra family called the death adder. This species has an appearance similar to the descriptions of the Olgoi-Khorkhoi, and it does spray its venom. Though death adders could conceivably survive in the Gobi environment, they have been found only in Australia and New Guinea.

Then there is the matter of the death worm's reputed ability to kill its victims from a far distance, without even shooting venom. Some have proposed that this might be performed with an electrical shock of some sort. This hypothesis might have arisen from an association with the electric eel, but the eel and all similar electricity-discharging animals are fish, and none of them could stay alive on land, much less in a desert. Most likely, the "death from a distance" component of the Olgoi-Khorkhoi legend is an exaggeration based on fear.

ONZA

For centuries reports of a large mystery cat have come out of the Sierra Madre Occidental range in northwestern Mexico. The Aztecs, who called it the *cuitlamiztli,* believed it to be a third species of felid, separate from the other native cats, the puma and the jaguar. It was thinner than the other cats, for one thing, and its ears were longer. The Spaniards, who noted its fierceness and its willingness to take on even armed men, gave it the name *onza,* after the Latin *uncia* (cheetah).

Though unrecognized by zoologists and little known to the larger world, its existence was taken for granted by locals. In the 1930s, an American hunting party seeking jaguars on La Silla Mountain treed an Onza and killed it. The hunters did not keep the remains, and later, when the guides told zoologists about it, they were met with disbelief. In the 1950s, however, Robert Marshall, who was researching a book on the Onza, interviewed them and conducted his own investigations in Mexico. Marshall's book *The Onza,* which appeared in 1961, was little noticed.

In the 1980s, **J. Richard Greenwell,** secretary of the **International Society of Cryptozoology,** contacted Marshall, who gave him part of an Onza skull. A University of Arizona zoologist, E. Lendell Cockrum, directed them to two Sinaloa, Mexico, ranchers who had another skull. Yet another was located in the Academy of Natural Sciences in Philadelphia.

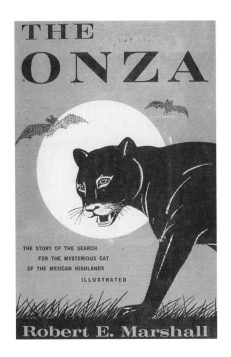

Robert Marshall's book on the Onza was the first effort to systematically collect all that was known of this cryptid. (Robert Marshall)

Then two deer hunters killed an Onza on the evening of January 1, 1986, in Sinaloa's San Ignacio District. Greenwell was alerted, and soon afterward he and University of New Mexico mammalogist Troy Best took photographs of the body before dissecting it at the Regional Diagnostic Laboratory of Animal Pathology in Mazatlan. Greenwell would write that "the cat, a female, appeared to be as described by the native people"—in other words, long, thin, and large-eared.

It would be more than a decade before results of the many analyses on the remains were published. In 1998, the final test results were reported in the journal *Cryptozoology:* tissue samples from this Onza were not from a distinct species of cat but were indistinguishable from those of North American pumas.

ORANG PENDEK

The Orang Pendek ("wild short man") or *sedepa* of Sumatra is a small, unknown primate that some cryptozoologists say may be related to the orangutan. Others, such as W. C. Osman Hill, have pointed to a possible link to the fossils of the Java man, *Homo erectus.*

Sightings of the Orang Pendek have been logged for decades. The definitive incident for Westerners took place in October 1923, on the island of Poleloe Rimau in Sumatra. The witness, a Dutch explorer named Van Herwaarden, had been hunting for wild pig when he was startled to see a slight movement in a lone tree. When he investigated, he spotted a creature clinging motionless to the tree. In *Tropical Nature* 13 (1924), Van Herwaarden gave one of the most detailed descriptions of these creatures ever, noting that the unknown primate

> . . . was also hairy on the front of its body; the color there was a little lighter than on the back. The very dark hair on its head fell to just below the shoulder blades or even almost to the waist. It was fairly thick and very shaggy. The lower part of its face seemed to end in more of a point than a man's; this brown face was almost hairless, whilst its forehead seemed to be high rather than low. Its eyebrows were frankly moving; they were of the darkest color, very lively, and like human eyes. The nose was broad with fairly large nostrils, but in no way clumsy. . . . Its lips were quite ordinary, but the width of its mouth was strikingly wide when open. Its canines showed clearly from time to time as its mouth twitched nervously. They seemed fairly large to me; at all events they were more developed than a man's. The incisors were regular. The color of the teeth was yellowish-white. Its chin was somewhat receding. For a moment, during a quick movement, I was able to see its right ear, which was exactly like a little human ear. Its hands were slightly hairy on the back. Had it been standing, its arms would have reached to a little above its knees; they were therefore long, but its legs seemed to me rather short. I did not see its feet, but I did see some toes which were shaped

in a very normal manner. The specimen was of the female sex and about five feet high. There was nothing repulsive or ugly about its face, nor was it at all apelike. . . .

Van Herwaarden put his gun down again and climbed the tree. This caused the Orang Pendek to run out on to a branch, which dropped some nine feet to the ground. Van Herwaarden dashed back to the ground, but as he raised his gun to shoot the creature, he found himself unable to fire. Watching the flowing hair from the fleeing Orang Pendek, he realized he would feel like a murderer if he killed so human-like a creature.

Like so many before him, Van Herwaarden was to return to Europe with a good sighting but no proof. One museum curator even rejected Van Herwaarden's account on the grounds that it was "too exact."

Reports of the Orang Pendek have continued. Since the 1980s, British travel writer Deborah Martyr has led various expeditions into the Kerinci region of southwestern Sumatra. According to reports, the Orang Pendek of that region has a large potbelly and various colors (dark gray or black in some cases, yellow or tan in others). Martyr's success and funding from British flora and fauna society created a wave of media attention. Reporters were expecting a discovery any day.

Early in October 1997, newspapers from London to Melbourne related the following sensational story, supposedly about the Orang Pendek:

> The creature stumbled across the wire, triggering the camera shutter, capturing its image on film. . . . This was a picture of an ape walking almost erect, a creature with a long red mane that could be man's nearest cousin, a new species of primate that could re-write the books on evolutionary theory. As the pictures filtered out to the world's zoologists and anthropologists, the debate began.

Unfortunately, the newspapers got the story wrong. Expedition members informed **Loren Coleman** that they had seen and cast footprints, but they had no clear photograph. Indeed, the two earlier fuzzy pictures referred to in other press reports were suspect from the beginning, though expedition members had to investigate for months to confirm that they were fakes. An Orang Pendek had not walked through a camera trap.

Other researchers have been conducting inquiries in Sumatra for years, and their underpublicized efforts should be noted. Claude Petit, professor and biologist, has been looking into the reports since 1980. As the personal friend of Kerinci National Park director Kurnia Rauf, Petit was able to examine the plaster casts that were held by the national park office before it was burned. This unfortunate fire was the result of arson, and status of the "Orang Pendek footcast collection" is now uncertain. Petit says that this cast was "about thirty centimeters [one foot] long, six to seven centimeters [2.5 inches] broad, the toes were not noticeable and no arch of the foot was evident." Petit was skeptical of its authenticity, suspecting it was something concocted "for the tourists." On the positive side, he collected a fair amount of compelling and consistent testimony from witnesses, who agreed that the creature of the forests east of Lake Kerinci is four feet tall and bipedal. Additionally, south of Lampung, in the area of Liwa, a huge earthquake in 1995 caused some disruptions in the wildlife population. According to Petit, the local people reported that animals looking like Orang Pendek came out of the forest briefly, frightened by the seismic activity.

Meanwhile, in the more believable "discovery" reports of October 1997, Martyr stated she found footprints she considers valid, apparently made by the same individual Orang Pendek. Various people showing off "footprints" of the Orang Pendek, Martyr cautions, may, in fact, be looking at "handprints." In 1998, back into the same area, she and one of her expedition members saw a large primate in a tree. Her effort, supported by grants from Fauna and Flora International, is the most well established and respected by cryptozoologists.

Another researcher, French botanist Yves Laumonier, has also collected convincing reports from the area during the 1990s.

Martyr, Petit, and Laumonier are continuing their respective quests, hoping all the while for a physical discovery or clear-cut photographs that will end the controversy. The Orang Pendek might become the next "official" large primate discovery during the coming decade, and the unfolding drama deserves cryptozoology's ongoing attention.

OUDEMANS, ANTOON CORNELIS (1858–1943)

Born in Batavia, into an educated family with many scientific and intellectual interests, Antoon Cornelis Oudemans developed an early interest in natural history. At the University of Utrecht he specialized in insects and worms. Not long after securing his doctorate in 1885, he assumed directorship of the Royal Zoological and Botanical Gardens at The Hague.

The love of his zoological life, however, was of something much larger than worms: the fabled **Sea Serpent.** He started collecting reports in his teenage years and was still a university student when he published his first article on the subject in 1881. He had concluded that the creatures not only existed but were **zeuglodons,** snakelike whales thought long extinct—a theory another biologist, **Roy Mackal,** would revive decades later as a possible explanation for **Lake Monsters.**

By the time Oudemans's magnum opus, *The Great Sea Serpent* (1892), had appeared, however, after an exhaustive analysis of the accounts he had come to a different reading of the 187 credible reports in his collection. The animals, he theorized, were giant, long-necked seals. In 1933, when stories of a strange beast at Loch Ness, Scotland, drew wide attention, Oudemans was sure it was one of his seals (he did not even consider the possibility that more than one—a breeding population—might exist in the loch), and he expected that the creature would soon be killed or caught.

Oudemans, who remained a respected figure in European science through his long career, resigned his directorship of the Royal Zoological and Botanical Society in 1895. He taught, conducted research into a variety of zoological matters, and wrote prolifically. Besides his pioneering cryptozoological work, he is best remembered for a classic book on extinct birds. He died before he could write an intended sequel to *The Great Sea Serpent.*

P

PADDLER

In the early 1940s, near Coeur d'Alene, Idaho, **Lake Monsters**—or at least reports of them—began to show up in Lake Pend Oreille. Typically, the sightings were of a large, not clearly visible object moving rapidly through the water. Some of the earliest printed accounts, heavily laced with ridicule, appear in U.S. Navy publications from the Farragut Naval Training Station at Bayview, Idaho, a top-secret submarine sonar research facility.

Monster stories became so frequent that before long locals had given the creature a nickname: Paddler. As North Idaho College professor **James R. McLeod** told science writer **Patrick Huyghe** ("Deep Secrets," *The Anomalist,* 5, 1997), the navy may have been satisfied with the stories of a monster at Lake Pend Oreille for decades and used it as a cover story for their alleged top-secret nuclear submarine and submarine sonar tests. McLeod and his college-based cryptozoological research group conducted a much-publicized investigation in 1984, concluding that a majority of the sightings could have been of a huge, prehistoric-looking sturgeon—not native to the lake but possibly an occasional visitor. Additionally, however, McLeod learned, "Every once in a while we would get someone who also saw a submarine, and the word nuclear kept coming up. That started bothering me." It bothered McLeod because no nuclear subs are ever supposed to be in an American lake.

Idaho anthropologist Duke Snyder says, "I'm inclined to think that a lot of events that occurred on the lake are really the result of navy activity of one kind or another. . . . If somebody begins a story about a monster in the lake, then that's a pretty handy explanation for strange things that go on. Of course, that raises the question [of] what the heck is the navy doing in the lake."

The navy denies it has ever used manned submarines or minisubs in the lake, but in the 1960s two navy contractors, Vickers and the International Submarine Engineering (ISE) groups of Canada, used a minisub, *Pisces I,* to train personnel in torpedo recovery in some American lakes. The very deep Pend Oreille appears to have been one of them. McLeod was able to confirm that the *Pisces I* was at Pend Oreille in 1965, but his questions to Vickers and ISE have gone unanswered.

PANGBOCHE HAND

In 1957, Texas oil millionaire **Tom Slick** launched a series of expeditions in search of the **Yeti.** Slick was aware of the works of **Bernard Heuvelmans,** had personally traveled to Nepal, and was intrigued by the reports of the **Abominable Snowman** coming from the area. Slick decided to sponsor more efforts along with another Texas oilman, F. Kirk Johnson, and these included a 1958 expedition that located the alleged bones of a Yeti's hand enshrined at a monastery in Pangboche, Nepal.

The monks refused to let an expedition member remove the hand from the premises. In 1959, a member of the Slick-Johnson expedition secretly replaced a few modern human finger/thumb bones for similar bones of the Yeti hand, wiring the fakes to the Pangboche Hand before a discovery could be made. The removed Pangboche originals were taken from Nepal, then with the valuable assistance of actor Jimmy Stewart transported from India to England. Stewart was a friend of Johnson. Stewart and his wife, Gloria, who were traveling in India at the time, agreed to wrap up the stolen bones in their underwear inside their luggage.

Jimmy Stewart assisted in transporting the Pangboche Hand back to London. He is pictured here with his old fishing and hunting buddy, F. Kirk Johnson, the Ft. Worth, Texas, oilman who was involved with the Slick-Johnson Snowman expeditions. (Deborah Johnson Head Collection)

British primatologist W. C. Osman Hill initially told Slick privately that the bones were of human origin, but then he changed his mind and declared them unidentifiable as any known primate, as had other scientists who quietly examined some of the first samples. Later Hill revised his opinion yet again, telling **Ivan T. Sanderson** that the Pangboche Hand must have belonged to a **Neandertal.** Unfortunately, the sample bones were lost and cannot be reexamined today.

Sir Edmund Hillary, the explorer who climbed Mount Everest in 1953, embarked on a highly publicized debunking expedition in 1960–61. Sir Edmund, who was also taking with him military men to spy on Chinese rocket experiments in Tibet, accused the Sherpas of being a superstitious people who did not distinguish between fantasy and reality and further insinuated that their Yeti sightings went hand in hand with heavy drinking. He obtained a "Yeti scalp," which he decried as being a fake made out of the skin of a goatlike animal, the serow, without understanding that the artifact was a common skullcap fashioned in imitation of the Yeti—or, as writer Donald Trull drolly observed, "These Yeti scalps were no more deceptive than the sugary pastry we figuratively call a bearclaw."

Hillary also ridiculed the Pangboche Hand still on display in the monastery, which he characterized as "essentially a human hand, strung together with wire, with the possible inclusion of several animal bones"—not knowing, of course, how perfectly accurate that description was, considering the quiet reconstruction the Slick-Johnson expedition had performed on the bones just a year earlier. The "animal bones" of the Pangboche Hand actually were those of the Yeti.

During the 1980s, explorers were still being shown and photographed with the Pangboche Hand. Dr. Marc Miller, in his 1998 book, *The Legends Continue: Adventures in Cryptozoology,* has a photograph of himself with the Hand from his 1986 trek to Pangboche. An NBC-sponsored analysis of the skin from the Pangboche Hand in 1991 revealed the Hand to be of "near human" origin. But further analysis may never occur. Late in 1992, the Pangboche Hand was stolen from the monastery where it had safely remained for over three hundred years, apparently a victim of the international trade in illegally obtained antiquities.

PANTHERA ATROX

Since colonial times residents of what is now the eastern United States have reported giant **Black Panthers** and Mystery Maned Cats. Zoologists reject such creatures as impossible. Pumas are not known to be melanistic, and African lions do not roam North American forests. Nonetheless, sightings, tracks, and livestock kills point to the possibility that "Black Panthers" and "black mountain lions" are thriving in wild America. Some cryptozoologists argue that these may be survivors from the Pleistocene era.

Panthera atrox, the American (Ice Age) lion, is the phrase used in felid cryptozoological circles to describe the large unknown maned cats and their kindred black mates, reported throughout North America. The idea originally was suggested by **Mark A. Hall,** developed by **Loren**

This illustration is a size comparison of the dark figure representing Panthera atrox *with the modern lion.* (Loren Coleman)

Coleman, and added to the master checklist of cryptozoology by **Bernard Heuvelmans** in 1986.

Panthera atrox supposedly died out at the end of the last glacial period, but accounts of unknown mystery cats may indicate that some survivors do remain. *Panthera atrox* and the modern African and Asian lion, *P. leo,* were identical, except for a larger size in the Americas. *Panthera leo* survived past the last Ice Age in Europe. An unbroken range of lions fringed the northern realms of the Pleistocene world. The great American lion (*P. atrox*) is merely a Western Hemisphere version of the European cave lion (*Panthera leo spelaea*). *Panthera leo leo,* the modern lion, is seen as the reduced remainder of *spelaea.* But some observers suspect that the cave lion persisted into historic Europe. Draft camels that accompanied Xerxes' expedition through Macedonia in 480 B.C. fell victim to lion attacks. Such ancient Greek authors as Herodotus, Aristotle, Xenophon, and others wrote of contemporary lions. Paleomammalogists see no difference between the cave lion and the modern lion. Bjorn Kurten and others hold that *spelaea* (the European cave lion) and *atrox* (the giant American lion) are identical.

Fossils of *P. atrox* have been uncovered in forty sites, from Alaska to Peru, from California through Nebraska to northern Florida. This giant lion was killed by Paleo-Indians, and Kurten points to evidence that it was around until as recently as 10,370 years ago, plus or minus 160 years.

"Modern reports indicate that the American lion is now dispersed across the continent of North America. If they in fact once lived in prides, as the lions of Africa today," writes Mark A. Hall, whose research on the 1948 Varmint (the local name for their mystery cats) accounts of Indiana appears to show, "these lions have had to adapt to a world that offers them marginal habitat and scarcer resources."

PATTERSON FILM

Capturing the fleeting sight of a seven-foot apelike creature retreating into the northern California wilderness, the Patterson **Bigfoot** Film is among the most renowned artifacts in the field of **hominology.** The footage has achieved iconic status even among the public at large, and forms the foundation of many Bigfoot hunters' beliefs.

This is a frame from the Patterson Film of a Bigfoot, taken October 20, 1967, at Bluff Creek, California. (Roger Patterson/Robert Gimlin; © René Dahinden in color)

The controversial reel of film was shot by Roger Patterson, a former rodeo rider who had become fascinated with Bigfoot after reading press reports about the creature in 1957. He wrote and self-published a book, *Do Abominable Snowmen of America Really Exist?* (1966). He then set out to film a documentary about sightings of Bigfoot.

On October 20, 1967, Patterson and Bob Gimlin were riding on horseback into California's Bluff Creek to shoot some background film footage. Patterson and Gimlin spotted a robust, dark-furred, bipedal creature crouched in the middle of a small

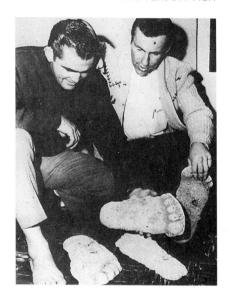

Roger Patterson and Robert Gimlin examine footprints on the Bigfoot cast shortly after the October 20, 1967, encounter that resulted in their film. (Roger Patterson/Robert Gimlin)

stream. The beast stood up to a height that Patterson estimated to be seven feet, four inches (some researchers, upon further analysis, say the creature may have been only six feet, six inches tall) and proceeded to walk toward the woods. Patterson's small Welsh pony smelled the creature and reared, bringing both pony and rider to the ground. But Patterson got up, grabbed his camera from the saddlebag, and while running toward the creature, took twenty-four feet of color film with the rented 16mm handheld Kodak movie camera. The creature walked steadily away into the forest, turning its head once toward the camera. Gimlin, meanwhile, remained on his horse, a 30.06 rifle in hand, fearing his friend might be attacked. But the Bigfoot soon disappeared into the woods. The men then tracked it for three miles, but lost it in the heavy undergrowth. Nine days later, casts were made of a series of ten footprints—14.5 inches long by 6 inches wide—found in the sandy blue-gray soil.

In the ensuing three decades, the 952 frames of Patterson's Bigfoot film have been submitted to all manner of examination and analysis by Canadian, Russian, English, French, and American experts. Because of its apparent breasts, the creature has been classified as female, being nicknamed "Patty" among Bigfoot researchers. These same individuals conclude that this filmed creature could not be a man in a suit due to the detailed muscle movement visible under the hair of the beast. The faking of such minutiae seems unlikely to those who consider the film a genuine piece of evidence.

Many others feel just as certain that Patterson's Bigfoot was a fake. They argue that as a man established in the "Bigfoot business," Patterson stood to profit from fabricating film footage of the creature. Bigfoot expert John Napier pointed to what he thought to be physiological inconsistencies in the footprint casts between the height of the creature and the length of its stride as shown in the film. If the creature was a fake, everyone agrees that it was a remarkably skillful one.

The only known source of such high-quality costumes and makeup in 1967 was the movie special-effects industry, and in fact there is circumstantial evidence that this Bigfoot came from Hollywood. After lengthy investigations and interviews, journalist Mark Chorvinsky has found that the consensus among special-effects professionals is that the film depicts a prankster in a skillfully crafted costume. In fact, many state that the falsity of the Patterson Film has been common knowledge in the business for years. The makeup artist Chorvinsky found most frequently associated with the Bigfoot film is John Chambers, a legendary elder statesman in the field of monster-making.

Chambers is best known as the famed makeup artist behind the *Planet of the Apes* films. His innovative, highly articulated ape *masks, not* suits, won him an Academy Award in 1968. Chambers, however, created monster costumes for dozens of other movies and TV shows, including *The Outer Limits* and *Lost in Space*. Chorvinsky reports none of the makeup professionals he spoke with had firsthand knowledge that Chambers had created the Patterson Bigfoot, but a large number of them either felt that it was widely accepted that he was responsible for it, or else reasoned that Chambers was the only artist at the time skillful enough to have crafted such a costume. Chambers, who currently resides in a Los Angeles nursing home in frail health, has recently told interviewers, including **Bobbie Short,** that he had nothing to do with the Bigfoot seen in Patterson's film.

In October 1997, upon the thirtieth anniversary of the Patterson

Film, new reports seemed to surface to confirm that Chambers had constructed the creature. But this was merely the earlier story recycled. This time, movie director John Landis stepped forward to "verify" what he said had been known among Hollywood makeup artists for years. "That famous piece of film of Bigfoot walking in the woods that was touted as the real thing was just a suit made by John Chambers," Landis said.

But the case is far from being closed. A number of Bigfoot authorities, including **John Green, Loren Coleman,** Bobbie Short, **René Dahinden, Mark A. Hall,** and others, reject the Chambers theory because of the investigation mentioned above and hold that the creature in the film is an unknown primate. A new $40,000 study by the North American Science Institute has concluded that the Patterson Film's Bigfoot is genuine, and computer enhancement analysis suggests that the creature's skin and musculature are what one would expect to find in a living animal, not in a hairy suit however innovatively constructed. In December 1998, Fox-TV's *World's Greatest Hoaxes* dismissed the film with claims that primates don't have dark ridges down their backs like the creature shown and that Patterson was an employee of American National Enterprise in 1967; both claims are laughable. The testimony of the Patterson Film remains strong, despite years of challenges.

PEREZ, DANIEL (1963–)

Daniel Perez, born in Norwalk, California, became interested in **Bigfoot** in 1973. In 1979, he founded the Center for Bigfoot Studies and started issuing a newsletter, *Bigfoot Times. Bigfoot Times* developed a reputation for

Daniel Perez. (Daniel Perez)

its hard-hitting and controversial critiques of the most prominent Bigfoot researchers and their works.

While Perez's fieldwork has taken him from Utah's High Uinta Mountains to California's Humboldt County, he is best known for his role as a chronicler and bibliographer. His contributions to the field include *The Bigfoot Directory* (1986), *Bigfoot at Bluff Creek* (1994), and *Big Footnotes: A Comprehensive Bibliography Concerning Bigfoot, the Abominable Snowman and Related Beings* (1988). Perez is at work on a new Bigfoot book.

PIASA

The Piasa, roughly translated from the Illini as "Giant Bird that Devours Man," is today known from the lore that issued from near the present-day city of Alton, Illinois, in the 1600s–1700s. In 1673, the French explorer Father Jacques Marquette, in recording his famous journey down the Mississippi River with Louis Jolliet, was the first to describe this beast from his contacts with the Indians who lived along the Mississippi River. Immortalized in a rock bluff painting near Alton, the monster was shown with huge wings, horns, and scales.

According to Marquette's diary, the Piasa "was as large as a calf with horns like a deer, red eyes, a beard like a tiger's, a face like a man, the body covered with green, red and black scales and a tail so long it passed around the body, over the head and between the legs."

There are many legends regarding its origin. One of the more popular accounts goes like this:

> Many moons ago, there existed a birdlike creature of such great size, he could easily carry off a full grown deer in his talons. His taste, however, was for human flesh. Hundreds of warriors attempted to destroy the Piasa, but failed. Whole villages were destroyed and fear spread throughout the Illini tribe. Ouatoga, a chief whose fame extended even beyond the Great Lakes, separated himself from his tribe, fasted in solitude for the space of a whole moon, and prayed to the Great Spirit to protect his people from the Piasa. On the last night of his fast, the Great Spirit appeared to Ouatoga in a dream and directed him to select twenty warriors, arm them each with a bow and poisoned arrow, and

conceal them in a designated spot. Another warrior was to stand in an open view, as a victim for the Piasa.

When the chief awoke in the morning, he told the tribe of his dream. The warriors were quickly selected and placed in ambush. Ouatoga offered himself as the victim. Placing himself in open view, he soon saw the Piasa perched on the bluff eyeing his prey. Ouatoga began to chant the death song of a warrior. The Piasa took to the air and swooped down upon the chief. The Piasa had just reached his victim when every bow was sprung and every arrow sent sailing into the body of the beast. The Piasa uttered a fearful, echoing scream and died. Ouatoga was safe, and the tribe saved.

An artist's fantastic interpretation of the Piasa. (Philip Hemstreet)

Modern reports of **Thunderbirds** have been recorded from the same area as the Piasa.

Late in the 1990s the Piasa, through the efforts of citizens, government, and business advocates, was repainted and restored to its former pristine state. It can be seen on the bluff just north of Alton, Illinois, on the Great River Road.

PORSHNEV, BORIS F. (1905–1972)

Boris Fedorovich Porshnev, a Soviet historian with a particular interest in human origins, became interested in the problem of "relict hominoids" in the 1950s. He created a study group with several Soviet scientists as a formal Commission of the Academy of Sciences of the U.S.S.R. (the so-called Soviet Snowman Commission). It was most active in 1958–59, when such individuals as **Tom Slick** flew to Moscow to meet secretly with the group. The author of many articles, Porshnev also coauthored a book with **Bernard Heuvelmans** (*L'homme de Néanderthal est toujours vivant,* 1974) that was published after his death. He advocated the revolutionary, and highly controversial, theory that **Neandertal** Man survives to the present—a hypothesis also argued by other students of **hominology** in Russia.

PROTO-PYGMY

Ivan T. Sanderson called the unknown hairy little people of the world "Proto-Pigmies." The term now used in the work of **Mark A. Hall, Patrick Huyghe, Loren Coleman,** and others is "Proto-Pygmies."

The phrase Proto-Pygmy describes the smallest of the world's unknown hominoids. Proto-Pygmies inhabit tropical forests down to seashores and swamps and range from southern Asia to Oceania, Africa, North America, and Latin America. They are known by the locals of these areas by such names as *alux,* **Agogwe, Teh-lma,** *sehite, menehune, sedapa,* **Orang Pendek**, and *shiru.*

Proto-Pymies vary from tiny to a little above five feet in height. They have black or red fur, different from their often long, flowing head hair. There is a strange "ancient" look to their face, which is "human-like" but not human, according to witnesses. They have small feet, no longer than five inches, and very small, sharp heels. Their five toes are not even across the end of the foot, so they do not match what would be found in a human child.

What are the Proto-Pygmies? Some North American Bigfoot researchers suggest they are simply "baby Bigfoot," even though their tracks are small with pointed heels and an uneven toe line—features that are diagnostically distinctive of the Proto-Pygmy. British primatologist W. C. Osman Hill felt the Proto-Pygmies of Sri Lanka were a small form of *Homo erectus.* **Bernard Heuvelmans** thinks that some of the little-people reports out of Africa could be relict populations of *Australopithecus.*

But others, like Sanderson, believe that some Proto-Pygmies might simply be unclassified pygmy *Homo sapiens* that have retreated into the rainforests and tropical mountain valleys of Africa or Asia. In general, the elusive nature of the Proto-Pygmies has given us little firm evidence of their fossil affinities and species relationships.

PYGMY ELEPHANT

The pygmy elephant (*Loxodonta pumilio*) of Africa is an animal whose reality as a genuine new species most cryptozoologists and some zoologists agree is a valid assumption. A few more restrained zoologists dispute its existence even as a subspecies. The latter zoologists think pygmy elephants are merely misidentified forest elephants.

Today, elephants live in India and Africa. The two widely acknowledged subspecies of African elephants are the forest elephant (*Loxodonta africana cyclotis*) and the bush or savanna elephant (*Loxodonta africana africana*). The forest elephants are somewhat smaller than the bush variety.

In 1906, the German zoologist Theodore Noack formally detailed what he called a "dwarf form" of the African elephant and scientifically described it as a separate species, *Loxodonta pumilio*. Science writer **Patrick Huyghe** has learned that the remains of the pygmy elephant upon which Noack based his description, kept at the Bronx Zoo until it

Pygmy elephant. (FPL)

died in 1915, survive in the collection of the American Museum of Natural History. The skull and skeletal material of specimen no. 35591 (pygmy elephant) are gathering dust in the museum archives, waiting further study.

Early twentieth-century expeditions and collecting trips to the Congo captured pygmy elephants and took them to zoos in Europe and America. In recent years, zoological parks in Africa have exhibited the pygmy elephant. From 1960 through 1970, Zaire's Kinshasa Zoo and Liberia's private presidential zoo at Totota housed pygmy elephants with mature tusks. Though observed for several years, the animals never grew, thus undercutting the skeptical view that these are merely immature forest elephants.

Finally, in 1990, then–West German ambassador Harald Nestroy photographed a herd of four adult and two juvenile pygmy elephants in the Congo. Using a great egret (*Egretta alba*) as scale, he determined that the mature female and tusked mature adult male pygmy elephants were no more than five feet tall at the shoulders. The juveniles, in Nestroy's words, were the size of sheep dogs. Nestroy also photographed a group of forest elephants and forest buffalo soon afterward. The forest elephants were definitely larger in size than the just-observed pygmy elephants, and the buffalo compared in size to the pygmy elephants.

Conservative zoologists offer a unique theory to explain the riddle of the pygmy elephant. Jonathan Kingdon expresses it in *The Kingdon Field Guide to African Mammals* (1997), writing that elephants maintain "family traditions" and evolve "subpopulations." Kingdon lists only two kinds of elephants in his book, the bush elephant, and the other, exactly noted as the "forest (pygmy) elephant," clearly establishing that he feels the pygmy elephant does not really exist as a species.

Cryptozoologists, however, say the evidence suggests the existence of this third type of elephant, known throughout central Africa to the natives as the "red" elephant versus the "blue" forest elephant. The pygmy elephant is hairier, redder, and no taller than 6.5 feet tall, compared to the 7.5- to 9-foot height of the supposedly "smaller" variety of African elephants, the forest elephants, or the much taller, nine- to thirteen-foot-tall bush elephants. Also, the pygmy elephants inhabit a vastly different type of habitat from the other two, living in the dense swamps of central

Africa, especially of the Congo. **Bernard Heuvelmans** theorizes that pygmy elephants may be much more aquatic than the two larger types.

PYGMY HIPPOPOTAMUS

In the late nineteenth century, Karl Hagenbeck, a famous German animal dealer, established a zoological garden near Hamburg, the prototype of the modern open-air zoo. In 1909, Hagenbeck sent German naturalist-explorer Hans Schomburgk to Liberia to check on rumors about the *nigbwe,* a "giant black pig." After two years of jungle pursuit, Schomburgk finally spotted the animal thirty feet in front of him. It was big, shiny, and black, but the animal clearly was related to the hippopotamus, not the pig. Unable to catch it, he went home to Hamburg empty-handed. In 1912 Schomburgk returned to Liberia and, to the dismay of his critics, captured a pygmy hippopotamus on March 1, 1913. He returned to Europe in August with five live pygmy hippos.

A full-grown pygmy hippopotamus (*Hexaprotodon liberiensis*) weighs only about four hundred pounds, one-tenth the weight of the average adult hippopotamus (*Hippopotamus amphibiu*s).

QUEENSLAND TIGER

Reported from the Queensland rainforests of Australia, the Queensland Tiger is not to be confused with the wolflike Tasmanian Tiger, or **Thylacine,** another **cryptid.** Queensland Tigers are medium-sized carnivorous marsupial striped "cats" known to the Aborigines for many centuries and to Euro-Australians since the 1600s. In the 1940s and 1950s, a wave of sightings erupted to the south of North Queensland's tropical rainforests. Witnesses told of encounters with a striped tiger-like beast around Maryborough and Gympie, just to the north of the Sunshine Coast. Expeditions in pursuit of the Queensland Tiger have tried to catch one for decades with no success. The Queensland Tiger is a

The Queensland Tiger here is based upon eyewitness accounts. (Frank Lane)

large, German shepherd–sized animal with stripes across its whole back, a catlike head, and a nasty habit of using its sharp front claws to rip the guts from animals that it attacks. It is said to do the same thing to kangaroos and animals it wishes to eat.

Bernard Heuvelmans relates the Queensland Tiger to the fossil marsupial "lion," *Thylacoleo.*

R

RAYNAL, MICHEL (1955–)

Michel Raynal is today's most communicative European cryptozoologist, maintaining a global network of contacts while working from France with **Bernard Heuvelmans** and **Jean-Jacques Barloy.** Raynal is the webmaster of the acclaimed French/English Internet site entitled Virtual Institute of Cryptozoology (http://perso.wanadoo.fr/cryptozoo/welcome.htm).

The Internet site was born on April 9, 1997. On April 10, Wanadoo, Raynal's Internet access provider, mentioned the site on its own home page, which generated about one thousand hits that day alone!

Raynal has authored more than thirty cryptozoology articles that have appeared in various scientific magazines. He has written on the controversial and possibly racist origins of a hoaxed southern American ape photograph, and the possible **Giant Octopus** remains found on a beach in St. Augustine, Florida, having even analyzed some samples. In recent years Raynal has done extensive bibliographical research in cryptozoology. He is the author of a multimedia program on cryptozoology for the Cité des Sciences et de l'Industrie of La Villette (Paris).

REBSAMEN, WILLIAM M. (1964-)

Arkansas wildlife artist Bill Rebsamen continues the long tradition of cryptozoologically inspired illustrators that includes **Bernard Heuvelmans**'s partner/artist Alika Lindbergh.

Rebsamen studied as a teenager under renowned Arkansas wildlife artist Susan Morrison, traditional naturalist Professor William McKim, and Sea World muralist Robert David Walters. Rebsamen has worked with Ducks Unlimited of Arkansas, and after becoming popular painting sporting dogs, he began doing "Pet Portraits" (a trademarked name). Because of his interest in cryptozoology and the desire to educate others about the authenticity of cryptozoology as a true endeavor of science and zoology, he has begun to illustrate the possible appearance of unknown animals. He has created original cryptozoology artwork for **Scott Norman, Karl Shuker, Loren Coleman,** and **William Gibbons.**

ROESCH, BEN S. (1980-)

Ben S. Roesch, a young cryptozoological writer, is webmaster of an active site entitled Cryptozoology—Searching for Hidden Animals (http://www.ncf.carleton.ca/~bz050/HomePage.cryptoz.html), and the editor of *The Cryptozoology Review*. One of the first of the wave of new cyber-cryptozoologists, Roesch is a university student in Toronto, Ontario, with a keen interest in cryptozoological studies and research. He is studying marine biology (mainly sharks), animal predatory behavior, and general zoology. Roesch is intrigued by rumors of a giant cookie-cutter shark, genus *Isistius,* and debunking reports of the survival of the giant fossil shark **Megalodon,** which he believes died out 1.5 million years ago, though it has attained a rekindled status in the 1990s. Roesch is also credited with assisting in the "discovery" of the eleventh **megamouth.**

RUSSELL, W. M. "GERALD" (1911–1979)

Gerald Russell, best known for his role in important Himalayan **Yeti** expeditions of the 1950s, was an adventurer and explorer who always seemed available for whatever cryptozoological pursuit came his way from the 1930s through the late 1950s.

Born in New York, Russell attended Cambridge University in England 1928–31, where he met and became lifelong friends of schoolmates **Ivan T. Sanderson** and later **Abominable Snowman** and **Buru** investigator Ralph Izzard. In 1932, Russell went with Sanderson as a member of the Percy Sladen expedition to Africa. While there, in the high forests of the British Cameroons, at Mainyu River near the Mamfe Pool, they encountered a large unknown animal, called *mbulu-em'bembe* (or **Mokele-mbembe** in the cryptozoological literature of today). Two months later, in the Assumbo Mountains, they witnessed the overflight of a giant batlike animal, known locally as an *olitiau* (more commonly known as the **Kongamato**).

During 1933–34, Russell participated in the William Harvest Harkness Asiatic Expedition to Tibet in pursuit of the **giant panda.** While this particular expedition was unsuccessful, he returned in 1936–37, with the **Ruth Harkness** Asiatic Expedition to Tibet, and assisted in capturing the first giant panda. Richard Perry, in his book *The World of the Giant Panda,* writes, "W. M. Russell obtained a half-grown tame beisung [giant panda], which was wandering free on a Wassu farm and apparently thriving on grass and other vegetation."

In 1939, while living in New York, Russell was one of the first Americans to volunteer for service with the British Royal Navy, and saw action in the Mediterranean and the Normandy landings.

During the three years after World War II, Russell journeyed to China to attempt to capture a rare, little-known animal, the golden takin, but was forced to abandon his efforts because of advances by Chinese Communist armies. The early years of the 1950s found Russell making a series of films on native methods of catching wild animals in Asia and Europe. He also became known for the care and patience he employed in finding specimens. When the planners of the 1954 *Daily Mail* expedition to Nepal in search of **Yeti** began picking the members of their group, they naturally chose Russell as one of the leaders. He was able to collect good sightings and droppings of the smallest type of Yeti, **Teh-lma,** seen in the montane forests of Nepal.

Tom Slick, who would sponsor serious but quiet efforts to find the Yeti, heard of Russell's abilities through Izzard's writings. In 1958, Russell led the Slick-Johnson Snowman Expedition to Nepal. Russell and his Sherpa companion Da Temba saw one of the little Teh-lma in the upper Arun Valley of Nepal.

Suffering serious health problems, Russell left the Slick-Johnson Snowman Expedition. He died two decades later in New York City.

S

SABER-TOOTHED CATS

In *The Cloud Forest* (1966), Peter Matthiessen relates a story told him in Paraguay by a seaman named Picquet. Matthiessen wrote: "[He] described a rare striped cat not quite so large as a jaguar and very timid, which is possessed of two very large protruding teeth: this animal, he said, occurs in the mountain jungles of Colombia and Ecuador, and he has glimpsed it once himself."

Matthiessen wondered if the saber-toothed tiger, like the puma, had long ago established itself in South America in a smaller subspecies and had thus survived the Ice Age extinction of its North American ancestor.

A September 1998 article in *Science Illustrée* mentions an observation in 1984, again in Paraguay, of a saber-toothed cat emerging from a cavern, apparently distinct from the 1966 report. This may be a recycling of the Matthiessen story or a new case.

Karl Shuker's *Mystery Cats of the World* mentions an alleged 1975 shooting of a "mutant jaguar" (as locals called it) in that South American nation. It is supposed to have weighed 160 pounds. Zoologist Juan Acavar, who examined it, measured its saber teeth, which were fully

Saber-toothed cats are a rare but intriguing cryptid. (Milwaukee State Museum)

twelve inches long. He thought it was a *Smilodon* (the Pleistocene saber-toothed tiger generally thought to be extinct for ten thousand years). So as not to disturb residents, however, the authories stuck with the jaguar identification. Nothing more has been heard of this specimen.

Bernard Heuvelmans notes that striped, saber-toothed cats have also been reported in the montane forests of Colombia and Ecuador. While Heuvelmans says members of the genus *Smilodon* might be involved, he feels more comfortable with thoughts that they may be related to survivors of the extinct saber-toothed marsupials of South America, the Thylacosmilidae.

SANDERSON, IVAN T. (1911–1973)

Ivan Terence Sanderson, one of the foremost pioneers of cryptozoology, was born in Edinburgh, Scotland. As a teenager, Sanderson led expeditions to some of the world's remotest jungles, gathering interesting tales on a wide variety of animals. His early books were keen portrayals of natural history that became extremely popular with the public. They included *Animal Treasure* (1937), *Caribbean Treasure* (1939), *Living Treasure* (1941), *Animal Tales* (1946), *Living Mammals of the World* (1955), *Follow the Whale* (1956), and *Monkey Kingdom* (1957). In the

1940s, Sanderson began to write articles in the *Saturday Evening Post* on topics ranging from sea monsters to living dinosaurs. One of these articles inspired **Bernard Heuvelmans**'s interest in pursuing cryptozoology.

In the 1950s and 1960s, Sanderson gained fame as a television talk show "animal man." He continued to write magazine articles on **Lake Monsters, Yeti,** and other cryptozoological wonders. His late 1950s popular features in *True Magazine* on "America's Abominable Snowman" gained many followers to the hunt for **Bigfoot/Sasquatch.**

Ivan T. Sanderson. (Ivan T. Sanderson)

His classic book *Abominable Snowmen: Legend Come to Life* (1961), an early and seminal work on the subject, remains a useful reference book. The 525-page book brought notice to the global nature of the re-

Ivan T. Sanderson's books have become classics in the field of cryptozoology. (Loren Coleman)

ports of Yeti, Bigfoot, and other giant hairy hominoid creatures. An associate of Sanderson's, **Mark A. Hall,** notes that the book is the basis for all work done since its publication in pursuit of mystery primates. Without this work, Hall senses that the awareness of Bigfoot/Sasquatch would have remained as regional as, for example, the many Lake Monsters.

In 1965 Sanderson established the Society for the Investigation of the Unexplained. He followed many leads to further adventures, tracking **Black Panther** reports, examining the **Minnesota Iceman,** and looking into **Thunderbird** accounts. His two rare paperback books, *"Things"* (1967) and *More "Things"* (1969), contained his musings on his investigations of many cryptozoological topics. Sanderson's greatest achievement may be the legacy of cryptozoologists he passionately inspired who now follow in his footsteps.

Ivan Sanderson died on February 19, 1973.

SAOLA

The **"Lost World" of Vietnam** had a surprise for zoology in 1992; it would reveal an amazing new animal, known to the locals as the *saola*. In initial press releases this forest animal would get the name Vu Quang ox,

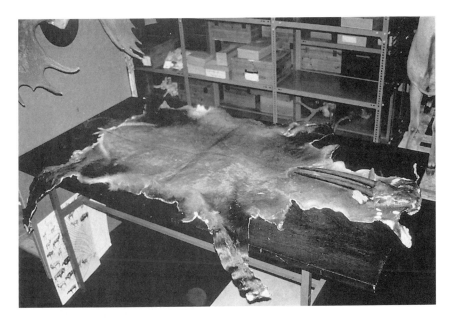

The skin and trophy skulls of the saola revealed that a new animal existed in Vietnam's "Lost World." (FPL)

but later it would be officially called by its native name, saola (*Pseudoryx nghetinhensis*). Though it was described in early media accounts as a goatlike species, examination of three available skins revealed it to be a living bovid. It is also the largest land mammal to be discovered since the **kouprey** in 1937. Since it was a part of the area's hunting lore, this discovery has significant implications for cryptozoology, for it was an animal familiar to natives but still a "hidden animal," unknown to science.

The June 3, 1993, issue of *Nature* makes it clear just how unique this animal is: "*Pseudoryx* differs significantly from all described genera in appearance, morphology, cranial and dental features and DNA. The long, smooth, almost straight, slender horns, elongated premolars, large face gland and distinctive colour pattern are diagnostic." The pattern mentioned is a series of black and white markings on the face, neck, feet, and rump.

It is noteworthy that the saola was found near the Mekong River in Cambodia-Laos, in the same general region of the kouprey. The saola, according to locals, inhabits the pristine evergreen montane forests of northern Vietnam, bordering Laos. Until the spring of 1994, Vietnamese and American biologists had not encountered a living specimen, though they had noted signs of twenty individual animals.

Finally, a female saola calf was captured just outside the Vu Quang Preserve and moved to an eight-acre, forested botanical garden preserve. The new specimen has a thin, dark brown stripe running down its back, distinctive white markings on its face, large eyes, and a short, fluffy tail.

In March 1994, Vietnam's Vu Quang Preserve yielded up evidence of yet another genus: the giant muntjac, or barking deer (*Megamuntiacus vuquangensis*). The largest muntjac ever found, this one has a red grizzled coat and weighs ninety to one hundred pounds. Not long afterward, the World Wildlife Fund reported the capture of a live specimen in Laos. Another new species of muntjac deer, *Muntiacus trungsonensis,* has been identified in the heavily war-damaged but dense scrub forest of the region. In 1994, word reached the West that a new bovid had been described from Vietnam and Cambodia. The animal, which resembles a small kouprey, was named *Pseudonovibos spiralis*.

The discovery of the saola appears to herald the discovery of other "hidden" animals in Vietnam's Vu Quang Nature Preserve, and cryptozoologists are paying attention.

SASQUATCH

In the 1920s, Canadian journalist J. W. Burns coined the word "Sasquatch" in order to describe the British Columbian version of unknown hairy giants. His Native Canadian informants called these beasts by various names, including *sokqueatl* and *soss-q'tal,* and Burns decided to invent one term for all of them. Sasquatch and **Bigfoot** denote the same creatures, although since 1958 **Bigfoot** has been the more popular name.

This Native Canadian mask carved in the early 1800s closely matches the descriptions of the Sasquatch. (Loren Coleman)

SCHAFFNER, RON (1951–)

An active midwestern field investigator, Ron Schaffner has researched unusual phenomena, especially those associated with cryptozoology, since 1975. He became interested in the subject while doing a part-time radio show, where he found a copy of John A. Keel's paperback *Strange Creatures from Time and Space.* This led to Schaffner's search over two decades for the answer to these mysteries. Schaffner was highly active in investigating the reported creature wave (increase of creature reports) of 1977 and 1980, and many of his cases have been documented in various publications.

Schaffner is one of the cofounders of the Bigfoot Researcher's Organization and a cocurator of the BFRO database, which maintains one of the largest websites of its kind (http://www.moneymaker.org/BFRR).

During the 1980s and early 1990s, he edited the newsletter *Creature Chronicles.* All back issues and additional investigations can be found on the web page with the same name (http://home.fuse.net/rschaffner).

SEA SERPENTS

Until the twentieth century no cryptozoological mystery generated so much wonder or sparked so much debate as the "Great Unknown"—the

Sea Serpent. Today such alleged beasts as **Bigfoot/Sasquatch,** the **Yeti,** the **Loch Ness Monsters,** and **Mokele-mbembe** have eclipsed the Sea Serpent in the popular imagination, but as late as the nineteenth century Sea Serpent sightings were reported and argued about in mainstream scientific journals.

Such creatures have a long history in the world's mythology. It was not until 1555, however, that an attempt was made to address them scientifically, when Olaus Magnus, the exiled Catholic archbishop of Uppsala, Sweden, wrote a survey of Scandinavian zoology. Besides more conventionally recognized marine animals, he said, the coastal waters housed serpents "of vast magnitude, namely two hundred feet long, and moreover twenty feet thick." They emerged from caves along the shore to devour just about anything in their paths, including the occasional sailor.

Other sources, including *Natural History of Norway* (1752–53), by the great zoologist and cataloguer Bishop Erik Pontopiddan, attest to the presence of large "serpents" in the North Sea. Magnus's estimation of the creatures' size is considerably exaggerated, however, and seems to owe more to the fabulous folklore surrounding the animals than to accurate observation.

During the seventeenth century, Americans in the Massachusetts Bay Colony remarked on Sea Serpents they allegedly were observing from both ship and shore. The first printed reference is in John Josselyn's *An Account of Two Voyages to England* (1674), in which the author recalled conversations in 1639 with locals who spoke of "a *Sea-Serpent* or snake, that lay coiled upon a rock at Cape Ann." In 1779, during the Revolutionary War, the crew of the American gunship *Protector* spotted and fired upon a Sea Serpent, which escaped apparently unharmed.

In May 1780, Captain George Little of the frigate *Boston,* in Broad Bay off the Maine coast, had this experience, as recounted in **Bernard Heuvelmans**'s *In the Wake of the Sea-Serpents*:

> At sunrise, I discovered a huge Serpent, or monster, coming down the Bay, on the surface of the water. The cutter was manned and armed. I went myself to the boat, and proceeded after the Serpent. When within a hundred feet, the mariners were ordered to fire on him, but before they could make ready, the Serpent dove. He was not less than from forty-five to fifty feet in length; the largest di-

ameter of his body, I should judge, fifteen inches; his head nearly
the size of that of a man, which he carried four or five feet above
the water. He wore every appearance of a common black snake.

The most spectacular of all the American Sea Serpent sightings occurred over several years in the second decade of the nineteenth century,
along the northeastern tip of Massachusetts. Numerous well-regarded
citizens spotted serpents in the ocean. A typical sighting is that of Samuel
Cabot, who on August 14, 1819, saw "an object emerging from the water at the distance of about one hundred or one hundred and fifty yards,
which gave to my mind at the first glance the idea of a horse's head. . . . I
perceived at a short distance eight or ten regular bunches or protuber-
ances, and at a short interval three or four more. . . . The Head . . . was
serpent shaped[;] it was elevated about two feet from the water. . . . [H]e
could not be less than eighty feet long."

An investigation launched by the Linnean Society of New England
in 1817, two years before Cabot's and others' sightings, had already
demonstrated a striking consistency in witness descriptions, which were
nearly all of a giant snakelike animal, dark on top, lighter beneath, which

*Detail from a 1940s map shows a fanciful interpretation of the New England Sea Serpent that
was routinely sighted off the coast of Maine and Massachusetts 1817–1819.* (Loren Coleman)

moved in an undulating fashion. Unfortunately, the society, which believed the animal to be a reptile, judged a three-foot snake killed in a field near Cape Ann to be a baby Sea Serpent. When it was proved to be simply a mutated specimen of the common black snake, scoffers used the mistake to discredit the society's larger conclusions, which were based on sightings of much bigger, oceangoing animals unrelated to the smaller land-based black snake.

That embarrassing blunder aside, the society's puzzlement about the sightings is understandable and justifiable. As even **Richard Ellis,** a writer on oceanography and a mostly skeptical commentator on cryptozoological claims, observes, the Massachusetts sightings remain among "the great unsolved mysteries of Sea Serpent lore."

Though by the nineteenth century ridicule had begun to surround the subject, some well-positioned scientists, including *Zoologist* editor Edward Newman, championed the Sea Serpent even though, as he acknowledged in an 1847 editorial, "It has been the fashion for . . . many years to deride all records of this very celebrated monster." The very next year, when the captain and crew of the frigate *Daedalus* reported a twenty-minute sighting of an "enormous serpent," some sixty feet of which were visible above the waterline, off the Cape of Good Hope, the controversy was revived in spectacular fashion. Captain Peter M'Quhae publicly disputed the theory advanced by the admiralty's consultant on Sea Serpent sightings, Sir Richard Owen, that M'Quhae and his crew had seen no more than a large seal.

The captain's vigorous defense of his and his men's good sense and observational skills won many admirers, but Sea Serpents continued their decline into unrespectability as the century passed. An 1892 book by the respected Dutch biologist **A. C. Oudemans,** *The Great Sea Serpent,* had a wide readership, though his theory about giant seals as the "true" Sea Serpent would be largely ignored by subsequent writers on the subject.

The twentieth century turned its collective attention to another variety of monster, namely those said to dwell in freshwater settings such as Scotland's Loch Ness. Still, though they were much less noted, Sea Serpent sightings continued. Some of the most impressive were off the coast of British Columbia, where a creature given the tongue-in-cheek name "Cadborosaurus"—soon shortened to **Caddy**—figured in a number of reports. One witness, Major W. H. Langley, a barrister and clerk of the province's legislature, observed a serpent-like beast near Chatham Island on October 8, 1933. Greenish brown in color, its body serrated, approximately eighty feet long, it was, Langley judged, "every bit as big as a whale." In the 1980s and 1990s, University of British Columbia oceanographer **Paul LeBlond** and Royal British Columbia Museum marine biologist Edward Bousfield conducted a comprehensive investigation that convinced them of the reality of Caddy-like uncatalogued sea creatures.

On May 31, 1982, a video was taken of an apparent Sea Serpent, estimated to be thirty to thirty-five feet long but only a foot in diameter, in Chesapeake Bay. In August of that year, seven scientists from various disciplines convened at the Smithsonian Institution to analyze the video. In a report summarizing their conclusions, George Zug of the Smithsonian Museum of Natural History declared, "We could not identify the object," though it appeared "animate." He went on, "These sightings are not isolated phenomena, for they have been reported for the past several years."

The most important book on the subject since Oudemans's is Bernard Heuvelmans's massive *In the Wake of the Sea-Serpents* (1968), which examines 587 reports; 358 of these, in his opinion, represent sightings of genuine unknowns. Heuvelmans believed that "Sea Serpents" were most likely at least nine different types of uncatalogued marine animals. Besides a few sightings of what he took to be a **Giant Turtle,** a very small number of reports may be, he writes, of "a surviving thalattosuchian, in other words a true crocodile of an ancient group, a specifically and exclusively oceanic one, which flourished from the Jurassic to the Cretaceous." The others, which form the bulk of the sightings, can be attributed to pinnipeds, cetaceans, and fish. He gave the names "long-necked" and "merhorse" to the first of these. Among the cetaceans were "many-humped," "many-finned," and "super-otter." The fish he called "super-eels." In other words, "Sea Serpents" are not serpents at all.

SHORT, BOBBIE (1954–)

Bobbie Short, a registered nurse by occupation, is a native Californian with a particular interest in the world's unrecognized primates. Her involvement was born in personal experience. While backpacking with friends deep in the Humboldt Forest–Trinity Alps region of northern California in the early morning hours of September 8, 1985, she saw a seven-foot-tall **Bigfoot** pass directly in front of her. Since then, she has traveled extensively in the Pacific Rim in pursuit of cryptids. During March 1999, for example, Short trekked the jungles of the Philippines to interview natives about their sightings and tales of unknown hairy, upright hominoids. Language was, at times, a barrier, but she utilized Harry Trumbore's illustrations contained in *The Field Guide to Bigfoot, Yeti, and Other Mystery Primates World-wide* (Avon 1999), as a tool. The illustrations were carefully examined by native islanders when sign language failed, and as a result Short, for the first time, obtained accurate composites from the field of what the Kapre, Waray-Waray, and **Orang Pendek** are reported to look like to the Filipino natives. She carried on a technique employed by **Tom Slick** when he used a small booklet of drawings as an identikit in the course of asking native Sherpas how the Yeti appeared to them.

Bobbie Short (Loren Coleman)

Short sat on the North America Science Institute's short-lived research board in Oregon and is a life member of the San Diego Zoological Society. She works to preserve Bigfoot literature, research documents, and memorabilia for the Willow Creek [California] Museum, specifically the **Bob Titmus** Bigfoot resource section, which contains Titmus's large collection of files and plaster casts of **Sasquatch** prints. Short has one of the major state-specific Bigfoot websites. Short is also a member and contributing writer for the Western Bigfoot Society and a member of the **International Society of Cryptozoology** and the **British Columbia Scientific Cryptozoology Club.**

SHUKER, KARL P. N. (1959–)

It all began for Karl Shuker when, aged thirteen, he walked into a bookshop near his home in the West Midlands, England, and noticed a copy of the Paladin paperback edition (1972 reprint) of **Bernard Heuvelmans**'s classic book *On the Track of Unknown Animals*. Receiving it soon

Karl Shuker holds a cast of a dinosaur foot-print, which he feels closely resembles that left by a Mokele-mbembe. (Karl Shuker)

as a birthday gift, he read it from cover to cover many times and was hooked. He began collecting news clippings, articles, and books on cryptozoology. In 1979, during his first year as a zoology undergraduate, Shuker began to lose weight suddenly and was quickly admitted to a hospital. A week later, he reemerged, at the start of a whole new phase of his life, as an insulin-dependent diabetic. He went on to finish his studies in zoology at the University of Leeds and obtained a Ph.D. in zoology and comparative physiology at the University of Birmingham, but he had to forgo the rigors of stressful scientific research. He decided to turn his life-long interest in cryptozoology into a writing career. Soon he was writing articles for minor magazines and sending in proposals for book ideas. Through many years of hard work, he finally was able to see many of his thoroughly researched books come to print. His books include *Mystery Cats of the World* (1989), *Extraordinary Animals Worldwide* (1991), *The Lost Ark: New and Rediscovered Animals of the 20th Century* (1993), *From Flying Toad to Snakes with Wings* (1997) and, acting jointly as consultant and contributor, *Man and Beast* (1993), *Secrets of the Natural World* (1993), and *Almanac of the Uncanny* (1995).

Shuker now works as a zoological consultant, lecturer, and writer. He appears regularly on television and radio, journeys throughout the world in the course of his researches, and is today widely recognized as one of the leading experts in cryptozoology because of his attention to scientific detail.

SHUNKA WARAK'IN

In the wilds of the upper midwestern United States lives a frightening-looking, primitive wolflike beast known to Indians and early western pioneers. The Ioway, as well as other tribes, even have a name for it: *shunka warak'in* ("carrying-off dogs"). Little has been written about this animal because records of it are relatively rare and the existence of the otherwise well-known timber wolf has often confused the picture. Nonetheless, evidence does exist for this new addition to the cryptozoological menagerie.

The story of the Shunka Warak'in begins in the 1880s, when members of the Hutchins family traveled west by covered wagon to settle in the Madison River Valley, near the West Fork, in the lower part of Montana. Their ranch left its mark on the geography of the region. The name Hutchins Ranch, located about forty miles north of the little town of Ennis, still appears on Montana road maps.

Shortly after the Hutchinses settled in the area, they and other locals encountered an unusual animal. As Ross Hutchins would write years later (in his 1977 book, *Trails to Nature's Mysteries: The Life of a Working Naturalist*):

> One winter morning my grandfather was aroused by the barking of the dogs. He discovered that a wolflike beast of dark color was chasing my grandmother's geese. He fired his gun at the animal but missed. It ran off down the river, but several mornings later it was seen again at about dawn. It was seen several more times at the home ranch as well as at other ranches ten or fifteen miles down the valley. Whatever it was, it was a great traveler. . . .
>
> Those who got a good look at the beast described it as being nearly black and having high shoulders and a back that sloped downward like a hyena. Then one morning in late January, my grandfather was alerted by the dogs, and this time he was able to kill it. Just what the animal was is still an open question. After being killed, it was donated to a man named Sherwood who kept a combination grocery and museum at Henry Lake in Idaho. It was mounted and displayed there for many years. He called it *"ringdocus."*

The younger Hutchins, who had a Ph.D. in zoology, had no idea what the animal was, though he advanced the speculation that perhaps it was a hyena that had escaped from a circus. He noted, however, that the "nearest circus was hundreds of miles away." Probably, he thought, this mystery would never be solved.

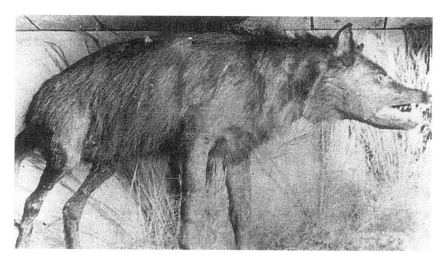

This is a mounted example of the Shunka Warak'in that was reportedly exhibited at various times in the west Yellowstone area and at a museum near Henry Lake in Idaho. Its whereabouts today are unknown. (Ross Hutchins)

In recent years, according to cryptozoologist **Mark A. Hall,** reported sightings of mean-looking, near-wolflike and hyena-like animals have come from Alberta, Nebraska, Iowa, and Illinois. The reports appeared to be without historical precursors, and thus caution seemed a wise response. On the other hand, the discovery by Hall of the Hutchins story now reveals that a photograph of the taxidermically mounted hyena-like animal, the so-called *ringdocus,* exists.

In 1995, Lance Foster, an Ioway Indian, told **Loren Coleman**: "We had a strange animal called *shunka warak'in* that snuck into camps at night and stole dogs. It was said to look something like a hyena and cried like a person when they killed it. Its skin is said to be kept by someone still."

Foster, who had heard of the mounted *ringdocus,* thought it was an example of the Shunka Warak'in, which he knew from his own experiences and those of relatives in Montana and Idaho.

The animal seems too small to be a "dire wolf," or cave hyena. The cave hyena was an Old World animal. Possibly the species existed here but was sufficiently rare that examples do not exist in the fossil record. This, of course, is purely speculative.

A prehistoric mammal that may fit these observations is the *Borophagus,* an ancient hyena-like dog found during the Pleistocene in North America. While the Shunka Warak'in has been described by various witnesses as a "hyena" or a "mean-looking" hyena-canid cross, the mounted animal has a decidedly doglike or wolflike appearance with the hyenid characteristics visible but not overwhelming.

The present whereabouts of the mounted Shunka Warak'in, Hutchins's so-called *ringdocus,* are uncertain, though some reports claim it has moved to the West Yellowstone area. Once it is located, it is essential that DNA testing on samples of the hair and skin be conducted. Only then will we know for certain whether we are dealing with a truly new animal or a taxidermist's very bad mount.

SISEMITE

The Sisemite is a **Bigfoot**-like creature reported in Central America. **Ivan T. Sanderson** notes traditions that associate these larger-than-man-sized, hairy upright beings with the abduction of women for purposes of procreation and companionship.

Among the Guatemalan Chorti Indians, it is said that the creatures have hair that grows to the ground and take notably long strides when they walk. They live in uninhabited hills, where secluded screams far from human habitations can be heard. The Chorti consider the Sisemites the guardians of wild animal life. Accounts of Sisemites attacking single hunters on lonely trails have been recorded.

As often happens, the Sisemite has various localized names. For example, analogous stories of the Ulak or Uluk are found along the Mosquito Coast of Central America. The tailless anthropoid ape Ulak is said to live on unexplored mountain ridges. Erect, about five feet tall, and covered with black hair, the Ulak is greatly feared; like the Sisemite, it is supposed to carry off human beings of the opposite sex. The Rama and the Creoles call this ape Yoho or Yuho, while the Paya and Ladinos apply to it the Spanish-Mexican name Sisemite, or Chichimite. Some Indians claim that this mysterious being has been seen on occasion over the last forty years around the Guarunta Mountains, which extend north of the lower Rio Coco.

SKUNK APE

"Only one big hairy monster can rightfully claim to be the stinkiest: the Skunk Ape of the Florida Everglades," writer Donald Trull remarks. True enough. The only problem is that there seems to be more than one kind of Skunk Ape.

From records of pre–World War II encounters through the early 1970s, the Skunk Apes seen were described as chimpanzee like short, hairy, and smelly. These chimplike Skunk Apes are related to accounts and traditions of the **Napes** reported throughout the southern bottomlands of the U.S. Like Napes, Skunk Apes leave anthropoid knuckle prints with a large toe extending out to the side. Witnesses said the apes moved around on all fours. Reports of these smaller animals were generally not from the Everglades but instead from Brooksville, Holopaw, and western coast sites in Florida. A few rare reports came from Broward County. Researchers **Ramona Clark, Robert Morgan, Ted Ernst,** and **Loren Coleman** have investigated Skunk Ape accounts through the years.

Loren Coleman has been to Florida several times searching for the unknown anthropoid Skunk Apes. Here he is in the Everglades in 1978. (Libbet Cone)

Since the late 1970s, however, the Skunk Ape that has attracted the most attention is said to be bipedal, seven feet tall, weighing three hundred pounds, covered in a dark brown, red, or black fur, and bearing a distinct and far-ranging aroma redolent of an unholy mixture of skunk, rotten eggs, and cow manure. "It stunk awful, like a dog that hasn't been bathed in a year and suddenly gets rained on," Charlie Stoeckman said of the Skunk Ape he saw in the Florida Keys in 1977.

Some accounts indicate that the Skunk Ape has been a part of Florida lore for decades, but it has been widely reported only since the 1970s, when developers began their encroachment into the Everglades. Dozens of sightings were reported in that decade; almost all of them mentioned the creature's strong, unpleasant odor. A few of them involved multiple creatures. In November 1975, for example, seven young men allegedly saw three in Citrus County, Florida. In February 1977, three, including one ten-foot-tall specimen, allegedly appeared near

Moon Lake, Florida. Nevertheless, single sightings of single individuals are the more common experience in Florida.

Although Skunk Ape sightings have been less common in recent years, the creature enjoyed something of a comeback in 1997. A guided bus tour group of foreign tourists in Ochopee saw a large, apelike animal ambling through the outskirts of a swamp. Soon afterward, Ochopee fire chief Vince Doerr saw a similar creature cross the road near his home and rush into the swamp. Doerr managed to take a distant snapshot of the supposed Skunk Ape before it disappeared. This "first-ever photograph" of the Everglades monster stirred a great deal of publicity, but Doerr himself denied that he had captured proof of anything extraordinary. The fire chief believed it was simply a prankster in a gorilla suit. "I just think someone's playing games. I just looked at it and laughed," Doerr said. "If I thought it was real, I would have run in there, beat it to death, and sold it to the *National Enquirer.*" Others were not so certain it was a hoax.

SLICK, THOMAS BAKER (1916–1962)

Tom Slick, early cryptozoological expedition supporter, inventor, innovator, and successful oil and beef businessman, led an adventure-filled life until he died in a mysterious midair plane explosion over Montana in 1962. He possessed a personality meant for Hollywood and indeed, Nicolas Cage and 20th Century Fox are currently making a movie, tentatively entitled *Tom Slick: Monster Hunter,* based on Slick's life (due out in late 2001 or 2002). Early reports say it may be a comedic farce, and if true, that would not be an accurate portrayal. Slick's quiet and steadfast nature is remembered and respected by those who knew the early leader's grounded and thoughtful demeanor.

Slick had been raised in Oklahoma and was a teenager living with his widowed mother's new husband, Charles Urschel, when on July 22, 1933, Machine Gun Kelly kidnapped Urschel. The kidnapping made Machine Gun Kelly a household name, and his capture after Urschel was released was national news. The Urschel kidnapping had much to do with the way Slick would later deal with his public image. Many chroniclers do not understand why Slick in the years of his cryptozoological pursuits was so publicity-shy, but his family's involvement with the FBI, Machine Gun Kelly, and its subsequent desire to maintain a low profile explain a lot.

Slick traveled in 1957 to Nepal, where he investigated **Yeti** reports. Trekking into the mountains himself, he was nearly killed in a bus accident, but continued on. Slick located fifteen self-identified eye-witnesses. He showed each a series of twenty photographs of animals that scientists had said might be confused with Yetis, and was able to build an identikit of the creature's appearance. While others found footprints in the snow on that expedition, Slick and his Sherpas found Yeti tracks in the mud. Photographs of the cast (see page 24) of one of those prints today show it is similar to the print found by Sir Eric Shipton in 1951. His sponsorship of the 1958 and 1959 Slick-Johnson Snowman Expeditions produced more results that were long hidden until rediscovered in the 1980s by **Loren Coleman.** Some of these included the details of the **Pangboche Hand,** analysis results on unknown parasites in **Teh-lma** feces, and heretofore undisclosed sightings. Slick's theory that more than one type of Yeti was involved in the sightings was a groundbreaking idea in the late 1950s. It caused **Bernard Heuvelmans** and **Ivan T. Sanderson** to reexamine some of their data.

An Indian journalist photographed a bandaged Tom Slick at the New Delhi Airport shortly after the return of his first Yeti expedition to the Himalayas. He was battered on the way there when a bus accident near Dharan, Nepal, left him injured in March 1957. (Times of India)

The 1957 release of the film *The Abominable Snowman of the Himalayas* has a character that may have been inspired by Tom Slick. **Abominable Snowman** hunter "Tom Friend" is portrayed by well-known American actor Forrest Tucker, and the film appears to have been loosely based on the unwanted publicity Slick's search for the Yeti was receiving at the time.

Slick also took trips to investigate Alaska's Iliamna **Lake Monsters** and the **Giant Salamander** said to inhabit California's Trinity Alps and Sacramento River. In 1960, he launched the Pacific Northwest Expedition, one of the best-funded of all hairy-hominoid hunts. The group included many notable hunters and researchers, including **René Dahinden, John Green, Bob Titmus,** and Ivan T. Sanderson. Many still active researchers became involved because of their association with Slick.

Before his death Slick also funded cryptozoological expeditions that sought **Orang Pendek** and other **cryptids.** He was involved in efforts with rhinos and other rare animals as well.

Slick's life was as mysterious as his many pursuits. It was little-known, for example, until his biographer discovered it, that the Texan had gone looking for the **Loch Ness Monsters** during the summer of 1937. Ignored by most cryptozoological histories until *Tom Slick and the Search for the Yeti* was published in 1989, Slick is now recognized for his quiet support of the quest for unknown animals. His legacy lives on through the further efforts of the now-seasoned fieldworkers he hired to do the searching in the 1950s and 1960s.

Tom Slick founded the Southwest Research Center in San Antonio.

STORSJOODJURET

Sweden's most famous monster is the Storsjoodjuret, which translates as the "Great Monster of Storsjön" or "The Great Lake Monster." Storsjoodjuret remains of interest to the citizens around Storsjön, county of Jämtland, in central Sweden. The number of persons who have sighted Storsjoodjuret is said to be in the hundreds, or maybe even thousands, and more are added to that number yearly.

Witnesses describe the rapidly swimming, log-shaped, overturned-boat–like beast as having three or more humps. Various accounts have it anywhere from nine to twenty-four feet in length. Its color is black, gray, or shades of red-yellow-brown. Some observers say they see feet, a horse-like head, a long neck, large eyes, and a large mouth. A few people have heard a seemingly bizarre sound, said to be like "two pieces of wood, clapped against each other," emitting from the creature.

"Every year we hear of people who have seen this beast," remarks Sten Rentzhog, president of the Östersund Society for the Scientific In-

vestigation of Lake Storsjön, who has collected hundreds of sighting accounts dating back to 1635. "There are probably also a lot of witnesses who never tell anybody about their sightings, for fear of ridicule. There are even people who have seen the beast while they were diving."

In July 1996, Storsjoodjuret was recorded on video by Gun-Britt Widmark, sixty-seven, while boating on the lake off Östersund. The creature had humps and was thirty-three to thirty-nine feet long. Two years later a well-publicized expedition became the focus of worldwide media attention. The

An old rune mentions the ancient tale of the Storsjoodjuret. (FPL)

expedition consisted of Adrian Shine, a longtime investigator of the Loch Ness Monster, and a group of Swedish researchers who had been studying the mysterious events at Storsjön. Their inquiries produced no significant results.

Storsjoodjuret has been explained in a number of ways—as logs, ripples, gas bubbles, or misidentification of known animals—but none cover witnesses' descriptions adequately, in the judgment of the area's researchers.

I

TAYLOR, DAN SCOTT (1940–)

The waters calmed, the surface appeared as a finely polished mirror, and the wait was finally over for the man in the yellow submarine. The sponsor, *World Book Encyclopedia,* had wanted this moment to take place for months. The year was 1969, and Dan Scott Taylor, Jr., in a one-person minisub he personally built, amid terrific fanfare, was diving to the bottom of Loch Ness. Down and down Taylor sank. Finally on one of his last dives, Taylor was bumped by what he believes must have been Nessie. As he gave chase, Taylor clocked the beast at about fourteen knots (sixteen miles per hour). But the minisub was too slow, and ever after he was haunted by a sense of failure.

Late in September 1998, Taylor announced his intention to return to Loch Ness. As J. R. Moehringer of the *Los Angeles Times* wrote, "Dan Taylor wakes up two hours before dawn and stares at the dark, thinking about the monster. When the swirling sky above the ocean looks like the creamy frosting on a birthday cake, the clouds like pink roses, he brews a pot of coffee and wakes Margaret, his wife of twenty-two years, and together they sit by the window, watching the sun rise and talking about the monster."

Dan Taylor took his minisub, the Viperfish, down to the bottom of Loch Ness in 1969. (Daniel Scott Taylor)

As Moehringer, a continent away from Taylor, who lives in South Carolina, would observe about this man who is building a new vessel for his quest: "Something in him needs that monster."

Taylor learned about submarines as a crew member in the navy and about building them at Georgia Tech. He built the original "yellow submarine" to seek the **Loch Ness Monster** in that 1969 expedition headed by University of Chicago biologist **Roy Mackal,** and is now building a four-man sub to finish the job he set out to do in '69. He calls his new expedition the Nessa Project.

The *Nessa,* as the submarine will be christened, takes its name from the Gaelic Goddess of Water, Nessa, after whom the River Ness, Loch Ness, and the monster, Nessie, were named. The Nessa Project plans to launch the minisub in June 1999. The Nessa Expedition will attempt to return with film, sonar, and tissue-sample proof of the creature's existence.

Taylor has sold his house and spent a quarter of a million dollars on the new sub. He has been busy working on completing the construction. It will be forty feet long, weigh thirty tons, and have a five-hundred-horsepower motor pulled from a locomotive, which will help him reach speeds of twenty knots, or about twenty-three miles an hour. "It'll sound like a freight train a-comin'," Taylor says. "But it'll move like a freight train, too! This thing is going to be a cross between a research submarine and a locomotive, because that's what it will take."

In September 1998, Taylor chose **Loren Coleman** to join his search for the Nessie. Coleman was named the project's cryptozoologist. He may be a technical observer on the dives and may participate as a formal crew member.

The Nessa Project website can be accessed at http://www.nessa-project.com

TATZELWURM

For hundreds of years, sightings in the Alps of Austria and Switzerland have told of a stubby lizard-like reptile two to six feet long. The name most often associated with this alleged animal is the one most favored by Austrians and known throughout the cryptozoological literature: *Tatzelwurm* ("claw worm"). But there have been no confirmed captures or classifications of this fabled beast. The creature is known by a host of regional names, including *Stollenwurm* ("tunnel worm") as it is known in the Bernese Oberland in Switzerland, and the *Bergstutzen* (mountain stump), *Springwurm* ("jumping worm"), *Daazelwurm,* and *Praatzelwurm,* as it is called in other Alpine regions. In the French Alps it is called the *arassas.*

The earliest account of the "modern" Tatzelwurm is that of Hans Fuchs, who saw two of these creatures suddenly appear in front of him in 1779. Badly frightened, he suffered a heart attack from which he subsequently died, though not before telling family members of his encounter. A painting by a relative commemorated his death, depicting two large, lizard-like creatures lurking in the background. German cryptozoologist Ulrich Magin has remarked, "This depiction of the two monsters is still the best we have of the creature."

Two other famous illustrations of the creature exist. A Bavarian hunting manual called *Neues Taschenbuch für Natur- Forst- und Jagd-freunde auf das Jahr 1836* (*New Pocket Guide of the Year 1836 for Nature, Forest, and Hunting Enthusiasts*) contains what **Bernard Heuvelmans** notes is "a curious picture of a sort of scaly cigar, with formidable teeth and wretched little stumps of feet." A more probable drawing of the Tatzelwurm was published in the 1841 Swiss almanac *Alpenrosen*. It shows a long scaly creature with two tiny front legs.

In late 1934, a Swiss photographer named Balkin allegedly came upon a small creature near a log and photographed it. The interest aroused by the photograph's publication inspired the *Berliner Illustrierte* to sponsor an expedition in search of the Tatzelwurm. But the winter expedition was disappointing and interest quickly waned. Today, most cryptozoologists regard this photograph of a Tatzelwurm as almost certainly a hoax.

Besides Swiss Tatzelwurms, reports of similar animals from Spain, France, and Italy have been recorded through the years. The most recent report on an alleged Tatzelwurm was published by Georges Hardy in the Swiss newspaper *La Tribune de Genève* on February 6, 1970.

Bernard Heuvelmans believes that the Tatzelwurm is related to the Gila monster of the American Southwest. It has been suggested that the Tatzelwurm might be an unrecognized variety of otter or some sort of amphibian, quite possibly an unknown European relative of *Megalobatrachus,* the famous **Giant Salamander** of China and Japan.

Reports have been infrequent in recent years, leading many to consider that if the Tatzelwurm ever existed, it may be extinct today.

TCHERNINE, ODETTE (n.d.–n.d.)

When Odette Tchernine was growing up in England, she fell in love with writing and had her first stories published in a local weekly when she was a teenager. Her career as an author had begun.

Tchernine called herself a "mixed Briton," with cultural roots in the British Isles, France, and the Crimea. This mixed ancestry gave her a perceptive understanding of people from many lands and cultures. As an author-journalist, Tchernine worked for Fleet Street and for provincial newspapers on current news, as well as doing research assignments. A Fellow of the Royal Geographic Society, she dwelled on her favorite subjects, including natural history, geography, anthropology, and medicine, editing in 1959 an exploration book, *Explorer's and Travellers' Tales.*

Tchernine produced two of her most insightful books on the **Abominable Snowman**. At the same time that **Ivan T. Sanderson**'s now classic worldwide survey of unknown hairy hominoids, *Abominable Snowmen: Legend Come to Life* (1961), was being published in America, Tchernine's *The Snowman and Company* (1961) appeared in England. Tchernine's detailed and comprehensive book surveyed most of the centuries of accounts of **Yeti, Almas,** and related unknown primates all across Eurasia and the Orient. Though not so systematic in her discussions as Sanderson, Tchernine was aware of the developments just starting to be noticed in British Columbia and California. Tchernine flavors her stories of the early days of Yeti research with passion and romanticism. Her account of her work and meetings with such individuals as zoologist Vladimir Tschernezky, primatologist W. C. Osman Hill, expedition sponsor **Tom Slick,** and expedition leaders John Hunt and Ralph Izzard provides a valuable behind-the-scenes look at some important historical cryptozoological moments. Tchernine, for example, appears to have been present in 1958 when Slick and Hill discussed, secretly, the remarkable find of the **Pangboche Hand.**

In 1970 Tchernine's *The Yeti* was published in England. (It was published as *In Pursuit of the Abominable Snowman* in 1971 in the United States.) Tchernine wrote that her second book on the subject was the first's "logical continuation: new facts, and very occasional laughter." *The Yeti* delved deeper into Russian research and brought forth considerable information on the Almas and the **Minnesota Iceman,** with sidetrips to Borneo and California. It is a rich book that reflects the good-humored journey she took in researching her stories, or as she said, "as information unfolded from my hammering out through legend, superstition, deceit, fear, and FACT. Knowledge came, not in carefully compiled documentation, but from far-flung sources and unexpected news."

TEH-LMA

The *teh-lma* ("That There Little Thing") is the smallest of several kinds of **Yetis** reported from the Himalayas. These animals are generally said to be three feet to four and a half feet tall, with hunched shoulders and a sharply pointed head that slopes back from the forehead. They are covered with thick reddish-gray hair. They inhabit the steamy mountain valleys of Nepal and Sikkim, surviving on a diet of frogs and other small animals.

During the *Daily Mail* Himalayan Snowman Expedition of 1954, American naturalist **Gerald Russell** first heard about a small Yeti that locals called the Teh-lma. After examining Teh-lma droppings, he concluded that this frog-eating kind of Yeti lived in the more tropical valleys of Nepal. As a member of the 1958 Slick-Johnson Snowman Expedition, Russell would encounter the Teh-lma again. Russell's guide, Sherpa Da Temba, and another eyewitness saw a Teh-lma in the middle of a creek in the Chhoyang River Valley in April. Russell, though he did not observe the Teh-lma himself, was able to find its tracks on more than one occasion and gathered other valuable evidence of their existence.

The Teh-lma are akin but different from the other Asian **Proto-Pygmies** such as the probably extinct **Nittaewo.** Sir Edmund Hillary and Desmond Doig note that in Bhutan, Sikkim, and southeastern Tibet, they are called Pyar-them. Of all of the "kinds" of Yetis, these "little Yetis," **Ivan T. Sanderson** says, "are the least known and the most neglected by everyone."

TELEBIOLOGY

A major debate raging within cryptozoology is whether it is necessary to kill an animal to prove that an undiscovered species exists. This questions whether the old methods of collecting animals have a place in modern cryptozoology. The cryptozoological theorist **Mark A. Hall** has proposed a new technique for studying **cryptids.** He calls it "telebiology." He writes that if, for example, **Bigfoot** hunters could obtain temporary captives, we should conduct various biochemical and DNA tests, and then set them free. He envisions this approach, telebiology, as part of a means by which we can begin to study the cryptids that have been the object of cryptozoology. Writing in *The Yeti, Bigfoot & True Giants* (1997), Hall notes that by using telebiology we make "the effort to study animals at a distance, using our brains and technology, [and] we can succeed where others have failed in the past. If we can accept that starting to study a species with a dead animal can be difficult, then we can put that goal at the end of the process instead of making it a requirement to do anything at all."

TESSIE

Many **Lake Monsters** have names that take their inspiration from the **Loch Ness Monster**'s Nessie. Lake Tahoe in California claims Tahoe Tessie or simply Tessie.

Washoe Indian legends spoke of monsters inhabiting the lake. Skeptics claim that Tessie eyewitnesses are mistaking logs or waves for sea monsters. Scientists with the U.S. Davis Tahoe Research Group under Professor Charles Goldman came to the lake in 1984 to investigate Tessie, with inconclusive results. Bob McCormick, who thinks Tessie may be a sturgeon, says that witnesses "see something long, very long, usually at least twenty feet long, that moves in the water; it's very dark, smooth; it rolls through the water." Local author John Roush holds that Tessie is a rogue giant sturgeon.

According to a 1998 report, a new mapping project by the U.S. Geological Survey is surveying the crystal-clear waters of Lake Tahoe, with scientists probing under the surface to chart the bottom of the lake. Perhaps their efforts will solve the mystery.

The Tahoe Tessie Museum and phone hotline for sightings have been established in King's Beach on the north shore of the lake.

THOMAS, LARS (1960–)

Danish cryptozoologist, zoologist, author, and translator Lars Thomas was born in Copenhagen. After graduating as a marine biologist from the University of Copenhagen in 1986, Thomas specialized in fish morphology. He has since analyzed fish artifacts from Danish and Greenlandic kitchen middens, and from the stomach contents of various fish-eating animals. Thomas's interest in cryptozoology began in his early teens. He has written a number of cryptozoological books and many articles that have been published in English (in *Strange Magazine, Fortean Times, Fortean Studies,* and *Animals & Men*). Most of his output, however, is available only in Danish.

Thomas has traveled extensively in search of strange creatures. In 1990, Thomas organized and led the seven-person Operation Exmoor expedition to the south of Britain in search of the Exmoor Beast. Though it did not find the beast as such, it did collect a tuft of hair at the site of a killed sheep; that later analysis showed it to be hair from a puma.

Since then, Thomas has conducted research on Denmark's own mystery cats. He also conducted an eighteen-month search for **Thylacines,** Giant Monitor Lizards, **Moas,** Huia-birds, Giant Geckos, and an unknown, unnamed mystery bird in Australia and New Zealand.

Thomas's travels have also taken him to Lake Storsjön in Sweden looking for **Storsjoodjuret,** the monster that allegedly dwells there. In his judgment most of the sightings in that particular lake can be explained by swimming moose. He has also polished a study of Hans Egedes's original description of the **Sea Serpent** sighting, the same description on which **Bernard Heuvelmans** based his description of the Superotter. Thomas also found a Maya carving in Xunantunich, in western Belize, which local people claim shows the mysterious **Sisemite.**

THUNDERBIRD

"Thunderbird" is the name given to a large, condor-like bird reported throughout North America since the beginning of historic records. Most people are familiar with Native American folklore and traditions about Thunderbirds, but cryptozoologists have also collected current sightings and case material. **Mark A. Hall**'s *Thunderbirds—The Living Legend!* (2nd edition, 1994) is the only detailed discussion of modern sightings from Appalachia and the Black Forest of Pennsylvania to the plains of Illinois and the Ozarks of Arkansas.

From their descriptions as large dark-colored, gliding birds with wingspans over fifteen feet wide, Thunderbirds seem to be associated with the largest-known soaring birds accepted by ornithologists—the condors. The Andean condor, *Vulturgryphus,* lives from seven thousand to sixteen thousand feet up in the Andes, from Colombia south to Tierra del Fuego. It is the world's largest flying bird, with a wingspan of about ten feet (it can reach twelve feet in some specimens). The Andean condor is glossy black with white upper-wing coverts, a bald head, and a white collar of feathers around its neck. The condors are known to attack and kill sick and small animals for food, though their primary source of meals is carrion, namely dead deer, horses, sheep, and rabbits. Most bird experts state that the feet of this condor and its North American cousin are too weak to carry food even moderately far distances.

The California condor, *Gymnogyps californianus,* is smaller than the Andean condor. However, with a nine-foot wingspan, it is the largest flying bird in North America. The sooty black California condor lacks the white neck collar. The 1977 Illinois Thunderbird eyewitnesses, highlighted in the **Lawndale Incident,** noted white neck feathers, which would mean these cryptids are closer in appearance to the Andean condor than to the California specimen.

Each year in late March, early April, July, and August, from the Ozarks down the Ohio River Valley and into the Appalachian Mountains, an irregular and noticeable migration of big birds seems to be occurring, and these may be Thunderbirds. Similar appearances in the western mountain states show a comparable pattern. Thunderbirds are still found in the wilderness craggies of the Bald Mountains (in prehistoric times believed by Indians to be inhabited by Thunderbirds) and in the sheer cliff caves of the Smokies and Ozarks (where backwoods folk still tell of encounters with giant birds).

The most likely zoological candidates for Thunderbirds may be supposedly recently extinct Teratorns. Alan Feduccia in *The Age of Birds* (1986) writes: "Perhaps the most remarkable of the Ice Age vulturine birds found in the New World were the teratorns. . . . The very common *Teratornis merriami* had a wingspan of eleven to twelve feet, and *Teratornis incredibilis,* known from Pleistocene deposits in Nevada and California, had a wingspan that may have approached seventeen feet. But the real giant was an Argentine fossil . . . nearly twice the size of *Teratornis merriami,* [which] stood five feet tall and had a wing span of about twenty-four feet; it is the largest flying bird known to science."

Dr. Kenneth E. Campbell, one of the discoverers of the Argentine giant, has long studied the Teratorns. He disagrees with the common wisdom that they, like condors, were carrion-eaters. Campbell believes they were predators, based upon his investigation of *Teratornis merriami,* which are so numerous at the La Brea tar pits. "The long, narrow hooked beak and the type of mechanism found in this species are similar to those that grabbed small animals with their beaks and swallowed them whole," Campbell has said.

The bones of the Teratorns have turned up in deposits from California to Florida. Apparently they were found throughout the United States, as well as the northern parts of Mexico. This fits nicely with the reports of the Thunderbird, which are centered in the same geographical areas. Furthermore, the bones, some as recent as eight thousand years old, have almost always been found in conjunction with human habitation sites. Were Native Americans killing these condor-like birds for their feathers or in retaliation for kidnapping their stock and children?

Did the Teratorns look like the Thunderbirds? Interestingly, *National Geographic* and other official efforts to represent the Teratorns have shown them as condor-like with white ruffs around their neck, obviously modeling them after the Andean, not the California, condor. Still, as with all fossil remains, we really do not know what the Teratorns looked like.

THYLACINE

The thylacine or Tasmanian wolf or tiger is a scientifically accepted species, a large marsupial native to Tasmania, not to be confused with the **Queensland Tiger.** The thylacine is a strange doglike animal with brown fur and vertical dark stripes running down its lower back. Old film footage shows that it routinely walked on all fours (although some eyewitnesses mentioned that the thylacine could stand on its back legs). It would regularly open and close its mouth to be as wide as its dog-

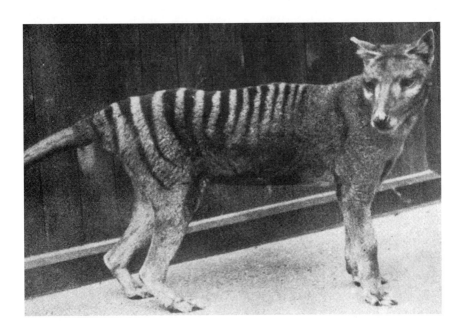

The last accepted living example of the Tasmanian wolf or thylacine was this individual, who died on September 7, 1936. (Hobart Domain Zoo)

shaped head. It is, however, a true pouched marsupial and a relative of the Tasmanian Devil. The word "thylacine" comes from its Latin name, *Thylacinus cynocephalus.* Most scientists believe the animal is extinct; however, each year a score of unconfirmed sightings are reported from the relatively uninhabited areas of Tasmania, Iran Jaya, New Guinea, and mainland Australia. Expeditions in search of the thylacine are frequent, and official wildlife departments in these areas take the sightings seriously.

TITMUS, ROBERT (1919–1997)

Robert Titmus of Harrison Hot Springs, British Columbia, was involved in **Bigfoot** events, or at least in unknown hairy hominid incidents, long before the modern American encounters began in 1958. While serving in the U.S. Marine Corps in the South Pacific during World War II, Titmus saw what he believed to be an unidentified hairy biped (though he did not realize it then), at a time when Bigfoot and **Sasquatch** were not household words.

Bob Titmus with a Bigfoot track. (John Green)

Titmus, an animal tracker and a taxidermist, was a friend of Jerry Crew, the construction worker who was one of the first to come upon huge unknown tracks at Bluff Creek, California, in August 1958. Titmus taught Crew how to work with plaster of Paris and how to make the first impression of the Bluff Creek "Bigfoot" track that was cast on October 1, 1958. Crew showed that cast to local newspaperman Andrew Genzoli (who first coined the phrase "Bigfoot") of Eureka's *Humboldt Times,* and pictures of Crew holding the Bigfoot footcast near his own foot were sent worldwide. Bigfoot had arrived, thanks in part to Titmus.

Titmus had always been the quiet focus of the North American unknown-hominid search effort. When **John Green** first came to investigate the Crew footprint finds, Green went to Titmus, and the two became friends. Titmus became a recognized authority who could find prints, recognize individual Bigfoots by their tracks, and show the casts of many Bigfoot tracks to the waves of searchers who came after him.

René Dahinden, Tom Slick, Ivan T. Sanderson, and many others visited Titmus over the years. On his Pacific Northwest Expedition, Slick hired him to be one of its "leaders" for several months in the late 1950s. When that effort changed directions, Titmus, who had become a close associate of Green and Dahinden, moved to British Columbia and spent the rest of his life delving into the mystery of the Bigfoot and Sasquatch from there. For a brief time Slick sponsored something he called the British Columbia Expedition in the early 1960s, and Titmus was one of its major members. Slick also sent Titmus to the University of Washington Hospital to study embalming techniques, in the belief that the 1961 Bigfoot/Sasquatch hunt would capture or kill a specimen.

From the 1960s until his death, Titmus would track the elusive Bigfoot/Sasquatch from Alaska to northern California. Nine days after Roger Patterson and Bob Gimlin took their film of an alleged Bigfoot in 1967, Titmus was there, tracking and examining the distances that the creature reportedly had covered. He would tell of having seen Sasquatch two times during these years and of having tracked the animals dozens of times. His collection of Sasquatch footprint casts is possibly the largest in existence. In 1987, the board of directors of the **International Society of Cryptozoology** recognized Titmus as one of its first honorary members.

Titmus never wrote about his work, instead sharing his discoveries down through the decades with others, including Green, Dahinden, Slick, **Grover Krantz, Jeff Meldrum,** and **Loren Coleman.**

Titmus, long ill, died of a heart attack on July 1, 1997, at Chilliwack, British Columbia.

TRAN HONG VIET (1942–)

Tran Hong Viet, the chairman of the Zoology Department of Teachers Training College–Vietnam National University, has studied Vietnamese fauna for more than a quarter of a century as part of an effort to preserve Vietnam's natural environment. His research has led to knowledge of **cryptids** and rare animals, including data on the **Nguoi Rung** ("Wildman") of Vietnam.

His Nguoi Rung investigation, which began in 1977, has yielded footprints and other evidence. In 1982, he found and made a cast of a broad but human-sized unknown hominoid footprint on the slopes of Chu Mo Ray near the Cambodian border in Kontum Province.

His studies of the Nguoi Rung continue currently through his position as director of the **Vietnam Cryptozoic and Rare Animals Research Center.** In 1998, the Vietnamese government awarded him a grant to publish his cryptozoological writings.

TRUE GIANT

In the late 1960s, **Bigfoot** hunter Roger Patterson wondered if something bigger than **Sasquatch** were not out there, leaving twenty-two-inch-long tracks. He called it a "Giant Hairy Ape." Other researchers, studying tracks nearly two feet long, harbored similar suspicions about the presence of an enormous non-Bigfoot primate. The Canadian researcher **John Green,** from tracks and eyewitness testimony he deemed persuasive, decided that a whole group of "giants" existed in Bigfoot country. **Mark A. Hall** gave this group of creatures the name True Giants after analyzing the growing body of evidence pointing to the existence of extremely large, hairy hominoids that routinely left long, *four*-toed prints.

For creatures said to be ten to twenty feet tall, the term True Giants is indeed appropriate. The big bodies of True Giants are remarkably lean, if not lanky, and are covered with reddish-brown or darker hair that is longer on the head and thinner on the arms. They appear to have no neck, and their facial features are flat. Their hands are enormous and flat. Their feet measure about ten inches wide by twenty-one inches long or longer, and they have four visible toes; if they have a fifth vestigial toe, it does not show up in most prints.

True Giants are reported in wooded mountain areas around the world, mostly in temperate zones, and are known by such native names as *gilyuk, misabe, chenoo, nyalmo, orang dalam,* and *ferla mohr.* Hall's analysis of old folklore and native traditions have convinced him that the True Giants were the cannibals of our past, although they were not man-eaters routinely; they have avoided contact with most humans in modern times.

Hall links True Giants to the fossil form known as *Gigantopithecus.* Besides Hall's discussions in his 1997 book, *The Yeti, Bigfoot, & True Giants,* **Loren Coleman** and **Patrick Huyghe** also write about this type of unknown primate in *The Field Guide to Bigfoot, Yeti, and Other Mystery Primates Worldwide* (1999).

U

UCU

Reports of South American creatures looking like **Bigfoot** of the montane forests of North America are hard to come by, except in the Andes. Creatures variously called the Ucu, Ucumar, and the Ukumar-zupai appear to be the South American equivalent of Bigfoot.

In May 1958, a party of campers at Rengo, fifty miles from Santiago, Chile, reportedly saw an "apeman." Police investigated and took affidavits. One witness, Carlos Manuel Soto, swore, "I saw an enormous man covered with hair in the Cordilleras."

Other evidence for such creatures has been recorded from about the same time in the region. In 1956, geologist Audio L. Pich found on the Argentinian side of the Andes, at a height of over sixteen thousand feet, seventeen-inch-long human-like prints. The next year, similar tracks showed up in La Salta Province, Argentina. Residents of Tolor Grande told newspaper reporters that a nightly chorus of "eerie calls" emanating from the Curu-Curu Mountains was frightening the community. The cries were attributed to a creature known as Ukumar-zupai.

In *The Evidence for Bigfoot and Other Man-Beasts,* Janet and Colin Bord write:

> In 1979, anthropologist Silva Alicia Barrios visited the mountainous regions of northern Argentina and heard about "a strange monkey" called Ucumar or Ucu. Don Pepe, who lives on the Argentina/Bolivia border and knows the countryside well, describes the Ucu: "The Ucu lives in the hills, there in back of El Chorro [the mountainous zone with tropical vegetation], and likes to scream at the cows and chickens. It's a 'zuncho' [robust and bulky] animal and even though it doesn't run a lot, it's very strong. It's never come close to me but it has some of my countrymen. I've seen Ucus, and Ucus trapping people. If the Ucu catches someone, the best thing to do is urinate because then it will let go. The Ucu likes to eat payo, the plant whose inside is similar to cabbage. It's big, the size of a fleecy dog, and walks erect. The noise they make sounds like uhu, uhu, uhu . . . ," which

[Ivan T.] Sanderson compared with the Ugh, Ugh, Ugh reported by Albert Ostman, who claimed to have been held captive by a family of Bigfeet in British Columbia in 1924.

According to Pablo Latapi Ortega, traditions of these giant apemen continue today in Argentina, where they are called Ucumar.

Ivan T. Sanderson and **Mark A. Hall** link the montane forest accounts of the **Sisemite** from near Mount Kacharul, Guatemala, to **Sasquatch,** Bigfoot, and the Ucu/Ucumar.

UFITI

The first chimpanzee (*Pan troglodytes*) to reach a zoo in England was brought to Bristol in the autumn of 1834 by a Captain Wood, who had picked it up on the Gambia Coast. Since that time, it has always

Ufiti was photographed in 1959, near Lake Nyasa, Africa, before she was captured in 1964. (Nyasaland Information Department)

been understood that chimpanzees exist in very specific locations in Africa. Three subspecies of chimpanzee have been identified: Central African chimpanzee, *Pan troglodytes troglodytes*; West African chimpanzee, *Pan troglodytes verus*; and the Eastern chimpanzee, *Pan troglodytes schweinfurthi.* Zaire's bonobo (*Pan paniscus*) which formerly was called the "Pygmy chimpanzee" is today seen as a separate species, with distinctive physical and behavioral characteristics.

Much confusion, however, still exists in Africa about just what kinds of apes live there. **Ivan T. Sanderson** reported on the remarkable unknown great apes, the Tano Giant of West Africa and the *muhalu* of the Ituri Forest, Congo. His friend, the animal collector Charles Cordier, found an unknown ape's track in the eastern forests of the former Zaire. Cordier also collected native traditions of a large undiscovered anthropoid in the area that was called *kikomba, apamandi, zaluzugu,* or *tshingombe* by different local peoples. Cryptozoologist **Bernard Heuvelmans** points out that in Kenya J. A. G. Elliot collected accounts of the *ngoloko,* another unique unidentified pongid.

Even when apes are caught in Africa, the picture sometimes gets muddled. In 1967, for example, the Basel Zoo received an alleged Koolokamba or gorilla-like chimpanzee (*Pan troglodytes koolokamba,* an unrecognized subspecies), which turned out to be a red-backed female gorilla. Jonathan Kingdon, in *Field Guide to African Mammals* (1997), suggests that there may be a mountain-dwelling version of the bonobo, as well as the fully recognized lowland type. The incident of *Ufiti* ("ghost") is also worth chronicling.

Ufiti was first seen near Lake Nyasa in August 1959. The Nyasaland Information Department recounts that first sighting in melodramatic fashion: "The first white man to see the strange monster opened fire with a revolver as it slunk eerily along the road in the misty moonlight." When Ufiti was finally photographed, experts could see that it was a chimpanzee, though a very out-of-place one. It was found along the Limpasa River in Malawi, almost five hundred miles from the nearest chimpanzee colony in Tanzania's Nkungwe Mountains.

In many ways Ufiti, a female, was no typical chimpanzee. She should have resembled the Eastern subspecies, but she was almost six feet tall and had a completely black face, ears, hands, and feet, which made her more like the West African forms. Ufiti also had a gray lumbar saddle (pale gray hair on her back), which is found among mature male gorillas (traditionally called "silverbacks"), but unknown (until Ufiti) in chimpanzees.

From this study of the findings made of the March 1960 Rhodes-Livingston Museum Ufiti Field Expedition, the cryptozoologist and primatologist W. C. Osman Hill concluded that while Ufiti was indeed a chimpanzee, it was a remarkable one. Hill collected other older reports of chimpanzee-like apes from Malawi's dense forests. From this evidence he theorized that Ufiti was an example of an undiscovered chimpanzee subspecies with more affinities to the Western than to Eastern varieties, though it lived closer to the known Eastern chimpanzees. He urged that more specimens be recovered.

The story, however, ends sadly, the mystery unsolved. The original female Ufiti was captured and sent to the Chester Zoo in England in March 1964. There she lived for a little over a month before her deteriorating health forced her keepers to euthanize her. The Ufiti saga has been documented in the writings of Ivan T. Sanderson, **Loren Coleman,** and **Karl Shuker,** but the long-neglected question of whether Ufiti might be a new subspecies of Malawi chimpanzees awaits an answer.

V

VIETNAM CRYPTOZOIC AND RARE ANIMALS RESEARCH CENTER

Ongoing endeavors in several countries seek to formalize and institutionalize the study of cryptozoology. Among the most remarkable and well-organized efforts is one occurring in Vietnam.

Vietnam is situated in a tropical transition zone for a variety of plants and animals spreading to the north (India, China) and to the south (Malay and Indonesian archipelago). As a consequence, Vietnam has rich and diverse fauna and flora.

Studies of Vietnam's fauna began long ago with the first publications by Le Quy Don in 1724–84 (regarding *Van dai loai ngu*), Dampier in 1703 (concerning some animals collected in Con Dao Island), and Linnaeus, 1758 (regarding the notice of jungle fowl *Phasianus gallus* found in Con Dao Island). Nearly three centuries later, many areas in the country still remain under investigation. After the Vietnam War, expeditions into the Vu Quang forest reserve in central Vietnam have found many new species, including **saola,** a robust muntjac deer, and a small muntjac species, the last of which was discovered in the forests of Quang Tri Province, a region that suffered heavy bombing during the war. These are the first new large mammals science has discovered since early in this century.

Vietnam's scientists are convinced that many species have yet to be discovered. Interestingly, Vietnam has no complete classification key for the country's fauna. But Vietnam's government and its scientists have decided that a general inventory of the fauna needed to be urgently addressed, and so the Vietnam Cryptozoic and Rare Animals Research Center was established on the first of May 1997 in the Teachers Training College–Vietnam National University, Hanoi, with this goal in mind. The director of the center is Professor **Tran Hong Viet,** chairman of the university's Zoology Department.

WAITOREKE

Next to the surviving **Moa** reports, the most discussed mystery animal of New Zealand is the Waitoreke. Maoris and early colonists on the nation's South Island frequently reported a small otter-like animal known as the Kaureke and also as the Waitoreke. The Maori word *waitoreke* comes from a root word for "water." Related words such as *waikeri* ("swamp") and *waikare* ("clear water") exist in the Maori language. Today, the word "Waitoreke" is the one used in cryptozoological contexts.

Theorists have speculated that the Waitoreke is an otter species, a seal species, and even a beaver. Others have mentioned that it may be of the order Monotremata (like the platypus and echidnas, egg-laying mammals). **Bernard Heuvelmans** writes of the Waitoreke in his 1986 checklist: "It is not excluded that it could be a species of monotreme (an archaic oviparous mammal-like platypus) rather than a new species of otter." The Waitoreke's true identity remains a mystery.

WALSH, DAVE (1973–)

Dave Walsh has this to say about himself:

> Dave Walsh spent what he has only recently realized to be a subtly odd childhood in the countryside of Co. Wexford, Ire-

land. His immersion in the study of cryptozoology, psychology, philosophy, and the paranormal probably began at a very early age, due to spending far too much time in his own company. After a brief and far too eventful academic career and a flirtation with microelectronics, Walsh settled into a rather eclectic lifestyle, working as an Internet communications specialist and website designer, part-time journalist, and occasional gentleman adventurer.

Walsh is a founding member and Chair of the Internet department at the Charles Fort Institute, a resource for scholarship and research in the understanding of strange experiences and anomalous phenomena. He has penned articles for numerous publications keeping a uniquely Irish perspective on reports worldwide and at home.

While the finding of a "real" animal at the end of the cryptozoology trail is the grail of many a researcher, Walsh's interest in Irish mystery animals does not rely on a tangible outcome, instead complimenting a concept of the poet John Keats: "Negative Capability, that is when man is capable of being in uncertainties, mysteries, doubts, without any irritable reaching after fact and reason."

In August 1998, Walsh traveled to Norway to take part in an expedition investigating claims of a lake monster in Seljord, Telemark. Accounts of that rather turbulent event can be read on-line in *Blather* and Kurt Burchfiel's account on the *Strange* website in addition to Walsh's articles in *Animals & Men* and *Fortean Times*. The expedition was captured on film for a Discovery Channel documentary.

WASSON, BARBARA (1927–1998)

Barbara Wasson Butler, using the name Barbara Wasson, was an insightful **Bigfoot** investigator. She lived in Bend, Oregon, and investigated cases throughout the Pacific Northwest.

Wasson received her bachelor's degree in psychology from the University of California–Berkeley in 1948, and her master's in psychology from Washington University, St. Louis, in 1962. She spent her professional career in clinical work in Missouri and Oregon. For years she maintained a private practice as a clinical member of the American Association of Marriage & Family Therapists, but in her spare time, she pursued Bigfoot passionately.

Wasson's initial book was the first to detail her thoughts on the researchers as well as the **cryptids** being researched. She was known for her pointed criticism of some fellow members of the Bigfoot community, whose disagreements prevented, in Wasson's judgment, the sort of teamwork essential to productive investigative efforts. Because of her clinical training and telling remarks, her book serves as one of the few examples of an attempt to analyze the field psychologically.

Barbara Wasson, 1977, in the Onion Lake area of California, searching for traces of Bigfoot. Fish Lake, noted on the sign, was the area where Tom Slick searched for Giant Salamanders. (René Dahinden)

She died on October 9, 1998, after a five-month battle with pancreatic cancer.

WINNIPOGO

The **Lake Monster** of Lake Winnipegosis, Manitoba, Canada, is called Winnipogo. It is described as serpentine and usually over twenty feet long. Sightings have been investigated by the University of Manitoba's Dr. James McLeod. In the 1930s, an unusual bone, apparently a huge spinal vertebra, was found by Oscar Frederickson on the shore of this lake, but was later lost in a fire. A wooden copy of the bone was shown to McLeod, who was surprised to see that it resembled the vertebra of a whalelike animal extinct for 4 million years. The **Loch Ness Monsters** investigator **Roy Mackal** finds the reports worthy of serious consideration based on his conversation with McLeod and his examination of the sightings evidence.

WOOD, FORREST G. (1919–1992)

Born in South Bend, Indiana, Forrest G. Wood graduated from Earlham College in 1940. After World War II, he studied marine biology at Yale, earning his master's degree, but falling short of his doctorate when he did not complete his dissertation. His plans to finish were interrupted in 1950 when he was appointed to be the American Museum of Natural History's first resident biologist on Bimini, in the British West Indies.

From there, Wood became the first curator at Florida's new Marine Studios (later renamed Marineland), the world's first oceanarium or marine park. During the 1960s and 1970s, Wood worked for the U.S. Navy, heading its marine mammal programs. He authored the now classic book *Marine Mammals and Man: The Navy's Porpoises and Sea Lions* (1973).

Wood was interested in cryptozoology for most of his life, specifically in its marine aspects—the **Sea Serpent** and **Giant Octopus.** It was while in Bimini in the 1950s that Wood first heard reports and tales of the Giant Octopus. Then, working at Marineland, Wood became interested in the St. Augustine, Florida, monster—thought by some to be the remains of a Giant Octopus—in 1957, and his investigation of the matter spanned a number of years. He tracked down a surviving sample of the St. Augustine specimen at the Smithsonian, and with biologist Joseph F. Gennaro, obtained an analysis of it. Wood and Gennaro's article on this affair in *Natural History* (March 1971) attracted attention and sparked a debate that continues to this day.

As one of its founding members, Wood was active in the **International Society of Cryptozoology** (ISC). Shortly before his death on May 17, 1992, he was named the ISC's first American honorary member.

WOODLAND BISON

When is the last time a new large mammal was "discovered" in North America?

According to zoologist **Ivan T. Sanderson,** a herd of wild woodland bison (*Bison bison athabasca*) was found unexpectedly in 1960, in a remote section of the Canadian Northwest Territories—even though the woodland bison had been supposedly exterminated throughout North America and reduced to a handful of nearly domesticated animals on a managed reservation hundreds of miles away. The discovery of this wild relict population of these Pleistocene-era bison, though not a new species, was quite a surprise to wildlife specialists.

The woodland bison of Canada is a little larger and darker, with more slender, longer horns than the traditional American bison (or "American buffalo") with which most people are familiar.

WRIGHT, BRUCE S. (1912—1975)

Born in Quebec City, Bruce S. Wright was an excellent athlete and marksman in his school and college days. His degree in forestry led him to a post with the Dominion Forest Service. He served with the Canadian navy during War World II. A 1968 book, *The Frogmen of Burma,* relates his part in the formation and commanding of the Canadian navy's Sea Reconnaissance Unit.

Subsequently, he carried out graduate study in wildlife management and became the director of the Northeastern Wildlife Station at the University of New Brunswick. His career as a writer began in 1938 with articles on conservation, and he continued to write articles and books on wildlife throughout his life.

Although a professional scientist, Wright routinely tackled cryptozoological subjects. One early all-consuming passion was research into the survival of the eastern mountain lion, including the enigma of Canadian **Black Panther** reports. Wright's 1959 book, *The Ghost of North America,* was published at a time when most zoologists were certain that the eastern mountain lion was extinct. (Today, the province of New Brunswick officially recognizes the reality of mountain lions within its borders; the animals have endangered-species status.) A revised, expanded edition of his original work, *The Eastern Panther: A Question of Survival,* appeared in 1972.

Wright investigated and wrote about other **cryptids,** including the survival of the West Indian monk seal in the 1960s, the **Lusca** of the Bahamas in 1967, and **Bigfoot/Sasquatch** in 1969 and 1971. He carried on an active correspondence with other cryptozoologists, including **Ivan T. Sanderson** and **Loren Coleman,** before his death in 1975.

There is a movement to honor his work to protect the mountain lion by naming a large area of the northern Maine and New Brunswick woods the Bruce S. Wright Nature Preserve.

XING-XING

Sightings of man-sized or smaller anthropoid apes recorded from southern China are often lumped with the body of traditions linked to the **Yeren** or Wildman. However, a distinctive animal, called by the locals the *xing-xing,* may be an undiscovered orangutan. In **Bernard Heuvelmans**'s view, these possibly are mainland orangutans that have survived from the Pleistocene era. They are, he says, similar in appearance to other unknown orang-like animals from Vietnam (*kra-dhan*), Burma (*iu-wun*), and Assam (*olo-banda, bir-sindic*).

Y

YAMENEKO

The *yameneko* is the name the Japanese first gave to a gray-brown, small domestic-sized felid, found on the 113-square-mile island of Iriomote-jima, at the southern end of the Japanese Ryukyu Islands. This attractive wild cat has dark spots in dense longitudinal rows that coalesce into bands. Before the rumors of the Yameneko, zoologists were confident that all the world's cat species had been described and named. Then in 1965, Japanese author-naturalist Yukio Togawa produced evidence, including at least one living animal, of a new cat from the remote, unexplored, rainforest-covered island of Iriomotejima.

Initially, the cat was placed in its own genus, *Mayailurus iriomotensis*. Today, the Yameneko or Iriomote cat is thought to be either a subspecies of the leopard cat *Prionailurus bengalensis* or a species in its own right, *Felis iriomotensis*.

As a point of interest, cryptozoologist **Karl Shuker** points out that a dwarf pig, unknown to science until found on this same island in 1974, hints that there may be yet more surprises in store at the home of the Yameneko.

YEREN

The *yeren* ("Wildman") has figured in central and southern Chinese folk traditions for centuries. Many encounters are recorded in the thickly forested regions of central and south China. The Yeren is said to be bipedal, a little over six feet tall with a heavy coat of red-brown hair. Large footprints, fourteen to sixteen inches in length, are found. In some locations, a second form of Yeren reportedly goes about on all fours and has longer red hair. Chinese researchers suggest that the first type of Yeren is a surviving *Gigantopithecus*, while other cryptozoologists sense the term Yeren may also apply to a second type of cryptid, which may be an undiscovered variety of mainland orangutan (**Xing-xing**), perhaps a relict population from the Pleistocene era.

YETI

The term "Yeti" comes from the Sherpa phrase *yet-teh,* which roughly translates into "That Thing." In the West, this creature is often called the **Abominable Snowman,** originating in the mistranslation of a generic term for these creatures in 1921.

The first known reference in English to the animal we now know as the Yeti is in an 1832 issue of the *Journal of the Asiatic Society of Bengal.* Mention is made of a sighting by native hunters in a northern Nepal province of a hairy, tailless biped. The writer, a British resident in the court of Nepal, thought the natives had seen an orangutan. Orangutans, of course, are not known to exist in mainland Asia. In *Among the Himalayas* (1899), Major L. A. Waddell dismissed sightings of mysterious Wildmen in Tibet as either tall tales or observations of "great yellow snow-bears."

On an Everest expedition in September 1921, Lieutenant Colonel C. K. Howard-Bury and his companions found enigmatic footprints, three times the size of human tracks, on the mountainside. The Sherpa guides attributed them to the *meh-teh* ("manlike thing that is not a man"), but its mistranslation in the *Calcutta Statesman* account of the incident resulted in the unfortunate appellation "Abominable Snowman." Howard-Bury's belief that the tracks were "probably caused by a large 'loping' gray wolf, which in the soft snow formed double tracks rather like those of a barefooted man" did not match the descriptions of the footprints, or the fact there are no known wolves in the Himalayas.

In 1925, British photographer N. A. Tombazi saw, at fifteen thousand feet near a glacier in the Himalayan range, a naked "figure in outline . . . exactly like a human being" walking through the snow. Its tracks were "similar in shape to those of a man, but only six to seven inches long by four inches wide at the broadest part of the foot. . . . The prints were undoubtedly of a biped, the order of the spoor [i.e., tracks] having no characteristics whatever of any imaginable quadruped."

More recent sightings do occur. In September 1998, an American mountain climber, Craig Calonica, on his way back to base camp on the Chinese side of Mount Everest, encountered two bipedal creatures— Yeti—walking together. They had thick, shiny black fur, with long arms and large hands. Calonica's Nepali cook also saw the Yeti. Calonica was firm in his insistence that "what I saw was not human . . . not a gorilla, not [a] bear, not a goat, and it was not a deer."

Famous Italian mountain climber Reinhold Messner told reporters

Sir Edmund Hillary attempted, in 1960, to debunk the Yeti when he returned with a Sherpa who carried a ceremonial skullcap made in imitation of the head of the creature. Bernard Heuvelmans and others quickly identified the skullcap as a ritual object made from the skin of the serow, a goatlike animal. (Chicago Daily News)

that in 1986 and in 1997 he experienced a total of four Yeti sightings. In one case, he said, he was so close to one that he could easily have touched it. He also obtained a skeleton, and he took clear photographs of the animals. They were, he alleged, large bears that often walk on two feet. Messner's book, *Yeti: Legende und Wirklichkeit* (published in German in 1998), however, reveals nothing earthshaking.

So what is the Yeti? Messner's bear? Howard-Bury's wolf? The British resident's orangutan? A mythological creature? Or an unknown anthropoid? The controversy continues. At the heart of it, however, are sightings, prints, and even physical evidence that seem to resist mundane accounting. Indeed, the Yeti is not one creature, but several different types of unknown primates all known as Yeti.

Mountaineers from England, Canada, the United States, Germany, Switzerland, and other Western nations have registered intriguing sightings of large apelike animals and collected prints associated with them. Reports also come from the Sherpa, Nepalese, and Tibetan people who inhabit the region. Descriptions are sufficiently consistent that sympathetic investigators believe they can discern two or three different kinds of animals from them. One is the Meh-teh. Zoologist Edward Cronin, who found tracks of what he believed to be the animal during a 1972 scientific expedition, summarizes in his book *The Arun* witnesses' descriptions thus:

This 1950s reconstruction of Yeti appears to most closely match the eyewitness descriptions of the Met-teh. (Bernard Heuvelmans)

Its body is stocky, apelike in shape, with a distinctly human quality to it, in contrast to that of a bear. It stands five and a half feet tall and is covered with short, coarse hair, reddish-brown to black in color, sometimes with white patches on the chest. The hair is longest on the shoulders. The face is robust, the teeth are quite large, though fangs are not present, and the mouth is wide. The shape of the head is conical, with a pointed crown. The arms are long, reaching almost to the knees. The shoulders are heavy and hunched. There is no tail.

The Dzu-teh ("big thing"), another animal reported as a Yeti, is a big, hulking animal that is usually quadruped but can walk as a biped. It may be a heretofore-uncatalogued large bear. This is the animal that Reinhold Messner claims to have seen. He collected tales of the Chemo, another name for the Dzu-teh, which merely reinforced the conclusion that the animal is a bear. The fact that Dzu-teh raid small livestock holdings and leave behind clawed prints, one on top of another, is a certain indicator that this "Yeti" is a bear.

The third type of Yeti, the **Teh-lma**, seems related to other anthropoids, the **Proto-Pygmies**, reported from throughout some of the remoter tropical valleys of Asia. **Gerald Russell**'s experiences with the *Daily Mail* Expedition of 1954 and **Tom Slick**'s expeditions of 1957–59 produced much evidence for the reality of the Teh-lma's presence (footprints, sightings, and feces). Some forty years ago, the Teh-lma was the major Yeti that was seen and discussed by zoologists who thought it would soon be caught. Sadly, by 1960 most of the funding for Yeti expeditions had dried up. The Teh-lma still remains elusive.

Those who hold that the Yeti is an unknown anthropoid have proposed a range of theories, from the conservative (a small vegetarian ape) to the radical (a surviving *Gigantopithecus*). Of course, part of the problem with these theories and the Yeti is that few have realized there are so many types, and indeed, different theories may be valid with different "Yetis." But until a body is produced, the question—as with so many **cryptids**—remains open.

YOWIE

Australia has its own version of **Bigfoot**, the Yowie, which has been reported primarily in New South Wales and along the Gold Coast of Queensland. Like the word "Bigfoot," "Yowie" has come to indicate any unknown hairy hominoid seen in Australia, and thus the picture has become muddled Down Under. The creature's long history can be traced back to Aboriginal legends.

The earlier name for the creature was the *yahoo*, which according to some accounts was an Aborigine term meaning "devil" or "evil spirit." But more likely, the indirect source of the name was Jonathan Swift, whose *Gulliver's Travels* (1726) concerns, in part, a subhuman race called the Yahoos. Hearing the Aboriginal reports of this unknown primate, nineteenth-century European settlers may have applied the name "Yahoo" to the Australian creature. A hundred years of sightings followed.

Some encounters were vague and a few were detailed, as, for example, Charles Harper's sighting of 1912. Harper, a surveyor from Sydney, and his companions were camping in the jungle along the Currickbilly Mountain range in New South Wales. They heard some sounds and saw a "huge, manlike animal" in the light of their fire. It was beating its chest. This beast had a very small, chinless human face with deeply set eyes and long canine teeth. It was bipedal, covered with long red-brown hair, and stood almost six feet tall. It seemed to have large breasts or a potbelly hanging down between its legs. Harper and his party were happy when the animal moved away.

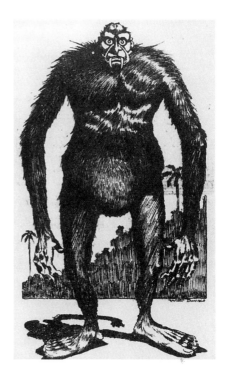

The Bombala Yowie, seen by Charles Harper in southeast Australia in 1912. This fanciful drawing is based on his description. (FPL)

Sometime in the 1970s, the term "Yowie" supplanted "Yahoo." The Yowie today is a popular figure in Australia, and toys and chocolates are made in imitation of what the Yowie is believed to look like. Newspapers report on each new sighting.

In 1997, for instance, a woman residing in Tanimi Desert was awakened at 3:00 A.M. by a horrendous animal-like sound. On searching for the cause of the disturbance, the startled woman became fiercely nauseated when she caught wind of a terrible smell, and then she saw a seven-foot hairy creature destroy her fence as it fled. The following morning, law-enforcement officers found a chewed piece of pipe and huge tracks.

The early accounts of gorilla-like creatures seem to have given way to tales of formidable beasts leaving enormously long footprints with four long toes. Accounts of four-toed **True Giants** may have been mixed in as well.

Z

ZEUGLODON

Zeuglodon is the most commonly used name for a type of long, serpent-like fossil whale. Also called *Basilosaurus*, this extinct genus of primitive whales of the family Basilosauridae (suborder Archaeoceti) is found in Middle and Late Eocene deposits in North America and northern Africa (the Eocene Epoch lasted from 57.8 to 36.6 million years ago). Basilosaurus had primitive dentition and skull architecture and ranged from fifty-five to seventy-five feet long, with a skull five feet in length. Zeuglodons, in recent years, have become the primary focus of several cryptozoology researchers, including Joseph Zarzynski, **Roy Mackal**, and **Gary Mangiacopra**, who theorize that the animal may be responsible for some modern reports of **Lake Monsters** and **Sea Serpents**.

ZUIYO-MARU MONSTER

In April 1977, thirty miles off the coast of Christchurch, New Zealand, the trawler's nets of a Japanese fishing boat, the *Zuiyo-maru*, snared a huge animal carcass of an unknown origin. The crew hauled the monstrous body out of the ocean onto the deck, and Michihiko Yano, the ship's assistant production manager, measured the creature and took some now-famous photographs. The creature was thirty-three feet long and weighed about four thousand pounds. It had a snakelike head at the end of a long, slender neck, giving it an unwhale-like appearance. Some of the crew thought it was a rotten whale, but others were not so sure.

The Zuiyo-maru Monster, which was netted by Japanese fishermen in April 1977. (FPL)

After great difficulty, the stinking Zuiyo-maru Monster was thrown overboard.

Media attention in Japan focused on the plesiosaur-like appearance of the creature. Interest in **Sea Serpents** rose. Toys were produced of the Zuiyo-maru Monster.

But Yano had taken samples of the "horny fiber" from one of the monster's fins. Tests determined the Zuiyo-maru Monster was a decomposed basking shark, although few today know that part of the story.

APPENDIX

CRYPTOZOOLOGY MUSEUMS AND EXHIBITIONS

Around the world museums and exhibitions of a cryptozoological nature educate and attract tourists, children, researchers, and the public. Some examples:

- The Smithsonian Institution's Natural History Museum in Washington, D.C., has an exhibit on the giant squid, traditionally known as the Kraken.

- At Washington State University, in Pullman, the Museum of Anthropology in College Hall holds a Bigfoot display.

- Willow Creek, California, has the giant Jim McClarin–carved statue of Bigfoot, and a museum with Bob Titmus's entire Bigfoot collection. Garberville, California, features the Legend of Bigfoot, which has a single life-size redwood Bigfoot, but not much more. The Michigan Magazine Museum is located in northeastern lower Michigan between Fairview and Comins on M33. One noteworthy artifact on exhibit there is a casting of an actual (or alleged) Bigfoot track cast, gathered by the Big Foot Investigation Association of Mayville, Michigan.

- China has opened a museum dedicated to the elusive Yeren apeman said to roam the Shennongjia Nature Reserve in Hubei province. The museum is displaying samples of reddish hair and plaster models of huge footprints collected. The museum, which opened in 1997, also features documents and pictures of various scientific and exploratory operations mounted over the years to track the creature.

- The Original Loch Ness Monster Visitor Center is situated near Loch Ness in the highlands of Scotland. It is credited as the official center publicizing the Loch Ness Monster in Scotland. Its website address is http://www.lochness-centre.com/exhibit/exhibit.html

- A competing similar site, the Official Loch Ness Exhibition Center, is situated right across the road from the above. Its website can be reached at http://www.lochness.co.uk/centre/exhibit/index.htm

Other wholly cyperspace museums can be "visited":

- The Beast of Bodmin Moor "exhibition" relates how the British Natural History Museum tracked down a mysterious big cat on Bodmin Moor in Cornwall, England: http://www.nhm.ac.uk/sc/bm/bm_01.htm

- The Unnatural Museum is a cryptozoology museum set up in cyberspace: http://unmuseum.mus.pa.us/lostw.htm

- The Virtual Institute of Cryptozoology is another such "museum" online: http://perso.wanadoo.fr/cryptozoo/welcome.htm

See also the entry "Cryptozoology Websites" for more places to visit, on-line.

CRYPTOZOOLOGY PERIODICALS
The following periodicals carry cryptozoological material in every issue:

- *Cryptozoology.* Published by the International Society of Cryptozoology (ISC), P.O. Box 43070, Tucson, Arizona 85733. A yearly (but actually infrequently published) scientific publication about 150 pages long. Membership to the ISC includes *Cryptozoology* and the *ISC Newsletter.*

- *ISC Newsletter.* Included in ISC membership along with *Cryptozoology.* Quarterly.

- *Strange Magazine.* Box 2246, Rockville, Maryland 20847. Twice every year.

- *INFO Journal.* The International Fortean Organization, Box 367, Arlington, Virginia 22210–0367. Listed as quarterly, but infrequent.

- *Fortean Times.* Dept. WWW, Box 754, Manhasset, New York 11030–0754. Monthly.

- *Exotic Zoology.* 3405 Windjammer Dr., Colorado Springs, Colorado 80920. Bimonthly.

- *CryptoNews.* British Columbia Scientific Cryptozoology Club, Suite 89, 6141 Willingdon Avenue, Burnaby, British Columbia, Canada V5H 2T9. Membership includes four issues (one year) of the club's newsletter.

- *Animals and Men.* 15 Holne Court, Exwick, Exeter, Devonshire EX4 2NA, England. Quarterly.

- *Cryptozoologist.* Box 360, Portland, Maine 04112. Annual, beginning in 2001.

- *The Nesspaper.* Official Loch Ness Monster Fan Club, 9 Burnbrae Place, Inverness, Scotland IV1 2TA, United Kingdom. Monthly.

- *Track Record.* Western Bigfoot Society, 225 NE 23rd Avenue, Hillsboro, Oregon, 97124. Monthly.

- *Crypto.* cheinselman@email.msn.com, Milford, New Hampshire. Monthly.

- *The Monthly Bigfoot Review,* P.O. Box 205, Newcomerstown, Ohio 43832. Monthly.

- *The Bigfoot Times.* Center for Bigfoot Studies, 10926 Milano Avenue, Norwalk, California, 90650. Monthly.

- *The Cryptozoology Review.* 166 Pinewood Avenue, Toronto, Ontario, M6C2V5, Canada. Irregularly.

- *Wonders.* Box 3153, Butler Station, Minneapolis, Minnesota 55403. Quarterly.

CRYPTOZOOLOGY WEBSITES
If there is only one cryptozoology site that you ever visit, go to Philip R. "Pib" Burns's ultimate links page at http://www.pibburns.com/cryptozo.htm

One of the most text-complete and scientific sites to visit is the webpage constructed by French cryptozoologist Michel Raynal. If you wish to dip into the French version or the English one, go find them and choose at http://perso.wanadoo.fr/cryptozoo/welcome.htm

Donald Trull, who assisted greatly with up-to-date entry information, and exchanged entry data, has a great site full of text and news stories at http://www.parascope.com/index.htm

These three are this handbook's top picks for the best cryptozoology webpages in all of cyperspace. See under **Globster** for our best pick for unique animal-specific site.

There are literally hundreds of other cryptozoology sites that should be mentioned, but a few of note can be found at:

http://www.agate.net/~cryptozoo/cryptohome.html
http://www.ncf.carleton.ca/~bz050/HomePage.cryptoz.html
http://www.moneymaker.org/BFRR
http://www.teleport.com/~caveman/wbs.html
http://www.planetc.com/users/bigfoot/scott.htm
http://www.n2.net/prey/bigfoot
http://coombs.anu.edu.au/~vern/wildman.html
http://www.netstra.com.au/~elek/Thylacoleo/thylo1.html
http://homepages.together.net/~ultisrch
http://www.nhm.ac.uk/sc/bm/bm_01.htm
http://www.geocities.com/RainForest/6232/cougar.html
http://www.geocities.com/RainForest/Vines/1318
http://www.serve.com/shadows/serpent.htm
http://www.princeton.edu/~accion/chupa.html
http://www.latinolink.com/news/0412chup.html
http://www.itv.se/boreale/utflykte.htm
http://members.aol.com/SSBN641Gld/index.html
http://www.floridaskunkape.com
http://www.cgocable.net/~rgavel/links/bigfoot.html
http://members.tripod.com/~cybersquatch/cybersquatch.htm
http://www.lorencoleman.com

NON-ENGLISH SITES

French
http://www.Generation.NET/~paul/crypto.htm
http://www.generation.net/~paul/bigfoot.htm
http://perso.wanadoo.fr/cryptozoo/welcome.htm
http://www.zigzag.be/cryptozoologia

Portuguese
http://www.utad.pt/~origins/bigfoot.html

Swedish
http://www.bahnhof.se/~wizard/crypto
http://www.itv.se/boreale/frosoc.htm

ON THE MATTER OF STYLE

The style of this book and the use of capitalization for cryptids (e.g., Bigfoot, Nessie, Yeti, Sasquatch, etc.), follows the "manual of style" that has been adopted by the International Society of Cryptozoology's editor, Richard Greenwell, and the ISC journal, *Cryptozoology*.

Greenwell details the proper capitalization of the cryptid names, before and after discovery, in a footnote in *Cryptozoology* Vol. 5 (1986), page 101. His formalization of this matter is furthermore based on what occurs in systematic zoology, firm ground indeed.

Greenwell is very clear in his example:

Native name: *okapi*; Western name for presumed, undiscovered animal: Okapi; common name after discovery and acceptance: okapi.

For our extended use, this translates into:

Native name: *yet-teh* or *yeti;* Western name for presumed, undiscovered animal: Yeti; common name after discovery and acceptance: yeti.

and

Native name: *oh-mah;* Western name for presumed, undiscovered animal: Bigfoot; common name after discovery and acceptance: bigfoot.

—Loren Coleman

Allen, Benedict. *Hunting the Gugu.* London: Macmillan, 1989.

Arment, Chad. *The Search for Enigmatic Animals.* Denver: Arment, 1995.

Bartholomew, Paul, Robert Bartholomew, William Brann, and Bruce Hallenbeck. *Monsters of the Northwoods.* Utica, NY: North Country Books, 1992.

Baumann, Elwood D. *Bigfoot: America's Abominable Snowman.* New York: Franklin Watts, 1975.

———. *The Loch Ness Monster.* New York: Franklin Watts, 1972.

Bayanov, Dmitri. *America's Bigfoot: Fact, Not Fiction—U.S. Evidence Verified in Russia.* Moscow: Crypto-Logos Books, 1997.

———. *In the Footsteps of the Russian Snowman.* Moscow: Crypto-Logos Books, 1996.

Beck, Horace. *Folklore and the Sea.* Middletown, CT: Marine Historical Association/Wesleyan University Press, 1973.

Benwell, Gwen, and Arthur Waugh. *Sea Enchantress: The Tale of the Mermaid and Her Kin.* New York: Citadel Press, 1965.

Beresford, Quentin, and Garry Bailey. *Search for the Tasmanian Tiger.* Hobart: Blubber Head Press, 1981.

Bernheimer, Richard. *Wild Men in the Middle Ages.* Cambridge, MA: Harvard University Press, 1952.

Berry, Rick. *Bigfoot on the East Coast.* Stuarts Draft, VA: Campbell Center, 1993.

Bille, Matthew A. *Rumors of Existence.* Seattle: Hancock House, 1995.

Bindernagel, John A. *North America's Great Ape: The Sasquatch.* Courtenay, British Columbia: Beachcomber Books, 1998.

Binns, Ronald. *The Loch Ness Mystery Solved.* Buffalo: Prometheus Books, 1984.

Bord, Janet, and Colin Bord. *Alien Animals.* London: Granada, 1980.

———. *The Bigfoot Casebook.* Harrisburg, PA: Stackpole Books, 1982.

———. *The Evidence for Bigfoot and Other Man-Beasts.* New York: Sterling Publications, 1984.

Bottriell, Lena Godsall. *King Cheetah: The Story of the Quest.* Leiden, Holland: E. J. Brill, 1988.

Bradley, Michael. *More Than a Myth: The Search for the Monster of Muskrat Lake.* Willowdale, Ontario: Hounslow Press, 1989.

Burton, Maurice. *The Elusive Monster.* London: Rupert Hart-Davis, 1961.

Campbell, Steuart. *The Loch Ness Monster: The Evidence.* Amherst, NY: Prometheus Books, 1997.

Carmony, Neil B. *Onza! The Hunt for a Legendary Cat.* Silver City, NV: High-Lonesome Books, 1995.

Carrington, Richard. *Mermaids and Mastodons: A Book of Natural and Unnatural History.* New York: Rinehart and Company, 1957.

Clark, Jerome, and Loren Coleman. *Creatures of the Outer Edge.* New York: Warner Books, 1978.

Coleman, Loren. *Curious Encounters.* Boston: Faber and Faber, 1985.

———. *Mysterious America.* Boston: Faber and Faber, 1983.

———. *Tom Slick and the Search for the Yeti.* Boston: Faber and Faber, 1989.

Coleman, Loren, and Patrick Huyghe. *The Field Guide to Bigfoot, Yeti, and Other Mystery Primates Worldwide.* New York: Avon Books, 1999.

Cooke, David, and Yvonne Cooke. *The Great Monster Hunt: The Story of the Loch Ness Investigation.* New York: Grosset and Dunlap, 1969.

Corliss, William R., ed. *Incredible Life: A Handbook of Biological Mysteries.* Glen Arm, MD: Sourcebook Project, 1981.

Costello, Peter. *In Search of Lake Monsters.* New York: Coward, McCann and Geoghegan, 1974.

———. *The Magic Zoo: The Natural History of Fabulous Animals.* New York: St. Martin's Press, 1979.

Dahinden, René, and Don Hunter. *Sasquatch/Bigfoot: The Search for North America's Incredible Creature.* Buffalo: Firefly Books, 1993.

Dinsdale, Tim. *The Leviathans.* London: Routledge and Kegan Paul, 1966.

———. *Loch Ness Monster.* London: Routledge and Kegan Paul, 1961.

———. *Project Water Horse.* London: Routledge and Kegan Paul, 1975.

Dong, Paul. *The Four Major Mysteries of Mainland China.* Englewood Cliffs, NJ: Prentice-Hall, 1984.

Dower, Kenneth Gandar. *The Spotted Lion.* London: William Heinemann, 1937.

Eberhart, George M., ed. *A Geo-Bibliography of Anomalies: Primary Access to Observations of UFOs, Ghosts, and Other Mysterious Phenomena.* Westport, CT: Greenwood Press, 1980.

———. *Monsters: A Guide to Information on Unaccounted-for Creatures, Including Bigfoot, Many Water Monsters, and Other Irregular Animals.* New York: Garland Publishing Company, 1983.

Ellis, Richard. *Monsters of the Sea.* New York: Doubleday and Company, 1994.

———. *The Search for the Giant Squid.* New York: Lyons Press, 1998.

Fairley, John, and Simon Welfare. *Arthur C. Clarke's Chronicles of the Strange and Mysterious.* London: Grafton Books, 1989.

Gaal, Arlene. *Beneath the Depths: The True Story of Ogopogo, Okanagan Lake Monster.* n.p.: Valley Review, 1976.

———. *Ogopogo: The True Story of the Okanagan Million-Dollar Monster.* Surrey, British Columbia: Hancock House, 1986.

Garner, Betty Sanders. *Monster! Monster! A Survey of the North American Monster Scene.* Surrey, British Columbia: Hancock House, 1995.

Gilroy, Rex. *Mysterious Australia.* Mapleton, Australia: Nexus Publishing, 1995.

Gordon, David George. *Field Guide to the Sasquatch.* Seattle: Sasquatch Books, 1992.

Gould, Charles. *Mythical Monsters.* London: Studio Editions, 1992.

Gould, Rupert T. *The Case for the Sea-Serpent.* London: Philip Allan, 1930.

———. *The Loch Ness Monster.* New York: University Books, 1969.

Grant, John. *Monster Mysteries.* Secaucus, NJ: Chartwell Books, 1992.

Green, John. *On the Track of the Sasquatch.* Agassiz, British Columbia: Cheam Publishing, 1968.

———. *Sasquatch: The Apes Among Us.* Seattle: Hanover House, 1978.

———. *The Sasquatch File.* Agassiz, British Columbia: Cheam Publishing, 1970.

———. *Year of the Sasquatch.* Agassiz, British Columbia: Cheam Publishing, 1970.

Grumley, Michael. *There Are Giants in the Earth.* London: Sidgwick and Jackson, 1975.

Guiler, Eric. *Thylacine: The Tragedy of the Tasmanian Tiger.* Melbourne: Oxford University Press, 1985.

Hall, Mark A. *Natural Mysteries.* 2nd edition. Minneapolis: MAHP, 1991.

———. *Thunderbirds—The Living Legend!* 2nd edition. Minneapolis: MAHP, 1994.

———. *The Yeti, Bigfoot, & True Giants.* 2nd edition. Minneapolis: MAHP, 1997.

Halpin, Marjorie, and Michael Ames, eds. *Manlike Monsters on Trial: Early Records and Modern Evidence.* Vancouver: University of British Columbia Press, 1980.

Healy, Tony, and Paul Cropper. *Out of the Shadows: Mystery Animals of Australia.* Chippendale, Australia: Ironbark, 1994.

Heuvelmans, Bernard. *In the Wake of the Sea-Serpents.* New York: Hill and Wang, 1968.

———. *On the Track of Unknown Animals.* London: Kegan Paul International, 1995.

Holiday, F. W. *The Dragon and the Disc: An Investigation into the Totally Fantastic.* New York: W. W. Norton and Company, 1973.

———. *The Goblin Universe.* St. Paul, MN: Llewellyn Publications, 1986.

———. *The Great Orm of Loch Ness: A Practical Inquiry into the Nature and Habits of Water-Monsters.* New York: W. W. Norton and Company, 1969.

Hutchison, Robert A. *In the Tracks of the Yeti.* London: Macdonald and Company, 1989.

Huyghe, Patrick. *Glowing Birds: Stories from the Edge of Science.* Boston: Faber and Faber, 1985.

Izzard, Ralph. *The Abominable Snowman Adventure.* London: Hodder and Stoughton, 1955.

Joyner, Graham C. *The Hairy Man of South Eastern Australia.* Canberra: Graham Joyner, 1977.

Klein, Martin, Robert H. Rines, Tim Dinsdale, and Laurence S. Foster. *Underwater Search at Loch Ness.* Belmont, MA: Academy of Applied Science, 1972.

Krantz, Grover S. *Big Footprints: A Scientific Inquiry into the Reality of Sasquatch.* Boulder: Johnson Books, 1992.

LeBlond, Paul, and Edward L. Bousfield. *Cadborosaurus: Survivor from the Deep.* Victoria, British Columbia: Horsdal and Schubart Publishers, 1995.

Ley, Willy. *Dragons In Amber: Further Adventures of a Romantic Naturalist.* New York: Viking, 1951.

———. *Exotic Zoology.* New York: Viking, 1959.

———. *The Lungfish, the Dodo and the Unicorn: An Excursion into Romantic Zoology.* New York: Viking, 1948.

———. *Salamanders and Other Wonders.* New York: Viking, 1955.

Mackal, Roy P. *A Living Dinosaur? In Search of Mokele-Mbembe.* Leiden, Holland: E. J. Brill, 1987.

———. *The Monsters of Loch Ness.* Chicago: Swallow Press, 1976.

———. *Searching for Hidden Animals.* New York: Doubleday and Company, 1980.

MacKinnon, John. *In Search of the Red Ape.* New York: Holt, Rinehart and Winston, 1974.

Markotic, Vladimir, and Grover S. Krantz, eds. *The Sasquatch and Other Unknown Hominoids.* Calgary, Alberta: Western Publishers, 1984.

Marshall, Robert E. *The Onza.* New York: Exposition Press, 1961.

McEwan, Graham J. *Mystery Animals of Britain and Ireland.* London: Robert Hale, 1986.

———. *Sea Serpents, Sailors and Skeptics.* London: Routledge and Kegan Paul, 1978.

McNeely, Jeffrey A., and Paul Spencer Wachtel. *Soul of the Tiger.* New York: Doubleday and Company, 1988.

Meredith, Dennis L. *Search at Loch Ness.* New York: Quandrangle/The New York Times Book Company, 1977.

Meurger, Michel, and Claude Gagnon. *Lake Monster Traditions: A Cross-Cultural Analysis.* London: Fortean Times, 1988.

Michell, John, and Robert R. M. Rickard. *Living Wonders: Mysteries and Curiosities of the Animal World.* London: Thames and Hudson, 1992.

Miller, Marc E. W. *The Legends Continue: Adventures in Cryptozoology.* Kempton, IL: Adventures Unlimited Press, 1998.

Moon, Mary. *Ogopogo.* Vancouver, British Columbia: J. J. Douglas, 1977.

Morgan, Robert W. *Bigfoot: The Ultimate Adventure.* Knoxville: Talisman Media Group, 1996.

Murphy, Daniel. *Bigfoot in the News.* New Westminster, British Columbia: Progressive Research, 1995.

Napier, John. *Bigfoot: The Yeti and Sasquatch in Myth and Reality.* New York: E. P. Dutton and Company, 1973.

Nugent, Rory. *Drums Along the Congo: On the Trail of Mokele-Mbembe, the Last Living Dinosaur.* New York: Houghton Mifflin Company, 1993.

Odor, Ruth Shannon. *Great Mysteries: Bigfoot.* Mankato, MN: The Child's World, 1989.

Opsasnick, Mark. *The Bigfoot Digest: A Survey of Maryland Sightings.* Riverdale, MD, 1993.

Patterson, Roger. *Do Abominable Snowmen of America Really Exist?* Yakima, WA: Franklin Press, 1966.

Perez, Danny. *Big Footnotes: A Comprehensive Bibliography Concerning Bigfoot, the Abominable Snowman and Related Beings.* Norwalk, CA: Danny Perez Publications, 1988.

———. *Bigfoot at Bluff Creek.* Norwalk, CA: Danny Perez Publications, 1994.

Place, Marian Templeton. *Bigfoot: All Over the Country.* New York: Dodd Mead, 1978.

———. *On the Track of Bigfoot.* New York: Dodd Mead, 1974.

Pyle, Robert Michael. *Where Bigfoot Walks.* Boston: Houghton Mifflin Company, 1995.

Quest, Mike. *The Sasquatch in Minnesota.* Fargo, ND: Quest Publications, 1990.

Reinstedt, Randall A. *Mysterious Sea Monsters of California's Central Coast.* Carmel, CA: Ghost Town Publications, 1993.

Sanderson, Ivan T. *Abominable Snowmen: Legend Come to Life.* Philadelphia: Chilton, 1961.

———. *Investigating the Unexplained: A Compendium of Disquieting Mysteries of the Natural World.* Englewood Cliffs, NJ: Prentice-Hall, 1972.

———. *The Monkey Kingdom.* Garden City, NY: Hanover House, 1957.

Searle, Frank. *Nessie: Seven Years in Search of the Monster.* London: Coronet Books, 1976.

Shackley, Myra. *Still Living? Yeti, Sasquatch and the Neanderthal Enigma.* New York: Thames and Hudson, 1983.

Shuker, Karl P. N. *Extraordinary Animals Worldwide.* London: Robert Hale, 1991.

———. *From Flying Toads to Snakes with Wings.* St. Paul, MN: Llewellyn Publications, 1996.

———. *In Search of Prehistoric Survivors.* London: Blandford, 1995.

———. *The Lost Ark: New and Rediscovered Animals of the 20th Century.* New York: Harper Collins, 1993.

———. *Mystery Cats of the World.* London: Robert Hale, 1989.

Slate, B. Ann, and Alan Berry. *Bigfoot.* New York: Bantam Books, 1976.

Smith, Malcolm. *Bunyips and Bigfoots: In Search of Australia's Mystery Animals.* Alexandria, Australia: Millennium Books, 1996.

Smith, Steven. *The Tasmanian Tiger—1980.* Sandy Bay National Parks and Wildlife Service, Wildlife Division Technical Report 81/1.

Snyder, Gerald S. *Is There a Loch Ness Monster? The Search for a Legend.* New York: Wanderer Books, 1977.

Soule, Gardner. *The Maybe Monsters.* New York: G. P. Putnam's Sons, 1963.

———. *The Mystery Monsters.* New York: G. P. Putnam's Sons, 1965.

———. *Trail of the Abominable Snowman.* New York: G. P. Putnam's Sons, 1966.

South, Malcolm, ed. *Mythical and Fabulous Creatures: A Source Book and Research Guide*. Westport, CT: Greenwood Press, 1987.

Sprague, Roderick, and Grover Krantz, eds. *The Scientist Looks at the Sasquatch*. Moscow, ID: The University Press of Idaho, 1977; rev. 1979.

Steenburg, Thomas N. *Sasquatch: Bigfoot—The Continuing Mystery*. Seattle: Hancock House, 1993.

Stonor, Charles. *The Sherpa and the Snowman*. London: Hollis and Carter, 1955.

Strasenburgh, Gordon R., Jr. *Paranthropus: Once and Future Brother*. Arlington, VA: The Print Shop, 1971.

Sweeney, James B. *A Pictorial History of Sea Monsters and Other Dangerous Marine Life*. New York: Bonanza Books, 1972.

Tattersall, Ian. *The Last Neanderthal: The Rise, Success, and Mysterious Extinction of Our Closest Human Relatives*. New York: Macmillan, 1995.

Taylor-Ide, Daniel. *Something Hidden Behind the Ranges: A Himalayan Quest*. San Francisco: Mercury House, 1995.

Tchernine, Odette. *In Pursuit of the Abominable Snowman*. New York: Taplinger Publishing, 1971.

———. *The Snowman and Company*. London: Robert Hale, 1961.

Time-Life editors. *Mysterious Creatures*. Amsterdam, NY: Time-Life Books, 1988.

Walker, Paul Robert. *Bigfoot and Other Legendary Creatures*. San Diego: Harcourt Brace and Company, 1992.

Wasson, Barbara. *Sasquatch Apparitions*. Bend, OR: Barbara Wasson, 1979.

Weidenreich, Franz. *Apes, Giants and Man*. Chicago: University of Chicago Press, 1946.

Wendt, Herbert. *Out of Noah's Ark*. Boston: Houghton Mifflin Company, 1959.

Whyte, Constance. *More Than a Legend: The Story of the Loch Ness Monster*. London: Hamish Hamilton, 1957.

Wignell, Edel. *A Boggle of Bunyips*. Sydney: Hodder and Stoughton, 1981.

Witchell, Nicholas. *The Loch Ness Story*. Baltimore: Penguin Books, 1975.

Wright, Bruce S. *The Eastern Panther: A Question of Survival*. Toronto/Vancouver: Clarke, Irwin and Company, 1972.

———. *The Ghost of North America: The Story of the Eastern Panther*. New York: Vantage, 1959.

Wylie, Kenneth. *Bigfoot: A Personal Inquiry into a Phenomenon*. New York: Viking, 1980.

Zarzynski, Joseph. *Champ: Beyond the Legend*. Updated edition. Montpelier, VT: Capitol City Press, 1988.

ACKNOWLEDGMENTS

Cryptozoology is my lifelong passion, and many have assisted me along the way. The forty-year journey that resulted in the writing of this book has involved thousands of eyewitnesses who have kindly allowed me to interview them, hundreds of librarians and resource specialists who have helped me with archival material, and scores of key researchers who have opened their files and hearts to my quest. I thank each and every one of those unnamed partners in this book. I wish I could have written a ten-volume encyclopedia that included every cryptozoologist from around the world, every new animal discovery, and numerous other cryptids that had to be left out.

For this volume, I wish to express my deep appreciation to the following people who have shared, supplied, and/or given their permission for images, quoted material, cryptid case information, and biographical data used in this specific book: Frederick Aldrich, Chad Arment, Dmitri Bayanov, Matthew A. Bille, David Bittner, Christina Bolgiano, Janet Bord, Pib Burns, Bufo Calvin, Mark Chorvinsky, Jerry Coleman, Terry W. Colvin, Scott Corrales, Paul Cropper, Cliff Crook, Ray Crowe, René Dahinden, Peter Darben, Mike Dash, Tod Deery, Jon Downes, Richard Ellis, Mark Erdmann, W. Henner Fahrenbach, Henry Fanzoni, Carol Fraser, Arlene Gaal, Ray Gavel, William Gibbons, Brian Goodwin, John Green, Dennis Jay Hall, Mark A. Hall, Jerome F. Hamlin, Craig Heinselman, Bernard Heuvelmans, Patrick Huyghe, Peter Hynes, Stephen Jones, Don Keating, John Kirk, Chris Kraska, Brad LaGrange, Richard La Monica, Paul LeBlond, Larry Lesh, Todd Lester, John Lutz, Jim McLeod, Scott McNabb, Ulrich Magin, Gary Mangiacopra, Debbie Martyr, Blake Mathys, Arnaz Mehta, D. Jeffrey Meldrum, Kyle Mizokami, Tom Moody, Robert W. Morgan, Allan Edward Munro, Scott T. Norman, Ray Nelke, Terry O'Neil, Chris Orrick, Andrew Peterson, Dan Porter, Michel Raynal, William M. Rebsamen, Robert Rickard, Ben S. Roesch, Clayton Rumley, Ivan T. Sanderson, Ron Schaffner, Wolfang Schmidt, John Setzer, Kevin Shepherd, Bobbie Short, Karl Shuker, Ian Simmons, Dan Scott Taylor, Lars Thomas, Roger Thomas, Tracy Torme, Joe Trainor, Doug Trapp, Donald Trull, David Walsh, Osamu Watanabe, Vern Weitzel, Bruce S. Wright, and J. Kevin Wells. My apologies to anyone whom I may have forgotten to include.

In the technical realm, I am most grateful for the labor of literary agent Daniel Greenberg, initial Simon & Schuster contact Sarah Baker, and tireless editor Carrie Thornton, all of whom assisted in steering this book to its birth.

As an endnote, I want to thank especially Leslie Abrons for her personal support through the passionate and sometimes lonely process that happens when one writes an encyclopedia like this one.

LOREN COLEMAN

I would like to acknowledge my appreciation to Helene Henderson.

JEROME CLARK

The authors also wish to thank:

Matthew A. Bille, Editor, *Exotic Zoology Newsletter,* for source material on cryptobears, other cryptids, and biographies; Janet Bord, for a quotation on the Ucumar-Ucu from her book *The Evidence for Bigfoot and Other Man-Beasts*; Mark Erdmann and Arnaz Mehta, for quoting their story of the Indonesian coelacanths, exclusively for this book; Patrick Huyghe, for material on hominoids and other primates from *The Field Guide to Bigfoot, Yeti, and Other Mystery Primates Worldwide*; Scott Norman, for source biographical data from his cryptozoological website (see appendix); Michel Raynal, for source cryptid and biographical material from his cryptozoological website (see appendix); Karl Shuker, for cryptid and autobiographical material; Donald Trull, from Parascope on-line news service (see appendix), for quotations and/or source material in various cryptid entries, especially Chupacabras; Dave Walsh, for direct quotation of his biographical sketch created for this book; and David Parnes and Libbet Cone for expedition-related photographs.